FLY
LIKE A PRO

D1361982

FLY
LIKE A PRO

DONALD J. CLAUSING

TAB BOOKS Inc.
Blue Ridge Summit, PA 17214

FIRST EDITION

SECOND PRINTING

Printed in the United States of America

Reproduction or publication of the content in any manner, without express permission of the publisher, is prohibited. No liability is assumed with respect to the use of the information herein.

Copyright © 1985 by TAB BOOKS Inc.

Library of Congress Cataloging in Publication Data

Clausing, Donald J.
    Fly like a pro.

    Includes index.
    1. Airplanes—Piloting. 2. Private flying.
I. Title.
TL710.C54 1985   629.132′52   85-12514
ISBN 0-8306-2378-7 (pbk.)

Contents

Introduction

People tend to think of flying as something an individual does, but the fact is that more often than not it is a group activity. As flying increased in complexity and sophistication from the days of the biplanes, the tendency was to put more and more people in the cockpit: copilots, navigators, flight engineers, radio operators and so on. At least one airline (Pan Am, with the original Clippers—the flying boats) even had a real Captain, like a ship's Captain, who was the aircraft commander, but didn't normally fly—they had pilots to do that. The Captain's job was command and control. It didn't work. The nautical model that served early aviation so well eventually reached its limits.

Ultimately, complexity and sophistication began to *decrease* the workload in the cockpit, instead of increasing it. The first casualty of aeronautical (note: *aero-nautical*) automation was the radio operator. Radio operation became simple enough that the copilot was able to take it on as an additional duty. Then, gradually, first over land and later over water, the navigator was dropped and the Captain assumed the navigational duties with the assistance of the copilot. Then the FAA allowed the smaller two-engine airliners to operate without Flight Engineers. The Boeing 737 was the "swing" airplane, some airlines voluntarily operating it three-pilot and others two-pilot. Finally, with the Super DC-9 (now the MD-80) and the Boeing 757 and 767, the Flight Engineer was replaced on the larger two-engine jets. The next logical step is to remove the flight engineer from all new airplanes, regardless of size or number of engines. But nobody is suggesting removing copilots from Transport Category airplanes—although there is no reason to think it couldn't theoretically be done.

Through all of this, the Private Pilot has been flying along by himself. It seems to me that there is a little bit of a contradiction here, but it's pretty obvious that, as a practical matter, requiring two pilots in private aircraft would effectively legislate personal flying out of existence. This is one of those inconsistencies that makes sense because it has to, and by and large it seems to work.

The reason it works for private aviation is because, in fact, two pilots are *not* necessary simply to operate Normal and Utility category aircraft (i.e., private aircraft). Having only one pilot doesn't work for Transport Category aircraft (airliners and business jets) partially because Transport Category aircraft still require more than one pilot to be operated safely, but mainly because it doesn't have to—the airlines and corporations that operate Transport Category aircraft can afford two pilots and the redundancy has come to be expected. But the best reason to operate a Transport Category aircraft with two pilots is the one nobody ever talks about: There is no other way to train copilots to be captains.

The two-pilot (captain-copilot) system is, in reality, an apprenticeship system. The copilot has duties, of course, as assigned by the captain, and these normally include handling the radios, reading the checklists, keeping track of the flight log, and taking care of the paperwork. But it is also customary to "swap legs"—to reverse these duties and let the copilot fly every other leg, under the captain's control and supervision, so he learns those duties too. It's not that copilots can't fly (in fact, being generally younger than captains, they sometimes can fly better than the "old men"), but that there is no better way to hone flying techniques and perfect procedures than under the watchful and critical eye of a more experienced senior pilot.

The copilot learns by observation, most of all. Flying isn't so much a matter of physically moving a large object through the air as it is a matter of making an endless series of decisions. A copilot is given the opportunity to spend many hours watching another— presumably more experienced—pilot make those decisions. He is able to test himself against the captain's decisions, to listen to and learn from the captain's line of reasoning, and he is able to learn from the example the captain sets. Copilots learn even when captains make mistakes, as they inevitably do. No other system has been devised which teaches copilots to be captains as well as this one.

The non-professional pilot doesn't get a chance to learn this way. Private Pilots are instant captains, turned loose after as little as 40 hours of instruction and one checkride to teach themselves, by trial and error, the lessons necessary to safely and routinely operate their aircraft under a variety of circumstances and conditions. Not only do they not have another pilot to learn from, but they also do not have a copilot to help. It's a very tough job.

I worked for a jet charter and aircraft management company for a while. The Vice President, who used to fly now and then as a copilot, told me a great story. He had recently convinced his wife that she ought to take flying lessons. She had just gotten home from doing some solo practice in the local area, and was complaining about what hard work learning to fly was. He listened, no doubt sympathetically, and explained that everyone feels that way in the beginning, but it wouldn't always seem hard, and, after all, it couldn't be all *that* hard—she *was* flying a pretty simple airplane, unlike the jets he flew. She smiled sweetly and said, "That's right. But you're just a copilot. *I'm* the Pilot-in-Command."

The Private Pilot has the toughest job in aviation and very little help in making it easier. No one is ever there to help him (or her) when he needs it—and it shows, unfortunately, in the accident record. (According to preliminary figures from the National Transportation and Safety Board, the accident rate for general aviation in 1984 was 9.8 per 100,000 hours flown. The corresponding figure for the commercial airlines was .164 per 100,000 hours flown.)

The reason professionals fly the way they do is because they were taught to fly that way by other professionals before them. The Private Pilot is not part of this loop. This book is an attempt to correct that—to put the non-professional pilot in the the copilot's seat for a while, and give him a chance to learn from the experiences and mistakes of others—in this case, mine.

Chapter 1

The Basics

There are no "amateur pilots;" some pilots get paid to fly and others don't, but that isn't important. The airplane doesn't know if the pilot is being paid or not, nor do the controllers, nor do the pilots of the other airplanes in the sky. Everyone is part of the same system and everyone has to operate in cooperation within that system. This means that *everyone* has to meet certain minimum standards of performance for the system to function properly and safely.

As far as the FAA is concerned, the pilot is just an element in an equation. The equation consists of airplanes, pilots, and ground support. The system as a whole needs all three elements to work properly, so each component has to meet certain minimum standards and each has to work with the others. These minimum standards are what I call The Basics.

In practical terms, The Basics are the things you need to know to be able to operate your aircraft on a daily basis, safely, routinely, and reliably. They include the Four Fundamentals: straight-and-level, turns, climbs, and descents, plus level-offs, airspeed control, and altitude control.

Within the instrument system this means being able to perform all of these maneuvers on instruments, without the aid of an autopilot or flight director. Besides the fundamentals of flying the airplane on instruments you must be able to fly approaches, holding patterns, and navigate using VORs and the Victor Airway system.

In addition to being able to fly the airplane, you need to know how to talk on the radio, be able to contact Flight Service in the air, and be able to quickly and accurately copy clearances and weather reports. You must know what a good weather briefing is and know how to get one. You have to be able to flight plan properly, and you must know and understand all appropriate regulations. Finally, you must be fluent with the contents of your approved Aircraft Flight Manual including the aircraft limitations and weight-and-balance, and you must know as thoroughly as possible the emergency and abnormal procedures for your aircraft. These are The Basics.

Most of these skills will be covered individually in this chapter. A few are important enough to warrant chapters of their own. As a whole they constitute the basic skills necessary to function properly in the system.

IFR VERSUS VFR

This book is primarily concerned with flying as transportation—the safe, routine, and reliable movement of people and things from point A to point B—and flying as transportation means flying according to Instrument Flight Rules (IFR). The problem with the alternative, Visual Flight Rules (VFR), is that in order to be safe the weather has to be excellent over the entire route, and it has to stay that way once you get there or you can't come home. This is seldom the case—not both ways, anyway—and it puts tremendous pressure on the pilot trying to make it work.

Even if you live in an area that always has great weather, the advantages provided in filing IFR—continuous radar monitoring, traffic advisories, separation, automatic avoidance of restricted areas, automatic opening and closing of flight plans, easy access to TCAs, flight following, terrain monitoring, and so on and so on—are so numerous that having an instrument rating is still an essential part of making flying safe, reliable, and routine.

Therefore, the first step in mastering The Basics is to get your instrument rating, even if you have just barely finished getting your Private Pilot's License. Don't worry about the 200 hours you need before you can take the test—by the time you finish your instrument training you will have very close to 200 hours anyway. It's fun, it's not half as hard as you think it is, and it will do wonders for your basic flying skills. The sooner you start working on it, the sooner you can start reaping the benefits.

STRAIGHT-AND-LEVEL

The most basic of The Basics is straight-and-level. Straight-and-level (S&L) means, specifically, being able to hold an altitude within 100 feet of the desired altitude (that's the "level" part), and being able to hold a heading within five degrees of the desired heading (that's the "straight" part). In smooth air you should be able to do better than that: 50 feet and two or three degrees is not unreasonable. Those are the standards for S&L and the system is predicated on an expectation that you can meet those standards.

TRIM

The better the airplane is trimmed, the easier it is to stay within those limits. To fine-tune the trim, start with the rudder. While physically holding the wings level, with your feet off the pedals (and both engines synchronized if you have two), watch the heading for two or three minutes. If the heading drifts off course, trim it out with the rudder trim. Trimming the ball to the center is a good start, but the only really accurate way to do it is to trim out the drift. (In any airplane with two needle-and-balls, I have yet to see the two balls agree.) Once the rudder is trimmed, trim out any aileron pressure you have been holding to keep the wings level. Then trim the elevator.

I like to use the manual trim for the elevator (when I have a choice—some airplanes only have electric trims). Most electric trims are just add-ons to the manual trim, and they usually jump and jerk around and generally don't work very well. They're okay for big trim changes, but not for fine-tuning. With the manual trim you can use little nudges to fine trim the elevator exactly where you want it. You want to smooth out the last little bit of fingertip pressure on the control column.

ALTITUDE CONTROL

Once the airplane is trimmed you should have very little trouble staying within plus or minus 100 feet of altitude, even in fairly rough air. Very few pilots realize how critical this 100 feet of leeway is. The maximum deviation the FAA can allow and still keep VFR and IFR airplanes separated is 100 feet—not 500, as you might otherwise assume. A little quick arithmetic will show why.

Suppose you have, on the one hand, a VFR aircraft with a desired cruising altitude of 9500 feet actually flying at 9600 feet—100 feet high (Fig. 1-1). Suppose you have, on the other hand, an IFR aircraft with an assigned altitude of 10,000 feet actually flying at 9,900 feet—100 feet low. Both are within the legal limits of plus or minus 100 feet of desired or assigned altitude. (Don't forget that the speed limit of 250 knots indicated airspeed stops at 10,000. If this IFR aircraft happens to be a jet, he could be indicating 390 knots at this point.)

So far so good. There is still a 300-foot separation between the two aircraft—9,600 feet for one, and 9,900 feet for the other. But don't forget that the FAA allows 75 feet of error in altimeters; the altimeter is a simple pressure-measuring device, and much greater accuracy than that is not practical. If both of the aircrafts' altimeters are off by 75 feet in the "wrong" direction—that is, if the VFR aircraft is really at 9675 feet and the IFR aircraft is really at 9825 (even though the altimeters read 9600 feet and 9900 feet respectively)—they will pass within 150 feet of each other and both be perfectly legal.

Every time you deviate from the proper altitude by more than 100 feet you reduce the separation even more. The errors may partly or even completely cancel, or if you are *real* lucky they may all go in the "right" direction, but they are just as likely to all go in the "wrong" direction, so think about that every time your altitude slips just a little above or below the allowable limit.

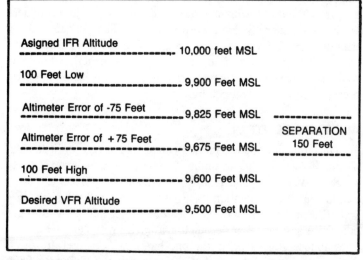

Fig. 1-1. Legal vertical separation between VFR and IFR aircraft can be as little as 150 feet.

TURNS

Turns are very important to smooth, safe instrument flight. In fact, *smooth* instrument flying and *safe* instrument flying are generally the same thing. Non-instrument rated pilots typically get in trouble in the clouds because the turns get out of hand. You just can't roll in and out of turns on instruments the way you can visually. Using the proper amount of bank for the situation is the key to avoiding control problems with turns, and it is also the key to fitting in with the instrument system: flying vectors, tracking airways, shooting approaches.

The smallest amount of bank possible, 1 or 2 degrees, is used for approaches and VOR tracking. A Flight Director (FD) is a computer that determines what the proper bank angle should be for a given situation. One of the things you can learn by watching it work is that once you have intercepted and established yourself on an inbound localizer course, and have bracketed a heading within 5 degrees, all corrections after that point will be small but continuous; the FD bars will be constantly moving, a little bit at a time, in order to maintain the aircraft exactly on the inbound course. The Flight Director will almost never command the wings to be exactly level, but neither will it command large corrections (again, assuming the inbound course has already been properly intercepted).

The same principle applies whether you have a Flight Director or not: Once established on an approach, use continuous corrections of 1 or 2 degrees to maintain yourself exactly on the centerline of the approach. These same bank angles will also work well for final corrections on non-precision approaches and for fine-tuning of headings when VOR tracking.

Enroute, at altitude, 10 degrees of bank should be the most you would ever use for routine turns to change heading or course, and 5 degrees of bank will normally be enough. Most passengers don't appreciate a big bank after sitting straight-and-level for awhile—it's upsetting to them. An older Captain I flew with told me that a passenger had said to him that he thought an airplane was like a canoe—if you tipped it too far over, it would flip upside-down. That's not true, of course, but that's the way many passengers feel about turns. In any case, there's no need for a big bank just to change heading a few degrees; 5 or 10 degrees is plenty.

When you do need a steeper turn—traffic avoidance, or a big change in heading, or a controller request for a tight turn (sometimes a controller will ask for a "good rate" to a new heading, which is the same thing)—do it; 25 to 30 degrees. If the request was for an "immediate" turn, make it 45 degrees of bank. A controller won't use the word "immediate" unless he means it. When you hear "immediate," act now, ask later.

After takeoff, on climbout, and on descent, 25 degrees of bank is about right. Twenty-five degrees of bank will be very close to a standard rate turn at most speeds, and it is easier to fly a constant angle of bank than it is to keep referring to a separate instrument in order to fly a perfect standard rate turn. Twenty five degrees is typical of the bank angle programed into most flight directors—which is a pretty good endorsement—and it seems to be about what the controllers expect in these circumstances. That's important, because a controller assumes you will turn in a predictable manner and has planned his other traffic accordingly. If you turn super-tight on him—something more than 30 degrees of bank—or drift around at 7 or 8 degrees of bank, he won't be expecting that and may be forced to move a lot of traffic around as a result.

Thirty degrees of bank is the steepest normal turn on instruments. It makes for a good rate of turn without getting into the control problems of steep turns. It is especially handy when circling to land. The key to a good circling approach is to stay in tight and not overshoot the final. Doing this usually requires tighter turns than normal. In fact, if your initial turns are done at 25 degrees, a 30-degree turn to final will generally ensure staying inside the final approach course—it is much easier to intercept the final approach course from the inside than it is to overshoot it and try to get back.

STEEP TURNS

Being able to do a good steep turn—45 to 60 degrees of bank—is one of the signs of a good pilot. I have always had trouble with steep turns. They are, however, very good exercises because they demand concentration, precision, and control, and they are not very forgiving. (That doesn't mean they are dangerous, just that small errors are readily apparent.) They also teach humility. But beyond their value as an exercise, there are times when a steep turn is necessary, and very often this happens close to the ground. The consequences of "losing it" in a steep turn close to the ground are probably fairly obvious, so the importance of practice should be pretty clear.

The most common mistake pilots make doing steep turns is to add back pressure too soon. You really don't need any back pressure until going through about 30 degrees of bank. I'm not sure whether this is because rolling into the bank generates a small amount of lift, or whether it's just a function of inertia, but whatever the reason, you don't need any back pressure initially. If you add it too soon, you will find yourself climbing.

The next mistake is to start chasing the altitude. Once the airplane starts "porpoising" (oscillating), you have pretty much had it. (Ask me how I know all this.) The key to maintaining altitude is not back pressure per se, but *attitude*. You need to experiment to discover what nose attitude results in zero altitude gain or loss for your airplane; that attitude is what you want to hold *exactly*. Back pressure is the inevitable by-product of attitude control, not an end in itself. Speed is controlled by power. If the bank and power are constant and the proper pitch attitude is held, the airplane will truck around the turn as if the altimeter needle were glued in place. Or so they tell me.

I used to think steep turns were dumb, but that was because I had trouble with them. I don't think they're dumb anymore, although I still have to work pretty hard at them. When you need to do a steep turn—on an unusually tight circling approach, for instance, or to avoid a collision, or to turn away from severe weather, or after an emergency on takeoff requiring an immediate return—you have to be able to do it right. You don't want to let a steep turn deteriorate into a spiral (not enough back pressure initially), nor do you want to "load it up" with back pressure, trying to gain altitude but just making the bank steeper instead, or zoom up, possibly into the clouds (too much initial back pressure), or become disoriented and progress into what the FAA diplomatically calls an "unusual attitude." It's a good idea to practice steep turns, at a safe altitude, regularly.

CLIMBS

Climbs are pretty simple and most pilots do them well, but a couple of points are worth mentioning. For the first 400 feet, the primary consideration in *any* airplane is to gain altitude quickly. For Normal and Utility Category aircraft, this means holding *best rate-of-climb speed* (abbreviated V_y) as accurately as you can, because that is the speed that most efficiently translates power into altitude. Until you have at least 400 feet of altitude (or whatever it takes to safely maneuver on one engine or to glide to an emergency landing area), you can't afford the luxury of a higher climb speed.

Carrying extra speed at this point may make you feel better—especially in a multiengine aircraft—but it won't translate into altitude if an engine quits. The extra speed will dissipate almost instantaneously with no appreciable altitude gain because the drag of the windmilling propeller will be greater at the higher speed. What you want, in *any* airplane, is altitude, and the way to get it is to climb at the best rate-of-climb speed.

This segment from liftoff to 400 feet is a critical time for any airplane, but it is especially critical for multiengine propeller-driven airplanes. To suddenly lose power on one engine at slow speed while close to the ground is an extremely marginal situation for a multiengine airplane. I won't try to teach you here how to fly a multiengine airplane, but just so we're all on the same wavelength, let's go over what happens to a multiengine airplane when one engine quits.

A multiengine airplane is a little like a rowboat: Lose an oar and a rowboat will go in circles, and the same thing will happen to a multiengine airplane when one engine quits, unless we do something about it. The farther out on the wing the engine is installed (which has to do with propeller clearance more than anything else), and the more power that engine is developing at the time, the greater the turning tendency will be.

An airplane has an advantage over most rowboats, though, in that airplanes have rudders. The rudder can, to a certain extent, counteract the tendency of the airplane to fly in circles on one engine. The ability of the rudder to do so is directly proportional to the speed of the airplane, because the faster the airplane is going, the more air flows over the rudder and the more "power" it has to do its job of straightening the airplane out. Conversely, the slower the airplane goes, the less ability it has to counter the turning force; as the airplane gets slower and slower it eventually reaches a point where it doesn't have enough rudder to keep the airplane from turning anymore, and the airplane at this point becomes uncontrollable. The speed at which control is lost with full takeoff power being developed on one side of the airplane and zero power on the other is called *minimum controllable airspeed* and is abbreviated V_{mc}.

If an engine quits abruptly when the speed is below V_{mc}, the airplane will both turn and roll into the "dead" engine, and if this happens close enough to the ground that a recovery can not be accomplished, the consequences are invariably disastrous. It generally takes several hundred feet to recover from an abrupt loss of power to one side when the speed is below V_{mc}, so the importance of maintaining adequate flying speed cannot be emphasized too much.

The problem you have in a multiengine airplane on takeoff is that you have no choice during the first 400 feet but to use maximum power and to fly fairly slowly (V_y) in order to gain a modicum of maneuvering altitude as quickly as possible, and that is exactly the combination of high power and low airspeed that makes V_{mc} a problem. This sounds like one of those situations where you can't win, but it's not quite as bad as it may sound: V_y, while slow, is still well above V_{mc}. If you don't go any *slower* than V_y, you won't have to worry about dropping below V_{mc}, and if you don't go any *faster* than V_y, you won't be giving away any altitude you might need later. This is why flying as close as you can to V_y for at least the first 400 feet is so important.

If you do lose an engine on takeoff and find that even at best single-engine rate-of-climb speed you are unable to climb, you may have to settle for mushing into the ground, but your chances of surviving this kind of crash are much, much better than your chances of surviving an uncontrolled, spiraling descent into the ground—and that is, unfortunately, nearly always the outcome when the airspeed is allowed to deteriorate below V_{mc} and an engine suddenly quits.

One of the many nice things about jets with engines in the rear is that their V_{mc}s are very low, which allows for a huge margin between V_{mc} and the slowest normal operating speeds. The engines are so close to the fuselage that there is little turning tendency when one quits. If an airplane with engines out on the wing is like a rowboat, then an airplane with engines mounted in close to the fuselage is like a canoe, and a single-engine airplane is like an outboard—it either goes straight ahead or it doesn't go at all. The Cessna Skymaster, with one engine in the front and another in the rear, both directly on the centerline, combined the best of both worlds: multiengine redundancy with single engine controllability. Unfortunately, it had a lot of problems with engine cooling. Too bad—they had the right idea.

All of this has to do with the first 400 feet, when the first priority is to gain altitude as quickly as possible for maneuvering in case of an engine failure—either the failure of the only engine or of one of the engines. Once you have some altitude and all the obstacles are clear, the most important consideration is visibility: Push the nose over where you can see something. This will also improve the engine cooling. The efficiency penalty in flying faster than best rate-of-climb is fairly small and the benefits are fairly large. If you are planning on climbing to within a few thousand feet of the service ceiling of your aircraft, you may have to drop back to V_y to keep the airplane climbing, but for most altitudes that won't be necessary. Below 10,000 feet, in visual conditions, maintaining a specific cruise climb airspeed is not as important as being able to see over the nose. Above that, or in the clouds, use the manufacturer's recommended cruise climb airspeed.

LEVEL-OFF

A nice, smooth level-off not only is easy on the passengers, but is essential to good altitude control. The key is to start leveling off early, trimming all the way.

Exactly what "early" means obviously depends on the rate of climb. There are various rules-of-thumb for this, but I think they unnecessarily complicate the issue. If you use common sense and err on the "early" side, you shouldn't have any problem.

For instance, if you are climbing at a good rate—1000 feet per minute (fpm) or so—start to level-off no later than 500 feet ahead of time. If the climb rate is more modest—say 200 or 300 fpm—150 or even 200 feet early would not be too soon. In any case, even if you are clawing your way the last couple of hundred feet, start slowly pushing the nose over coming up on the last 100 feet. Leave the power alone; let the airplane accelerate as you gradually push it over. Work on leveling off and getting trimmed. Then bring the power levers back. Ideally, the passengers won't even know when you have leveled off until the power is reduced. This is the smooth, accurate way; it's easiest on the engine, and it keeps ATC happy. Keep your finger by the trim wheel and just keep nudging it along.

I don't recommend using the autopilot to level off. There are very few autopilots with the power and smoothness to level off properly. The very newest and best systems for jet equipment will, but most won't. If yours does a decent job of it, fine, but you should still disengage the autopilot after it has done the leveling. Make sure all three axes are still in trim, and *then* you can put it back on again if you want.

DESCENTS

The subject of descents could fill an entire chapter, but the basics are fairly simple. The first priority is a descent that works out right; i.e., one that gets you down in time, but not early. The second priority is a descent that doesn't abuse the engine, and the third priority is a descent that is comfortable.

Most pilots use some kind of a rule of thumb to plan their descents. In pressurized aircraft, a common rule is to start down when the mileage is three times the altitude (in thousands) and maintain that relationship all the way down. Thus, from 33,000 feet you would start down 99 miles out and come down fast enough to keep that ratio constant all the way down.

Unfortunately, this rule won't work for unpressurized airplanes; the descent rates are too high—1000 fpm or more. A comfortable, unpressurized rate of descent is 300 fpm. This means from 9000 feet you will need 30 minutes to get down to a sea-level airport. (You need to descend 9000 feet, and you come down 300 feet for each minute; 300 into 9000 is 30.) This 300 fpm rate is probably slower than you are used to using, but it is what the major airlines commonly used for passenger comfort in the old, unpressurized days, and it doesn't shock cool the engine either. The little bit of extra true airspeed or tailwind that you give up by starting down a little bit early is not worth worrying about, and the advantages are considerable.

For maximum fuel efficiency in the descent you should bring the power back and keep the airspeed constant. As long as fuel isn't a problem, though, there's no reason not to push the nose over a little to regain in the descent some of the ground speed lost in the climb. Just don't overdo it; most passengers are very uncomfortable with anything that looks like a "dive," and in any case it is a good idea to avoid the yellow arc on the airspeed gauge. Smooth air has a way of suddenly becoming rough.

AIRSPEED CONTROL

In order to have complete control over the airplane, you must be able to maintain any assigned airspeed that is safe and within the limitations of the aircraft, and you must be able to do it for all configurations: clean, partial flaps, gear down, and full flaps. Until you can do all this, you haven't mastered the airplane.

The starting point is level flight. If you know ahead of time the amount of power necessary to maintain a given airspeed, airspeed control is a very simple matter: Simply set the power to the appropriate setting and wait for the airspeed to settle. A minor adjustment should be all that is necessary after that. If you can develop a rule of thumb for your particular airplane, so much the better; you won't have to memorize a bunch of power settings and airspeeds. A rule of thumb for Falcon 20s (just as an example) is: Total fuel flow "equals" airspeed; i.e., 2000 pounds per hour fuel flow will give 200 knots airspeed, clean. In a single-engine airplane, a useful rule might be something like an inch of manifold pressure (either way) equals plus or minus 10 knots indicated airspeed.

As you add flaps and drop the gear, additional power will have to be added to maintain a given speed. You should have a good idea ahead of time how much power is needed so the airspeed doesn't vary all over the place as the gear and flaps go out. You will have to experiment, but that in itself is good practice—a lot better practice than cruising around trying to find an airport with a coffee shop, for instance.

In the climb, power is not available to control airspeed, so in this case pitch controls airspeed: Faster equals nose down, slower, nose up. In the descent, set the airspeed first, and then adjust the power for the desired descent rate.

Airspeed control is one of the main ways controllers separate and sequence aircraft. If you want to operate in the system, you must be able to maintain any assigned airspeed within the limits of your airplane.

COMBINED MANEUVERS

Needless to say, you must be able to *combine* basic skills. In other words, you should be able to change your airspeed while descending, or change headings while climbing, or maintain a constant airspeed while changing altitudes. These are not "tricks"— they are basic flying skills. You should be able to perform these maneuvers both on instruments and visually. Actually, flying precisely on instruments is the easy way. Doing it visually is really much harder.

AUTOPILOTS

If you need an autopilot to do any of these things, you need more practice. This is not to say that an autopilot doesn't have its place, just that you must never allow yourself to become dependent on it. If you need an autopilot to be able to do a legitimate job of flying the airplane, then the most competent pilot in the airplane is the autopilot and the primary source of control is something other than a human being—and that's not good.

APPROACHES

You must be able to do the three basic types of approaches: ILS, VOR, and NDB. Since most aviation accidents occur during the approach and landing phase of flight, this is obviously a critical area. Each type of approach will be dealt with in some detail in the chapter on approaches; suffice it to say for now that the ability to fly a good approach is fundamental to safe flying.

HOLDING

Holding is easy—it's getting *into* holds that's tough. For me, the key to entering a hold is orientation: knowing exactly where I am, where the hold is, and what direction I am going to go around. Once I know all that, it is very easy to figure how to get myself from where I am to where I want to be.

There *are* pilots who don't use orientation to get into a hold; they use the directional gyro (DG), and depending on which sector the outbound heading falls, that tells them what kind of entry to use. I never have been able to figure it out. If you're interested, there are books that explain this method, and you can even buy little plastic overlays that go over the DG and divide it into appropriate sectors. (You can also buy holding pattern computers, but I am very wary of paraphernalia in the cockpit. It just adds to the clutter and is never there when you need it.) I think, ultimately, the hard way is the easy way.

Sometimes it helps to actually draw the hold on the chart with a pencil. (Make sure you get the turns depicted correctly—right or left.) If you know where you are on the chart, and the hold is drawn correctly on the chart, the preferred entry is usually fairly obvious. Sometimes all you have to do is "draw" the hold mentally, but in one way or another it helps to visualize it to get into it.

In any case, don't get rattled, take your time (slow the airplane down to give yourself more time if you want to—there's no point in going fast just to hold anyway), and when in doubt, at least stay inside the holding area. Keep in mind that the holding pattern is a large, protected area on the controller's scope that he expects you to stay in. A holding clearance is, in effect, an area restriction: "Go to your room and stay there until I call you." The whole point of the various entries is to keep you inside the area while you are in the process of getting established in the hold. Keep that in mind and the entry should be pretty obvious.

Technically, in radar contact, there is no longer a requirement to report entering the hold, but this was a requirement for so long that most pilots still think it is. As a result, it has become customary to report entering the hold anyway. Sometimes controllers will want to terminate the radar coverage once you are in the hold, so the report serves as a cue for them to terminate the radar coverage. This isn't anything to worry about. They still see you. It just makes their job a little easier. Once you're cleared out of the hold, they invariably ask for an ident and reestablish radar contact.

VOR TRACKING

Navigation means finding your way. In practice, this means tracking along VOR airways. Someday maybe all IFR-equipped aircraft will have inertial nav, or Omega, or Loran, or NavStar (satellite navigation), or some such wizardry, but in the meantime and for a while to come, tracking along airways described by VOR radials is the basic means of instrument navigation.

With practice, tracking along a given VOR radial can be as unconscious and habitual as driving a car—but it doesn't happen automatically. In the beginning you have to try.

To digress a little (bear with me; there's a reason for this), think back to when you were a student pilot and were first learning to do landings. At first, no matter how hard you tried, you probably found yourself all over the sky—too high, wide, then low, then wide the other side, and so on. As time went on, the errors got smaller and smaller, and the effort required seemed to be less and less. It wasn't. You actually worked more when the errors were small, but it seemed like less because you had learned to make many small corrections rather than let things get out of hand and then have to make one or two big corrections.

This insight is key to many things in aviation, including VOR tracking: It is much easier, in the long run, to make many small corrections than a few big ones. This doesn't mean overcontrolling, of course, or chasing after the VOR needle. But it does mean making a small correction just as soon as the needle moves off center. And then another one. And then another one. After about three corrections you should have a pretty good heading nailed down, and after that only an occasional small correction should be necessary. If it seems like a lot of work at first, that's only because it hasn't become a habit yet. Once you decide that you are *not* going to let the deviation needle get past the first dot on your VOR deviation indicator, you are on the road to accurate and easy VOR tracking.

When you do use the autopilot enroute, use the heading mode, not the nav mode. The nav mode has no brain; it will turn toward the needle and continue to do so until the needle starts back, which usually results in a huge overcorrection. Even when it finally succeeds in centering the needle, it will still follow every little swing after that, most of which are just random blips.

You can do much better than that with the heading mode, because you're smarter than that. It takes a little experience to get a feel for what to ignore and what to correct for, but in the end you'll get a much more comfortable ride this way than you would with the nav mode. (One of the many nice things about Omega and inertial and other area navigation systems is that they provide a steady signal. With these systems you can use the nav mode—but not with VORs.)

FLIGHT SERVICE

Being able to contact a Flight Service Station enroute is an important skill. Flight Service is the best place to get up-to-date weather information enroute. If the weather is deteriorating from what it was before you took off or what it was forecast to be, the sooner you know it, the better. Worsening weather may dictate a fuel stop or even a diversion to another airport if it looks like the destination is going below minimums. The sooner a decision to divert or make a precautionary fuel stop is made, the more choices you have available and the less time is lost.

To use Flight Service effectively, you have to know how it works and what frequencies to use for what. All Flight Service Stations (FSS) have a common frequency of 122.2. This is both good and bad. The good part is that it is easy to remember: basically all twos. As long as you know the name of a nearby FSS you can just call it on 122.2. (The common call sign for all Flight Service Stations is "Radio," as in "Concord Radio" for the Concord FSS.) The bad part is that everybody else can remember 122.2 also, so the frequency is usually congested.

It is much better to use one of the frequencies specifically assigned to the FSS you want. These will also be frequencies in the 122 range, such as 122.3, 122.4, 122.5, etc. (with one exception which we will get to in a minute). These specific frequencies are found on the charts—both Sectionals and Low Altitude Enroute charts—over the VOR identification boxes within that FSS's area. It takes a second to look them up, but it generally pays off.

When you do call, say loudly and clearly, "Washington Radio, Range Rocket 1234 Xray on 122.3," or whatever. With any luck, Washington Radio will answer. Sometimes you get a Flight Service Station specialist from another nearby station with the same frequency answering instead and cutting out the one you want. Usually "Foggy Bottom Radio please disregard; '34 Xray' is calling Washington Radio" will do the trick. If you go ahead and talk to the one that does answer, what usually happens is that then the first guy wakes up and blocks the second one out. It's not really their fault either—they're trying to help, but it's an old system. Do the best you can. Help is supposed to be on the way.

A general FSS can provide general services. Makes sense. If all you want is the most recent weather, try to call a Flight Watch station instead. All Flight Watch stations have a common frequency of 122.0; however, Flight Watches are much more spread out than regular Flight Service Stations, so interference is less of a problem. They're great, because they have all the weather you could want on a video screen right in front of them, and you won't have to wait ten minutes for some clown to file three flight plans before you get your chance to talk.

The only FSS frequency which is not a 122-"something" frequency is 123.6, which is reserved for Airport Advisory Service (AAS). Airports which have a FSS but not an operating tower have an AAS. All this means is that anyone who wants to can report his position from the airport and his intentions to FSS, and FSS will log all reports and keep everyone in contact informed of reported traffic. FSS doesn't "control," they just keep track of and relay the reported traffic. In order to keep a clear channel for information that is useless if it isn't passed on quickly, 123.6 is restricted to airport advisories and you shouldn't use it to ask for the weather or file a flight plan. If you do, you will probably be politely told to change to another FSS frequency.

LIMITATIONS

When you take a checkride for a type rating in a particular airplane, you prepare for the oral exam mainly by memorizing the Limitations section of the Aircraft Flight Manual (the AFM). You also have to be familiar with the aircraft systems and be able to work performance and weight-and-balance problems, but the main part of the oral exam for a type rating is usually a line-by-line quiz of the Limitations section of the AFM. For instance: "Mr. Smith, this aircraft is approved for what types of operations? What is the minimum flight crew? What is the maximum number of passengers? What is the altitude limit for takeoff and landing? What is the maximum landing weight? What is the maximum operating speed? What are the limits for takeoff power? For maximum continuous power?" And so on and so on.

The reason you must know these things, and the reason the FAA puts such emphasis on them, is because operation within the Limitations, as described in the AFM and supplemented by appropriate placards, is *mandatory*. It has the force of law. These are not recommendations, they are *requirements*. Failure to observe them can lead to fines, suspension of privileges, and voiding of your insurance.

To observe the Limitations, you must know them. The only way to know what the Limitations are for sure is to get your Aircraft Flight Manual out, flip to the Limitations section, read it, memorize it, and then quiz yourself until you know it cold. Whenever I have to take an oral exam, I have my wife quiz me first. I usually know the material pretty well before I give her a chance to find out I don't know everything.

It is important to differentiate between what the manufacturer *recommends* and what the FAA *requires*. The manufacturer may give you pages of information on how to set the power for various cruise conditions, or on how to lean the engine, or on what guidelines to use for setting the cowl flaps, and so on. These are the manufacturers' recommendations, and to the extent they were developed by a small army of engineers and substantiated by thousands of hours of operational experience, they are to be taken very seriously. But they are not mandatory. You do not *have* to set the power according to any cruise charts, unless those charts are found in the AFM. If the only limitation in the manual, markings, or placards is "Max power, all altitudes: 2700 rpm," you may, legally, run the engine at 2700 rpm, even if that means 95% or 100% power.

I think this is an important distinction, because it is vital to know where you have flexibility as a pilot and where you do not. Limitations are *mandatory,* recommendations are not. The only exception to the absoluteness of the Limitations is your emergency authority as pilot-in-command to deviate from any regulation (and therefore any limitation) if necessary—but the burden of proof as to the wisdom of that deviation will be on you.

There is an implied requirement that the necessary equipment to observe the limitations also be installed and functioning. Thus the Flight Manual may not specifically state that you must have a fuel pressure gauge, but if the Flight Manual has a maximum or minimum fuel pressure limitation, you must, by implication, have a working fuel pressure indicator; there is no other way to observe it. Another example: can you fly without an operating cylinder head temp gauge? No, not if a maximum cylinder head temperature is listed as limitation in the AFM; however, if no limitation is listed there, then you may.

The observance of the Limitations as listed in the Aircraft Flight Manual is one of The Basics. The Limitations define the safe, normal operating envelope of the aircraft. Outside of that envelope is the realm of the test pilot. If you exceed those parameters you run a significant risk of serious damage or injury, you jeopardize your license, you forfeit your warranty rights, and in all likelihood you invalidate your insurance. They may not always make sense, but there is always a reason behind every limitation. The smart set just accepts them.

WEIGHT-AND-BALANCE

Another very important part of the Aircraft Flight Manual (although one frequently published separately) is the weight-and-balance section. Ensuring that the weight and balance are within limits is an important part of flight planning, and is covered in that chapter. The part we're concerned with here is an understanding of the effect of excess weight and out-of-balance conditions on the performance and controllability of the airplane.

The problem with an overweight condition is not that the airplane can't handle a little extra weight—usually it can, if the truth be told. The problem is that the airplane may not be able to handle the additional stress. Normal Category airplanes are certified to 3.8 Gs. An extra 100 pounds may not be a problem for the airplane to lift, but in a 3.8 G maneuver that extra 100 pounds becomes 380 pounds, and the airplane may not be strong enough to handle that. The tail is usually what comes off first, and not just the elevator— we're talking the *whole* tail. In simple terms, when you overload the airplane you are reducing the structural integrity of the airplane—it will break with fewer Gs than it would otherwise.

Out-of-balance is even more serious than overweight. A

noseheavy airplane is stable but inefficient. It will be very difficult to flare and may result in a hard landing, but it is seldom the cause of serious accidents.

Tailheaviness, on the other hand, is very dangerous. The further to the rear the center of gravity is, the less stable the airplane. An airplane that is unstable will not recover from a stall without pilot input, and if the center of gravity is too far to the rear it will not recover from a stall at all, with or without the pilot's assistance—the nose will pitch up and stay there. This is what happened to the B-1A that crashed at Mojave in 1984, destroying the airplane and killing Rockwell's chief test pilot. The weight-and-balance of the B1 is particularly tricky because the sweep of the wing can be changed, but what happens when the balance is too far aft is exactly the same. A word to the wise.

REGULATIONS

You should know thoroughly the regulations that pertain to your operation. That means most of Parts 61 and 91. Fortunately, there aren't many. Unfortunately, they could be clearer and more specific. Because of this they are subject to endless interpretation and argument. For instance, in IFR conditions, a reserve of 45 minutes fuel at "normal cruising speed" is required. (FAR 91.23.) What is "normal cruising speed"? It isn't defined. Most people (including me), assume that it means whatever cruising speed you flightplan for. But I don't know that for sure. It might mean "but not long-range cruise, because that isn't 'normal'." This may seem like nitpicking, but if you ever have to declare an emergency because you are low on fuel, this question may assume larger proportions.

The best defense is a thorough knowledge of the regulations. (Being inherently skeptical of the self-serving interpretations of other pilots is also advisable.) Knowledge plus experience will result in the best interpretations. Discretion will minimize this ever being a problem.

CLEARANCES

Some pilots have trouble copying clearances, although with enough practice nearly everybody gets it sooner or later. Two things that help speed the learning process are: 1) Be ready; 2) Know what's coming.

Being ready means having a piece of paper and a pen or pencil handy, which in turn means always putting them in the same place. That is the only way they can really be "handy." You don't have to have whole reams of paper and boxes full of pencils, but you do need to develop some sort of system that includes a place to write clearances and a place where you always keep a pen or pencil. Then, when you hear "34 Xray, clearance," you will be ready to write. Naturally, if you're busy with something else, such as taxiing or an important checklist item, tell the controller to stand by. It can wait. But when you *are* ready, *be* ready.

If you know what's coming in the clearance, and the order it will come in, writing it down is very simple. The first item will be the routing, then the altitude, the transponder code, and the last item is usually the departure frequency. Sometimes you will get an additional remark of some sort such as a void time. I write them down on a line-by-line basis, according to the order given. Thus, a typical clearance after I have copied it would look like this:

V91 PWL FPR
60 Exp 350 10 min
3457 119.85
1522

This is my shorthand for a clearance that went: "34 Xray is cleared to SOP via V91 Pawling, flightplanned route, to maintain 6000; expect Flight Level 350 10 minutes after departure. Squawk 3457; departure frequency 119.85. Clearance void if not off by 1522 Zulu." I would read it back shorter than the full readout to me, probably something like: "34 Xray cleared to SOP, V91 Pawling, flight planned route, 6000, expecting 350 10 minutes after departure, 3457, 119.85 and void 1522." As long as the order is the same, the numbers are what count. Reading clearances ties up a frequency for a long time, so appropriate abbreviation is not only all right, but good.

If they throw you a routing you never heard of, write it down as you hear it, using whatever abbreviation comes in handy, and then make sure when you read it back you say the words exactly as you heard them. This gives the controller a chance to correct you if you heard a fix wrong. You don't have to look up the whole new routing before you read it back; read it back, then look it up on the chart. If it still doesn't make sense, or you just can't find a fix, go back and ask, but nine times out of ten it will make perfect sense when you look it up, and you won't tie up the frequency that way.

Whatever you do, don't *ever* take off if you don't fully understand the clearance. That is one of the stupidest things you can do in aviation—a lot more stupid than going back and admitting you can't find a certain VOR or intersection or airway on your chart.

Some sort of shorthand system for copying a clearance is necessary, but I don't think you need to memorize any one system, nor does it have to be extensive. Make up your own if you want. Something for altitude restrictions ("cross at or above" for instance), and short forms of the words and phrases you usually hear is all that is really needed. If something new comes up, either write it out or invent a short form on the spot. You only have to remember it long enough to read it back; you can always write it out fully after you have "hung up."

WEATHER REPORTS

Copying weather in the air is a lot like copying clearances, only the abbreviations are different. Most pilots use abbreviations based on the old teletype system of reporting, before "SCT," "BKN," and "OVC" were invented. That is, they use ⦶ for scattered, ⦷ for broken, and ⊠ for overcast. "Thin" or "light" is a dash after the symbol. Altitudes are in hundreds: Drop the last two zeroes. All other numbers, such as visibility and temperatures, are written out. "Indefinite" is W, and "obscured" is X, "partially obscured" a dash with an X (-X). Simple. The order is always the same: clouds from lowest to highest, visibility (miles and type: fog—F; haze—H; smoke—K), temperature, dewpoint, and winds. Thus "35 ⦶ 45 ⦷ 7H 67 63 2410" means "3500 scattered, 4500 broken, seven miles in haze, temperature 67, dewpoint 63, winds 240 at 10"—a nice spring day. You probably first saw this system when you were a student pilot. If you quit using it after that, try it again. With a little practice it becomes second nature and makes copying weather much easier.

These, then, are the basic skills needed to safely and routinely take your place in the system. If none of this presents a problem for you, great. If you do see any weak areas, this is the time to correct them. It isn't hard, but it doesn't happen by itself either. The main difference between a *pilot*, and someone who just happens to have a license is mastery of The Basics.

Chapter 2

Flight Planning

You can't *not* flight plan. Even if your flight plan consists of nothing more than making sure the tanks are full, the sky is clear and you know how to find the airport you want, you have flight planned. It isn't much of a flight plan, but it is a plan of sorts.

The question is not *when* to flight plan, but *how* to flight plan. What are the key elements? How can these elements be adapted to fit both short and simple flights and long, complex flights? How is the plan actually used in the airplane? In short, how do you plan a flight in such a way that there is no reasonable doubt that the flight will not be completed safely, routinely, and as planned?

It might be easiest to start with what flight planning is not. Flight planning is *not* just filling out a flight log, nor is a flight log something only student pilots use. Flight planning is the entire scheme of things: how you intend to get yourself from here to there, including cruising speed, departure time, altitude, routing, enroute time, fuel, alternates, weight-and-balance, and takeoff and landing runway lengths. The flight log portion of the flight plan is a specific, detailed breakdown of the enroute portion of the flight plan. It is not just an aid for student pilots, but an important part of most flight plans, regardless of pilot experience.

Another misconception is that flight planning for sophisticated and complex aircraft is different from flight planning for more typical general aviation aircraft. The process is exactly the same. The details will vary of course, depending on aircraft type, but the principles are the same. The only real difference—and it is a very minor one—is that turbine equipment is very often flight planned with the aid of computers. This is very advantageous for both operational and for economic reasons. With a computer it is a simple matter to change one variable (cruise altitude, for instance) and very quickly see how the change affects the flight, either time-wise (operational) or fuel-wise (economic). With the computer you can also run the problem "backwards"—that is, you can tell the computer to optimize the flight plan for fuel or time, and the computer will then figure out the best speed and altitude profile.

All this is very nice and saves the airlines and corporate flight departments who have this service large amounts of money, but it isn't anything you couldn't do by hand, given enough time. The advantage of the computer is that it works so fast that it can check out virtually all the variables for each flight and determine the exact profile—altitudes and speeds—for maximum fuel savings. Since the cost of fuel saved is so much greater than the cost of the computer, it makes sense for these operators to use the computer. Software for flight planning suitable for use on personal computers also is becoming widely available, bringing these same advantages to the private operator. But the result in every case is not something different, only something that is quicker, generally more accurate, and usually more economical.

One recurrent theme you will hear in this book is that flying for transportation is instrument flying. That means if you want to actually go somewhere (as opposed to just sightseeing or having fun in the local area), you file an instrument flight plan and follow instrument flight rules (IFR). You do this even though the atmospheric conditions may not require it.

Filing IFR solves all kinds of problems—and, I think, the more you fly, the clearer it will become that this is the smart thing to do. Whatever it costs to go IFR instead of VFR (Visual Flight Rules) in terms of time, trouble, or expense is irrelevant compared to the gains in consistency, security, separation, and potential assistance that the instrument system provides.

This isn't to say that pilotage (flying by reference to geographical features) or dead reckoning (estimated headings and times) isn't fun or won't work a good part of the time, but these basic navigational techniques just aren't accurate enough or reliable enough to use as a primary form of navigation and flight planning when the goal is reliable transportation. Lindbergh crossed the Atlantic using only dead reckoning, but he didn't have any choice—and at one point he had to circle low over some fishermen to ask the way to Ireland. Pilotage and dead reckoning do have a place as a backup in case of total electrical failure, but when we talk about flight planning in this chapter, we mean *instrument* flight planning.

MAJOR COMPONENTS

I think the easiest and most logical way to think about flight planning is to take a step back and look at the big picture. What are we trying to accomplish when we flight plan? It seems to me that what we are really trying to do is to be able to determine in advance that the successful completion of the flight is a virtual certainty. We can divide this task into two fundamental components: How to get there, and how much fuel to take. "How to get there" means we need a route and an altitude, and "how much fuel to take" means we need to know how long we will be in the air and how much fuel we expect to burn per hour.

For the simplest kind of flight—good weather to a nearby airport over a well known route—the flight planning might consist of nothing more than reviewing this information in enough detail to accurately complete a flight plan form and file an instrument flight plan (Fig. 2-1). But it is still flight planning. On a more complex flight, the flight planning would be much more detailed, with a written record made prior to takeoff, including the preparation of a flight log. But it still boils down to *how to get there and how much fuel to take.*

DESTINATION

I usually start my flight planning with the "there" in "how to get there"—the destination airport. One of the mistakes pilots often make is to automatically select the airport nearest to their ultimate destination. That is, if they are going to an office downtown, they select the nearest downtown airport. Or if they are going to visit a factory in a small town they automatically go to the airport listed for that town. This is very often a mistake, for several reasons.

The problem with using the nearest airport to the downtown business district—or the only airport for a small town—is that often these airports have less-than-optimum approach and landing aids. It doesn't make any sense to try to save time by using an airport with a VOR approach and fairly high minimums, miss the approach, and end up going to the "big" airport with the ILS and

Form Approved: OMB No. 04-R0072

DEPARTMENT OF TRANSPORTATION FEDERAL AVIATION ADMINISTRATION **FLIGHT PLAN**	CIVIL AIRCRAFT PILOTS. FAR Part 91 requires you file an IFR flight plan to operate under instrument flight rules in controlled airspace. Failure to file could result in a civil penalty not to exceed $1,000 for each violation (Section 901 of the Federal Aviation Act of 1958, as amended). Filing of a VFR flight plan is recommended as a good operating practice. See also Part 99 for requirements concerning DVFR flight plans.

1 TYPE	2 AIRCRAFT IDENTIFICATION	3 AIRCRAFT TYPE/ SPECIAL EQUIPMENT	4 TRUE AIRSPEED	5 DEPARTURE POINT	6 DEPARTURE TIME		7 CRUISING ALTITUDE
VFR					PROPOSED (Z)	ACTUAL (Z)	
IFR							
DVFR			KTS				

8 ROUTE OF FLIGHT

9 DESTINATION (Name of airport and city)	10 EST TIME ENROUTE		11 REMARKS
	HOURS	MINUTES	

12 FUEL ON BOARD		13 ALTERNATE AIRPORT(S)	14 PILOT'S NAME ADDRESS & TELEPHONE NUMBER & AIRCRAFT HOME BASE	15 NUMBER ABOARD
HOURS	MINUTES			

16 COLOR OF AIRCRAFT	CLOSE VFR FLIGHT PLAN WITH ____________ FSS ON ARRIVAL

FAA Form 7233-1 (5-77)

Fig. 2-1. Standard FAA Flight Plan form, available free of charge at all Flight Service Stations.

low minimums anyway. Since these smaller airports usually don't have any weather reports or forecasts, you really don't know what the weather is going to be when you get there, and missing the approach is a very real possibility in many cases. Sometimes you get in, but then the weather deteriorates below takeoff minimums. If you are operating Part 91 you can take off anyway, but you won't be able to see all the terrain and obstructions.

Why put yourself in that box? If you go to the major airport serving the area in the first place, you frequently end up *saving* time, and you almost always reduce the risks associated with non-precision approaches to minimums.

There are other operational reasons for not necessarily using the closest airport to your ultimate destination: The smaller and more remote airports and the secondary city airports tend to have major obstructions on the approaches (such as tall trees, power lines, and smoke stacks); they generally have shorter runways; they have more terrain induced turbulence; they are usually uncontrolled. The people may be friendly, the setting may be very picturesque, and they may be nice places to visit on a weekend or to go to an airshow, but in terms of safety they impose an additional element of risk that is unnecessary and not justified in most cases by the amount of time saved.

I know it's hard to overfly a close-in airport and drive a few extra miles for what often seems like no good reason at all. But, in fact, there are very *good* reasons. If you want your flying to be routine and safe, day in and day out, you have to put safety first, and in practical terms this means sometimes overflying less-than-completely-satisfactory airports. Everybody *says* "Safety first," but *doing* it when it involves a sacrifice of some sort is the real test. If you not only *say* "safety first," but also *mean* "safety first," you'll look for the best airport, not the closest.

Lastly, in practical terms, even when the weather cooperates and a safe arrival is accomplished, using smaller airports often does not even save time. Again and again I have seen passengers insist on going to the closest suitable airport to their destination, only to wait around for many minutes for a taxi to show up, or wait for the party being met (with the transportation) to find the airport, or count on getting a rental car only to discover that they don't have any. It's a fact of life that if the airport facilities are not all that great, the ground facilities are probably not all that great, either.

I am not saying that all small airports are bad; if the approach and takeoff minimums are satisfactory for the prevailing weather, the approaches are safe, the terrain non-precipitous, the runways long enough to provide a margin of safety, and you have called ahead to check on the services, fine. But check these things out. It is an important area of flight planning. If you're careful, you *can* make these airports work. My point is to remember that you usually have a choice—don't automatically plan on going to the airport that is closest to your destination.

The process I go through in selecting a destination airport is to first identify all the airports near my ultimate destination, and then automatically eliminate all those without instrument approaches. I then locate the closest one and check it out for suitability. If I have any question about it that I can't resolve with a phone call, I eliminate it—there is almost always a large metropolitan or regional airport fairly nearby, and I just don't want to take a chance on questionable facilities. The advantages of using these larger airports are so much greater than the disadvantages that they are generally the obvious choice. Selecting a major airport also makes the rest of the flight planning easier. We will go into that a little later.

If you are a little bit nervous about using the bigger airports—you aren't sure you can handle the traffic, or the controllers talk too fast, or you are hesitant to mix it up with airline traffic—there is no reason to be ashamed; we've all been there. You just need a little more dual with an experienced flight instructor. Then pick your time and plan your trip carefully, and try it. In all likelihood you will find flying to a major airport easier than to a smaller or less busy airport. Everything is predictable and smooth at the bigger airports, and you have company to show you the way. Pretty soon you'll wonder why you ever did it any other way.

PREFERRED ROUTES

Having selected a destination airport, the next step is to find the best routing. (We're assuming here that this is a trip you can easily make nonstop. We will go into longer trips requiring a planned stop further on in the chapter.) If you are going to one of the bigger airports around a major city, including one of the major general aviation airports, the first place to check for routings is the Preferred Routings section of your instrument charts. This section shows routings between a variety of major city pairs. If you are going from Boston to Chicago, for instance, the exact routing from takeoff to initial approach fix will be listed. Your routing problems are over for that trip.

Even if you are not leaving from a major airport, the preferred routings are still helpful. Look up the departure city that is near your actual place of departure, and use as much of that routing as you can. Generally you will have to figure out how to get on the routing after takeoff, but after that it will be the same. You can even use these routings to give you an idea of what ATC expects you to file if one of the routes goes over or near your departure point. For instance, the routing between Boston and Chicago goes right over Utica, Syracuse, Rochester and Buffalo. If you are departing from one of these cities, all you need to do is to get yourself onto the routing that goes overhead, and the rest of the preferred routing will still apply.

If you have done much instrument flying you have probably figured out by now that "preferred" really means "expected" or "normal." You can always file something else, but the preferred routing is what you are going to get. Once in the air, all kinds of changes are possible depending on the traffic and the controller, but the initial clearance will almost always be for the preferred routing. There is no point in trying to fight it. Naturally, if you have a good reason for wanting to go another way (and "because it's shorter" is not a good reason, but to avoid mountainous terrain or a line of thunderstorms would be), say so in the remarks section of the flight plan. But be prepared to wait until ATC can accommodate your request. Special requests generally go to the end of the line.

Actually, there are lots of preferred routings, but only a few are published. Practicality dictates that standard patterns of arrival and departure be established for all major airports, with appropriate transitions for the satellites.

One way to find out what those routings are is to go to a Center facility and ask a supervisor for a briefing on how the arrivals and departures are handled in that center—but he probably doesn't have the time for such a request, and at any rate it isn't necessary. Knowing what the routings are ahead of time can help in flight planning, but it isn't essential—you will be told what you need to know. Experience is the best way to find out what these routings are. After you have flown a particular route several times you will start to learn the patterns.

In the absence of experience, ask local pilots; they can usually tell you what the local arrival and departure patterns are. These patterns aren't normally published and probably won't be; there are just too many and they change too much.

One way to get a clue as to what the likely arrival routings are, if you are unfamiliar with the area and there is no one to ask, is to look for the published holding fixes around the major airport in the area. These will normally also be the major arrival fixes, because that is where the controllers stack the arrivals when the approaches are saturated. Enroute or departure holding fixes aren't depicted because they are only needed rarely and in a random fashion; arrival holds are fairly common. So if you see a published hold on a chart, it probably is part of an arrival routing.

When all else fails, don't worry about getting the exact preferred or expected routing. Just file the route that looks like it makes the most sense. Watch out for restricted areas and try to file using airways, with direct routings only as a last resort, and you may be pleasantly surprised and get the routing you file. This is good—your flight log will still be valid (more on this later). If you don't get it, you'll have to make the changes to the flight log in the air. Sorry, old man. Part of the game, you know.

DISTANCE

After you have a routing, the next step is to measure the distance between each fix and add them all up to get the total distance for the trip. Try to make this as accurate as possible (without being ridiculous). That is, take into account known vectors and circuitous routings after takeoff; don't just measure from the departure point to the first fix unless you expect to actually go directly to that fix. Account for each of the legs between VORs separately, and measure (with a plotter) the distances between direct fixes. From the initial approach fix to the airport measure the distance directly; there is no way to know which approach you will get or how you will be vectored, or even if you will get an approach, so greater accuracy here is impossible.

The result is total distance and that is what you will use for your initial flight planning. Remember the two main components of flight planning: How to get there, and how much fuel to take. You now know how to get there, and with the total mileage you can go to work on the fuel.

ALTITUDE SELECTION

To determine fuel consumption rates you need to know what altitude you intend to file for and at what percent of power you intend to run the engine or engines.

First, what altitude to file? If weather were never a factor and the winds were always calm, the only factor would be distance: The longer the trip, the higher the altitude, up to the practical ceiling of the aircraft. Altitude is where the greatest gain in aerodynamic efficiency is. You *could*, for instance, go on a long trip at 3000 feet, but would save time or fuel or a little of both by going at a higher altitude. Let's look at an actual example from real life, using the Beech F33A Bonanza, to see exactly what the savings are. These figures and illustrations come directly from the Beech *Pilot's Operating Handbook and FAA Approved Flight Manual*.

Referring to Fig. 2-2, and using the column for "Standard Day (ISA)," we see that at 3,000 feet the F33 will use 15.2 gallons per hour at 75 percent power while cruising 167 knots true airspeed. At a constant rate of fuel flow, the airspeed increases about 1 1/2 knots for each 1,000 feet you climb, up to 6,000 feet. After that point the speed starts to drop off, but so does the fuel flow, for a net gain. In fact, by climbing to 11,000 feet, the same airspeed can be achieved as at 3,000 feet while reducing the fuel flow to 13.1 gph. (The principle is the same for turbocharged aircraft, but the effect tends to be spread out over a wider range of altitudes.) Clearly, there is a gain in efficiency with altitude.

The question is: "How much of a gain is there?" You have probably been taught to take advantage of these gains in efficiency at the higher altitudes—and, to the extent winds and weather are not factors, that is correct. But the simple fact is that the gains are small. For a Beech Bonanza, climbing from 3,000 to 11,000 feet saves approximately 3.7 gallons on a trip of 300 nautical miles. At $2.00 per gallon, that's $7.40—less than you'll spend for a typical airport lunch. Alternately, stopping the climb at 7000 feet saves 0.8 gallons and two minutes on a 300 nautical mile trip. On shorter trips the savings are, of course, even less.

I'll say again: If winds and weather are not a factor, go high—it doesn't cost a thing and may save a little time or fuel or both. But winds and weather are almost always factors, and their importance almost always outweighs the small gains in efficiency that come with altitude. So altitude selection will normally be a process of picking the right altitude based on optimizing the tailwinds, minimizing the headwinds, and avoiding the unfavorable and hazardous weather.

From a practical point of view, what altitudes are available to choose from? The Bonanza Manual lists cruise figures from sea level to 16,000 feet. While the theoretical bottom of the bracket is

CRUISE POWER SETTINGS

75% MAXIMUM CONTINUOUS POWER (OR FULL THROTTLE) 2500 RPM
3200 POUNDS

PRESS ALT	ISA -36°F (-20°C)								STANDARD DAY (ISA)								ISA +36°F (+20°C)							
	IOAT		ENGINE SPEED	MAN. PRESS.	FUEL FLOW		TAS	CAS	IOAT		ENGINE SPEED	MAN. PRESS.	FUEL FLOW		TAS	CAS	IOAT		ENGINE SPEED	MAN. PRESS.	FUEL FLOW		TAS	CAS
FEET	°F	°C	RPM	IN HG	PPH	GPH	KTS	KTS	°F	°C	RPM	IN HG	PPH	GPH	KTS	KTS	°F	°C	RPM	IN HG	PPH	GPH	KTS	KTS
SL	27	-3	2500	23.9	91.4	15.2	159	165	63	17	2500	24.6	91.4	15.2	163	163	100	38	2500	25.1	91.4	15.2	166	161
1000	24	-5	2500	23.6	91.4	15.2	161	164	60	16	2500	24.3	91.4	15.2	164	162	96	36	2500	24.8	91.4	15.2	168	160
2000	20	-7	2500	23.4	91.4	15.2	162	163	56	14	2500	24.1	91.4	15.2	166	161	93	34	2500	24.6	91.4	15.2	169	159
3000	17	-8	2500	23.1	91.4	15.2	164	163	53	12	2500	23.8	91.4	15.2	167	160	89	32	2500	24.3	91.4	15.2	171	158
4000	13	-10	2500	22.8	91.4	15.2	165	162	49	10	2500	23.5	91.4	15.2	169	159	86	30	2500	24.0	91.4	15.2	172	157
5000	10	-12	2500	22.5	91.4	15.2	167	161	46	8	2500	23.2	91.4	15.2	170	158	82	28	2500	23.7	91.4	15.2	173	156
6000	6	-14	2500	22.2	91.4	15.2	168	160	43	6	2500	23.0	91.4	15.2	172	157	79	26	2500	23.5	89.7	15.0	174	153
7000	3	-16	2500	22.0	91.4	15.2	169	159	39	4	2500	22.6	89.7	15.0	172	155	75	24	2500	22.6	86.7	14.5	172	150
8000	-1	-18	2500	21.7	89.4	14.9	169	156	35	2	2500	21.7	86.5	14.4	170	151	71	22	2500	21.7	83.6	13.9	171	147
9000	-4	-20	2500	20.8	86.5	14.4	168	153	32	0	2500	20.8	83.7	14.0	169	148	68	20	2500	20.8	81.0	13.5	170	143
10000	-8	-22	2500	20.0	83.7	14.0	167	150	28	-2	2500	20.0	81.0	13.5	168	145	64	18	2500	20.0	78.3	13.1	168	140
11000	-12	-24	2500	19.2	80.9	13.5	166	146	24	-4	2500	19.2	78.3	13.1	167	142	60	16	2500	19.2	75.7	12.6	167	137
12000	-15	-26	2500	18.3	78.2	13.0	165	143	21	-6	2500	18.3	75.7	12.6	165	139	57	14	2500	18.3	73.1	12.2	165	133
13000	-19	-28	2500	17.6	75.4	12.6	163	139	17	-8	2500	17.6	73.0	12.2	164	135	53	12	2500	17.6	70.6	11.8	163	129
14000	-23	-30	2500	16.8	72.9	12.2	162	136	13	-10	2500	16.8	70.6	11.8	162	131	49	10	2500	16.8	68.3	11.4	162	128
15000	-26	-32	2500	16.1	70.4	11.7	160	133	10	-12	2500	16.1	68.2	11.4	160	127	46	8	2500	16.1	66.0	11.0	159	122
16000	-30	-34	2500	15.4	68.1	11.4	158	129	6	-14	2500	15.4	65.9	11.0	158	124	42	6	2500	15.4	63.7	10.6	156	118

NOTES:
1. Full throttle manifold pressure settings are approximate.
2. Shaded areas represent operation with full throttle.

Fig. 2-2. Cruise power setting chart for the Beech Bonanza at 75 percent power. (Courtesy of Beech Aircraft Corporation.)

therefore sea level, in practice the lowest IFR altitude available (Minimum Enroute Altitude—MEA) is 2,000 feet, and this is found only in flat country near the ocean; generally, MEAs will be higher. The first step in determining your altitude "bracket" is to scan your route for MEAs. The highest MEA found indicates the lowest altitude you want to file for. (It's not a good idea to file for an MEA lower than that allowed for any one segment of the trip if you can possibly help it. If both you and the controller forget to climb to the higher MEA prior to reaching it, the outcome could be disastrous.) So the *highest* MEA represents the *lowest* available altitude.

The theoretical top of the bracket is either the service ceiling or the highest altitude shown in the performance charts, which is 16,000 feet for the F33A Bonanza. The rate of climb upon reaching the service ceiling will be between 50 and 100 feet per minute (fpm), and that is not enough to hold altitude, even in smooth air. The slightest disturbance will result in more than 100 feet of deviation in altitude, which is not acceptable. You need at least a 200 fpm rate of climb remaining to maintain altitude, and 300 fpm is better. If your manual doesn't have a chart showing fpm remaining upon reaching a given altitude, it's easy enough to figure it out for yourself. Load your airplane up to max gross takeoff weight and climb as high as you can at best rate of climb speed. When the rate of climb has dropped to a steady 300 fpm, that is your maximum (practical) service ceiling. You could call this the Real Service Ceiling (as opposed to the Theoretical Service Ceiling.)

Without supplemental oxygen, I would limit the maximum altitude to 11,000 feet, regardless of the climb capabilities of the aircraft. I personally feel the regulations are too loose in allowing anything higher. (According to FAR 91.32, oxygen is required after 30 minutes between 12,500 and 14,000, and all the time above 14,000.) Even a healthy young pilot who doesn't smoke will start to get short of breath above 11,000, and the rest of us even lower. An older pilot who smokes probably shouldn't go higher than 8,000 feet without oxygen. If you want to flight plan higher than that, you should have oxygen available. You don't have to keep the mask on all the time at the lower altitudes, but you should at least have it available for regular use—maybe one minute every 10 or 15 minutes, and for several minutes prior to descent. At night I would halve these intervals; your eyes are very large consumers of oxygen.

I will admit to being skeptical as to the practicality of using supplemental oxygen for any length of time. I will also admit to not having tried it. All my flying has either been below 12,000 feet or in pressurized aircraft. If you have found it practical and comfortable, fine, but I remain skeptical. I think unpressurized high altitude flight, for normal civilian transportation, pushes the limits of practicality—and possibly safety.

To summarize, then: in a nonpressurized airplane, the maximum useful altitude range is 2,000 to 11,000 feet without supplemental oxygen, and with oxygen, whatever the highest altitude obtainable is with 300 fpm rate of climb remaining. For the F33A this is about 15,000 feet for most temperatures and weights. Acceptance of this bracket simplifies the altitude selection process considerably.

So where have we gotten? We have narrowed our range of altitudes down to no lower than 2,000 feet and normally (no oxygen or pressurization) no higher than 11,000 feet, and we have determined that the winds aloft and weather are much more important factors in determining a cruise altitude than efficiency per se. We still have to decide which of these two remaining factors—winds aloft and weather—is the more important.

No one wants to flight plan into horrendous winds at altitude, nor intentionally give up a nice tailwind. Most pilots fly because they like to go fast, and minimizing headwinds and maximizing tailwinds is part of the game.

But headwinds and tailwinds are factors of time and money. Weather involves safety, and that has to take priority. I think even comfort takes some priority over speed. I don't like flying in or under bumpy clouds, and most passengers hate it, regardless of what they tell you. I think getting on top is very desirable and worth a headwind penalty. I know staying out of the ice is worth a headwind penalty, and I know staying underneath towering CUs and out of heavy precipitation and turbulence and avoiding embedded thunderstorms is worth giving up a tailwind for.

So I think the first step toward selecting an altitude has to be a look at the weather—and especially any current pilot reports. Where are the tops? Where is the ice? What kind of turbulence can be expected in the clouds? What sort of convective activity can be expected? How high do I have to go to get on top or above the ice? How low do I have to go to stay out of the towering CUs or stay beneath the ice? These are the questions to ask first in selecting an altitude.

In some cases—maybe even in *many* cases—none of these limiting factors will exist. The weather gods don't always bring ice, turbulence, and thunderstorms. When they don't, you can go to the winds and maximize the tailwind or minimize your headwind. Since the winds almost always increase rapidly with altitude, the selection process becomes a simple one of going high with a tail-wind and low with a headwind. With no wind or a crosswind, you might as well go as high as is practical for the trip length.

The more performance and altitude capability your aircraft has the more complex the process of altitude selection is—which is one reason turbine powered aircraft are frequently flight planned with computers; fuel flows for turbines drop off very dramatically with altitude, but the headwinds can also increase very dramatically. When does the fuel saved get lost in going slower? This is a very tedious question to answer without a computer to do the legwork.

The problem for non-turbine equipment is of an altogether different sort. The basic question here is "What is the smartest altitude from a safety and comfort point of view?"

This is really a harder question to answer; you can't put numbers in a computer and wait for an answer. The way to answer the question is to organize it—develop a list of priorities. First, limit your choice of altitudes to a practical range. Second, look at the operational considerations—the weather. Basically, you are looking for a smooth, ice-free and preferably even cloud-free ride. If all the altitudes are problem free, then look at the winds: headwind low, tailwind high. When this happens it's like getting something for free. You go low one direction to duck under the strong headwinds, then go high the other direction to ride with it as a tailwind—nice work if you can get it.

POWER SELECTION

Exactly what percent of power to use is a question we are going to examine in some detail in the chapter on Cruise Control, so I'm not going to get into the specifics of how to go about deciding that question right now. The important point here is to select a given percent of power in order to determine what we can expect for a true airspeed and fuel flow. The ins and outs of exactly which power chart to use can wait, but without specific cruise information our flight planning is going to be a rough guess, at best.

ESTIMATING TIME AND FUEL

We now know where we are going, over what route, at what altitude, and have settled on a cruise power setting schedule. The remaining important questions are "How long will it take," and "How much fuel will we burn?" How long will it take is dependent on the groundspeed, which means we have to determine the headwind or tailwind component for the trip.

The accuracy of the groundspeed estimate will be directly proportional to the amount of time you put into analyzing the winds aloft information. The simplest and least accurate way is to "eyeball" an average headwind or tailwind component, using the closest winds aloft altitude (3,000, 6,000, 9,000, etc.) and as many stations as are available.

This is okay, but a little more effort will give much better results. For instance, mentally averaging as above, but then getting out a "whiz-wheel" to compute the actual *component* will result in a much more accurate average groundspeed estimate. (Winds of 270 at 100 is not a 100 knot headwind if the true course is 240—it's more like an 85 knot headwind.)

For *maximum* accuracy, you have to interpolate the winds aloft forecasts for your specific cruising altitude (unless it happens to be one of the altitudes for which winds aloft are forecast—3,000, 6,000, 9,000, etc.) for each station along your route of flight, and then compute a groundspeed estimate for each leg using the closest reporting point. This is a lot of work, but if you have the time, it will pay off in computer-like accuracy. With this kind of accuracy you can hit time estimates within a minute or two and fuel estimates within a gallon or two, even over max range distances.

The choice is yours, but the less accurate the groundspeed estimating method, the more conservative the fuel estimates have to be to compensate. The pilot who "eyeballs" a long trip and says it looks like he should land with about an hour's fuel is a fool looking for trouble, but the pilot who determines a specific groundspeed estimate for each leg and says he should land with 57 minutes of fuel probably will.

True airspeed comes from the performance charts; adding or subtracting the tailwind or headwind component (respectively) will give you estimated groundspeed. Groundspeed and distance will determine enroute time per leg; fuel flow (which you also know from your performance charts) and time will give you estimated fuel used per leg. Totaling the leg estimates results in total time enroute and total fuel required.

You now know all the important flight planning facts including time enroute and fuel required. Note that time enroute is really just a curiosity piece at this point; its only operational value is to provide fuel burn. But it will assume great importance as the flight progresses, because comparing estimated times to actual times will provide a valuable early indicator of whether you are using more or less fuel than planned.

RESERVES

Obviously we have to put on more fuel than just enough to get to our destination—there is an unpublished rule that says we must always land with *some* fuel. The regulations call for 45 minutes of additional fuel at "normal cruising power." If you flight plan for 55 percent power, then you must plan on having 45 minutes of fuel remaining based on fuel flow at 55 percent power. If you flight plan for 75 percent power, then the required reserve will be proportionately higher. The faster you go, the higher the fuel flows, and the more reserve required. Fuel flows for the Bonanza vary from 15.2 gph at 75 percent power to 9.6 gph at 45 percent. This results in an 11.4 gallon reserve at 75 percent, and 7.2 gallons at 45 percent. These are minimums—there is no law against carrying more. The point here is that 45 minutes of fuel is not an absolute. It depends on what cruise regime you follow.

Obviously you want to "err" on the high side. I don't believe in tankering around a lot of extra fuel "for mama and the kids" and all the rest of that nonsense, but there is nothing wrong with figuring a generous amount of fuel as your personal "standard minimum reserve." I assume that if I really end up needing this 45 minute reserve, I am probably going to be doing approaches, missed approaches and climbs, not just cruising along at altitude. Therefore, I assume a higher-than-normal fuel consumption during the entire 45 minutes. In the Falcon 20, for example, low-altitude flying at high power settings generally results in 3000 pounds of fuel burned per hour, so I automatically use 2500 pounds of fuel as a standard reserve. This is actually 50 minutes of fuel at 3000 pounds per hour, and more than an hour at any of the "normal" cruise power settings, but it is a nice even number well on the conservative side. Since it is already conservative, I don't feel any need to "throw a little more on," either.

The unnecessary fuel you carry around is not only uneconomical, but, more importantly, it robs you of performance you may need to climb above ice, clear obstacles, or get stopped safely in an aborted takeoff or maximum effort landing. A little extra reserve fuel is fine, but there *is* a safety tradeoff involved in carrying extra fuel; citing "safety" as the reason for loading on bunches of extra fuel is usually a cover-up for laziness and poor flight planning.

To continue the example of the Bonanza then, I would start with 45 minutes of fuel at 75 percent power. Figure 2-2 shows fuel flow of 15.2 gph at 75 percent power, which is 11.4 gallons for 45 minutes. I would add two gallons for a go-around or missed approach and "round it up" to 15 gallons as my standard reserve. Therefore, after figuring the fuel requirements to actually reach the destination, I would automatically add 15 gallons to that figure in order to determine my required fuel load, and in so doing I would feel very confident that I was both safe and legal.

ALTERNATES

What about an alternate? The regulations require an alternate if, for one hour before and one after the estimated time of arrival at the destination airport, the weather is forecast to be less than a ceiling of 2000 feet or visibility less than 3 miles. In other words, the destination weather has to be somewhat *better* than minimum VFR, or you must have an alternate. This includes any *possibility* that the weather will be less than 2000 and 3, which means the words or phrases "chance of," "occasional," or "variable" also apply. In the Northeast the forecasts almost always include something less than 2000 feet broken or overcast or visibility less than 3 miles, so I have gotten in the habit of always having an alternate. Besides, even good forecasts occasionally go completely belly-up, and airports are sometimes closed for reasons having nothing to do with the weather, the most common being disabled aircraft on the runways. In many countries an alternate is required to file IFR regardless of the weather, and that makes sense to me. Backups are always a good idea.

But the main reason I always like to have an alternate is because I almost ran out of gas once when I didn't have one and should have (even though it wasn't required). I was flying copilot on a Hawker-Siddeley 125-600. We were in Boston, the weather was good—high overcast with good visibility and forecast to stay that way—and we had a short deadhead hop to Westfield, Mass., about 20 minutes away. We didn't have a whole lot of fuel, but we did have enough to fly 20 minutes plus maybe 45 or 50 minutes reserve, so off we went. About halfway there, just over Worchester, we ran into a wall of snow—a regular blizzard. This was unexpected, but not much of a problem in itself since we had filed IFR anyway—but it did mean having to shoot an approach at Westfield.

We checked the weather there and it was snowing hard but well above ILS minimums—still no problem. Except at this point the controller told us to hold over the beacon at Westfield; we were number three for the approach. *That* was a little bit of a problem— waiting for two approaches would use up a good part of our 45 minute reserve.

Then the *really* bad news: no one was being cleared for any approaches. The hold was indefinite. We asked for an expected approach clearance time and he said he really didn't know, "call it an hour," but it might have to be extended.

The Captain said, "That's no good, ask him for a clearance to Bradley" (about 10 minutes south of Westfield). The controller said Bradley wasn't conducting any approaches either. We kind of looked at each other, and the Captain said—with some impatience— "Well, ask him for an approach back to Worcester."

This time the controller came back with: "Look, there aren't any approaches being approved anywhere in the approach area. I've got a guy lost in the clouds and we're trying to find him. Stand by."

Stand by? What does he mean, "Stand by"? We were less than an hour away from logging some multiengine glider time. But there was nothing to do but get to work and look up the max endurance power settings and compute the time remaining. Just as I picked up the mike to tell the controller that our time to fuel exhaustion was no more than 50 minutes, he said they had just found the lost pilot and had reopened the approaches. He cleared the number one aircraft holding for the approach, and we were, in turn, given vectors for the approach and ultimately landed safely, legally—and shaken. "Never again" I said, and never again have I.

It took a series of unlikely events for this to become a problem, which is the way problems in aviation usually happen. We were tight on fuel to start with, the forecast was wrong, and someone got lost. But I learned that a series of unlikely events *can* happen, and from that point on I have always planned on having enough fuel to get to an alternate, no matter what the weather is forecast to be. If you follow this rule, you can forget about the hour before and hour after business—the 3000 over and 2, or is it 2000 over and 3?—forever. Again.

To be a legal alternate, the alternate must be forecast to be at or above alternate minimums at the time of arrival at the alternate airport. Alternate minimums are 600 foot ceiling and 2 miles visibility if the airport has an ILS to 200 and 1/2, higher for others as published on the back of the Jepp chart. There is no "hour before and hour after" business, just "at the time of arrival at the alternate." These minimums are deliberately higher than required to complete an approach: 600 and 2 verses the usual 200 and 1/2 ILS minimums. This conservatism is intentional. It is meant to ensure that when you take off you will have somewhere to land. This extra margin means the alternate can be as much as 400 feet worse than forecast on the ceiling, and a mile and a half below forecast on the visibility, and still be at or above minimums.

The FAA doesn't specifically say so, but they really don't want you hopping from airport to airport, trying approaches until you finally make one—or run out of fuel, whichever comes first. Another unwritten rule is: "Once you miss an approach, don't fool around anymore—go to your alternate and land." It doesn't make sense to carry extra fuel just to keep trying approaches at different airports. If the fuel runs low before you find an airport you can get into, you've got a real problem on your hands. When you take off, barring very unusual circumstances such as an emergency or truly extraordinary weather, you should plan on landing at one of two airports: your filed destination, or your filed alternate. Anything else probably means you took a chance.

Once in a while, when a very powerful weather system dominates a large area, it can be very hard to find an alternate. If the entire area is forecasting low ceilings or visibility due to snow, heavy rain, or fog, sometimes the only airport without some mention of ceilings below 600 feet, or visibilities less than 2 miles, will be several hundred miles away. It hurts to have to file and fuel for an alternate so far away, especially when the weather has been low but still well above landing minimums all day, and you are virtually certain you will make the approach at your destination. And it *really* hurts when the nearest legal alternate is so far away that even with full fuel you can't go to your destination, proceed to your alternate and land with 45 minutes of fuel—and therefore can't go, even though the weather at the destination is above minimums. But that doesn't happen often, and that is the system and adhering to it has kept a lot of pilots from running out of gas for a long time.

The FAA also requires you to fuel for any "known" delays. Actual reported delays are very rare these days. Most known delays are absorbed on the ground and do not require extra fuel. But I like to interpret the rule broadly and conservatively, just for myself, by thinking of "known" delays as meaning "likely" or "expected" delays. Thus, I always assume there will be delays going into major metropolitan airports like LaGuardia, Kennedy, O'Hare, Atlanta, Houston, Denver, and LA. The delays are usually fairly short—20 to 30 minutes—but not at all unusual, so I put on an extra 30 minutes worth of fuel going to these airports. If you fly to an airport that regularly has delays, you should fuel for that expectation also.

To summarize reserve fuel planning then: 1). Always have a legal alternate. 2).Fuel your trip to be able to go to the destination, continue on to that alternate, and land with a "fat" 45 minutes of fuel plus an allowance for known or expected delays. 3). If you miss your approach at the destination, go to your alternate and land.

When the inevitable happens, and you do miss the approach at your destination airport, you are entitled to be a little irritated when you finally taxi in to your alternate, but you are also entitled to give yourself a little pat on the back—you completed another safe flight, under difficult circumstances, routinely and uneventfully, and that's what it's all about.

AIRCRAFT FUELING

We have now completed all the basic flight planning: destination, route, altitude, time, and fuel. One of the more important "numbers" that comes out of this exercise is the total fuel required, which varies depending on the conditions that prevail at the expected time of departure (in particular, winds aloft and the choice of an alternate). It therefore follows that the airplane cannot be properly fueled until the flight planning is complete.

This is contrary to common practice. Most pilots routinely fill the tanks after landing. This is more convenient, and it does minimize condensation in the fuel tanks (although condensation shouldn't be a problem in a frequently flown and thoroughly preflighted airplane), but the extra fuel you end up tankering carries a weight—and therefore a performance—penalty. (Extra weight also carries, of course, an economic penalty.) The proper way to do it is to complete the flight planning, and *then* fuel the airplane, putting on enough fuel to bring the total load up to the required amount. I guess you can make bigger mistakes than to overfuel an airplane, but it's still a mistake.

FLIGHT LOGS

We have been talking here about the general principles of flight planning, and for short trips over well known routes with good weather, the flight planning we have done so far is sufficient and provides reasonably accurate information for filing the instrument flight plan. We know how long the trip should take given the winds aloft that were forecast, we have designated a conservative alternate and have allowed for a substantial reserve, and we have fueled the aircraft accordingly. Checking our progress at the halfway and three quarters-way points for the effects of unforecast winds, changes in altitudes or routings, or the application of carburetor heat on our reserve fuel is usually sufficient to keep us aware of any impending problems in time to do something about it.

On a longer trip, or for a trip over a route that we don't know well or where the weather is questionable—and, in any case, for the first 100 hours in any new airplane—a flight log is essential. There is nothing like the peace of mind that comes with having a good flight log to refer to as the flight progresses, nor is there a better way to get to know an airplane.

A flight log is a detailed breakdown of the flight plan, fix by fix, showing your time and fuel estimates for each leg, which you update with actual times and fuel burns as you go. As you go along, entering and comparing actual time enroute to estimated time enroute, and actual fuel remaining to estimated fuel remaining, the times will either be early, right on, or late, and the fuel will either seem to "grow," stay the same, or "shrink." The figures and the trends are right there in front of you—no surprises. If the fuel consumption for the first leg is higher than expected, you are put on alert. Maybe it was just a fluke and the next leg and the next are right on. But if the next leg turns out high also, you'd better do some checking while you still have lots of fuel. Maybe the winds are stronger than forecast; maybe the airplane has something dragging (like a step that didn't retract or a baggage door that isn't closing tightly); maybe the airplane is out of rig; maybe you forgot to lean the engine—any of these factors would cause the fuel flows to be higher than "book." Or maybe you made a mistake reading the charts or a mistake in the arithmetic. *This* is the time to find out, not with 100 miles to go, no good airports underneath you, and the fuel remaining indicators bouncing around the bottom of the gauge.

I don't think a flight log has to be complex, or cluttered up with all kinds of navigational information like VOR frequencies or drift angles. The VOR frequencies can come right off the enroute chart; the drift angles will take care of themselves. "Keep it simple" is my motto. The main elements are distance, time, fuel burn, fuel remaining, and groundspeed. A sample flight log for a typical trip from Boston to Buffalo, using perfomance figures for the F33A Bonanza, is shown in Fig. 2-3.

There is nothing sacred about this particular format. If you have a format you are comfortable with, by all means use it. I kind of like this one because I invented it. (Little joke there.) If I had to defend it, I would say I like it because it is simple, it works from left to right in logical fashion, and the most important number— actual fuel remaining—is all the way on the right where it stands out and can be seen easily. It does take a little "sideways" adding and subtracting; if you want to be able to add or subtract directly under the appropriate number you will have to modify the form to combine those columns. This will make the arithmetic easier, but I think it adds clutter and a little bit of confusion to the form. It's up to you.

I just can't emphasis enough how important I feel it is to maintain a good flight log. Every time I have had a problem with a flight it has been because I took off relying on approximations and "rules of thumb" instead of careful flight planning, and I didn't have a flight log to tell me early on that a problem was developing. A minor problem can become a major problem when you fail to realize soon enough that you *have* a problem. Scrambling around trying to solve a problem at the last minute doesn't make sense any time, but *especially* not in an airplane. An airplane won't stand still—it has to keep moving or it falls down. The time you spend trying to solve the problem (once you are finally aware of the problem) is more time lost. This creates pressure, and pressure is not conductive to good decision making. The best prevention is information and the best way to organize that information is with a flight log.

LONG TRIPS

I said earlier that I would say something about long trips that can either be done in one long, max-range hop or broken up with a stop, and the pros and cons of each. In general, I always go with the planned stop. Too often when you try a long leg, you have to make a stop anyway when the winds don't work out as planned, or ATC needs you at a less fuel efficient altitude, or the weather deteriorates at the destination and your fuel reserves are no longer adequate. You end up getting the worst of both worlds this way: First you go slowly to stretch the range, and then you have to come

Dep. Point	Total Dist.	Total Time	Time Off	Total Fuel		Workspace
BOS	355	2+48	0700	Estimated : 64.0	Actual :	

Fix	Dist.	Dist. Rem.	Est. GS	Actual GS	ETE	ETA	ATA	Fuel Req.	Fuel Rem.	Actual Fuel
CTR	87	268	140	143	+37+05	0742	0742	10.7	53.3	54
ALB	48	220	140	144	+21	0803	0802	5.3	48.0	50
UCA	62	158	140	141	+27	0830	0828	6.9	41.1	43
SYR	46	112	140	139	+20	0850	0848	5.1	36.0	37
ROC	65	47	140	139	+28	0918	0917	7.1	28.9	30
BUF	47	0	140	138	+20+10	0948	0948	6.3	22.6	25
								41.4		

Workspace:

Route: BOS to BUF via direct CTR V203 ALB V2 BUF.
Altitude: 6000
Power: 75%
Winds: 270 at 32 (ISA)

Alternate: ROC

Fuel: BOS-BUF 41.1
BUF-ROC 4.6
Reserve 15.0
60.7

Notes: 1. The easiest way to allow for the additional time to climb to altitude is to add 5 minutes to the first leg.
2. On the last leg add 10 minutes to allow for an approach and traffic pattern.

Abbreviations: Dist.=Distance   Dep.=Departure   Rem.=Remaining
Est.=Estimated   Act.=Actual   GS=Ground Speed   ETE=Estimated
Time Enroute   ETA=Estimated Time of Arrival   ATA=Actual Time of Arrival

Fig. 2-3. Sample flight log, based on a typical trip in a Beech Bonanza from Boston to Buffalo. This example shows what the completed flight log might look like at the end of the trip.

down and make a fuel stop anyway and refile the next leg. If there is any question about the nonstop range I think it makes sense to plan a stop in the first place. (In the chapter on Cruise Control we will talk about what to do when a stop isn't possible or desirable.) A well-planned stop doesn't have to cost more than 15 or 20 minutes in ground time, and the break is usually appreciated. The time spent on the ground for the turnaround can very often be made up enroute—the two shorter legs can be flown faster since fuel is no longer a factor.

This isn't an absolute—I have planned long legs using long-range cruise techniques and they have worked and there is a certain satisfaction in maximizing the full range capability of an airplane. But it seems like nine times out of ten, if the leg is too long to be done at normal cruising speed, but *is* possible at a slower cruise speed, it ends up not working and requiring an intermediate stop.

WEIGHT-AND-BALANCE

The last part of flight planning is assuring that the weight-and-balance is within limits. This may not seem like a logical part of flight planning, but if you keep in mind that the purpose of flight planning is to provide a highly probable assurance that the flight can be successfully accomplished, then you can see that weight-and-balance is a part of flight planning. Assuring that the weight is below max gross, that any zero fuel weight limitations are observed, and that the balance is within the normal envelope is an integral part of the flight planning scheme.

If you were operating under Part 135 or 121, the regulations that cover Air Taxi and Airline Operations respectively, you would have to actually do a weight-and-balance computation for every flight. The airlines use computers for this, of course; air taxi companies frequently develop a "system" to simplify the task—charts that list all possible combinations of fuel, baggage, and passengers—but one way or another it is done for every leg, showing loaded weight of the aircraft and the location of the CG. These guys fly the same airplane day after day, and the FAA still requires them to do a weight-and-balance for each leg—but you almost never hear of an airline or charter flight crashing due to improper weight-and-balance.

Every year airplanes operating under Part 91 do crash because of overweight or out-of-balance conditions, and these crashes are completely avoidable. I think it is fairly easy to see how they happen, though. Most of the time airplanes are automatically within the weight-and-balance limits. Airplanes are designed to be in balance in normal use, and the typical load doesn't exceed the max weight limit. But it is very easy to have the exceptions sneak by.

For instance, if you verified at one point that your airplane is within limits with full fuel and two passengers, and you have flown the airplane that way any number of times without a problem, you may not think to recheck the weight-and-balance when your two passengers for a particular flight are big guys with heavy bags and they both sit in the back with the bags behind them. It just kind of sneaks by until you take off and notice the airplane doesn't handle right and is not performing well—or worse. To simply say, "If there's any doubt I always check," really doesn't get it, because you don't always doubt when you should. If you include weight-and-balance as a *regular* part of your flight planning, those situations that exceed the limits won't get by you.

FLIGHT PLANNING AS PLANNING

I flew for several years for a corporation that went from being a $100 million company to a $1 billion company in ten years. Their flight department started with a Cessna 401 and now consists of a Citation, a Falcon 10, and a Falcon 50. (The Falcon 20 has been traded in.) When the Chairman was asked in an interview for one of the leading financial journals what his secret was, he said simply, "There's no secret. Everything is done according to plan." This company didn't just set a goal of $1 billion and then tell everyone to work real hard and hope it happened. It had a specific plan describing for itself exactly how it intended to go about becoming a $1 billion company. It put the plan into action, monitored its own progress, and made changes as necessary to stay "on plan."

This is what *flight* planning is all about, with the significant advantage that in the case of flight planning you have enough information to determine in advance whether your plan is achievable or not. Develop a plan, put it into action, monitor its progress, and make changes as necessary to assure its successful and uneventful outcome.

"Everything according to plan." It's the only way to go.

Chapter 3

Cruise Control

The cruise portion of flight usually takes the most time and receives the least attention. This is not all that surprising; once the aircraft has been leveled off, trimmed, and leaned out, there normally isn't too much to do other than keep track of the flight log, watch the VORs go by, check in and out with the controllers, and get an occasional update on the weather. But that's not to say that the cruise portion isn't important, nor does it mean that it requires no thought or advance planning. The cruise portion of the flight may be less demanding than the takeoff, climb, descent, and approach segments, but it is not without its nuances and subtleties.

The phrase *cruise control*, in the literal, technical sense, relates to the optimization of long-range cruise techniques; specifically, "cruise control" is the gradual reduction of power, as fuel is burned off, for the purpose of maintaining the most efficient angle of attack. I will cover long-range cruise techniques in some detail, and will describe why and how power and airspeed are reduced as weight diminishes, if maximum range is desired. But the phrase "cruise control" is more widely and popularly used to mean simply the control of cruise power (and therefore airspeed and fuel flow) during the cruise portion of the flight. In this chapter, unless I am specifically referring to long-range cruise, I am using "cruise control" in this more general sense.

47

ENROUTE PERFORMANCE

The amount of power we use in excess of the amount of power needed to maintain altitude determines our enroute performance: how fast we go, how much fuel we burn, and what kind of "mileage" we get. ("Mileage" is called either "specific distance" or "specific range" in aviation, and instead of being expressed in terms of miles per gallon, it is expressed in terms of *nautical* miles per *pound* of fuel. For avgas, multiplying by 6 will convert to nautical miles per gallon, and multiplying that number by 1.15 will convert to *statute* miles per gallon—what your car gets. This is all part of the conspiracy to make flying seem more difficult than it really is.) The choice as to the actual percent of power used is normally left to the pilot, and the process of determining and managing the available power is what we are going to call "cruise control."

ENROUTE OPTIONS

The simplest and most common form of cruise control is to always use the same power setting. A pilot might, for instance, always cruise at 2400 rpm and 22 inches of manifold pressure, regardless of altitude or winds. For flight planning purposes he simply assumes an average value for true airspeed and fuel flow. This method has only one thing going for it—simplicity—and almost everything going against it. Accurate flight planning is nearly impossible with this kind of simplification. The pilot can compensate for this inaccuracy by carrying extra fuel, but that will not always solve the problem; in the absence of good flight planning, it is very possible that any problem that does arise won't surface until it's too late. Because it is not only inaccurate but also inefficient, the pilot who uses this method also makes unnecessary fuel stops, sometimes flies too *slowly*, and frequently burns large amounts of fuel for very small gains in speed. It may be possible to "get away with" using rules of thumb in place of accurate cruise control, but you can do a lot better.

For the pilot willing to make the effort, cruise control pays dividends both in terms of safety and in terms of optimum performance. The range of choices begins with long-range cruise—the slowest but most fuel-efficient schedule, resulting in the maximum nonstop range—and ends with maximum cruise, the exact opposite: maximum speed without regard for fuel consumed. Between long-range cruise and maximum cruise lies the "normal range," and several choices exist here: low-power cruise, normal cruise, and high-power cruise. We will look at each of these cruise regimes in this chapter, and we will also take a look at a fairly new cruise concept known as lowest cost cruise—neither fastest nor farthest but *least expensive*. The arrangement will be from slowest to fastest, with lowest cost cruise last.

LONG-RANGE CRUISE

Long-range cruise is seldom used in its pure form, for the simple reason that long-range cruise is excruciatingly slow. It is *so* slow, in fact, that most general aviation owners' manuals don't even carry a schedule for it. In the absence of a long-range cruise schedule, you can approximate long-range cruise airspeed by substituting best rate of climb speed: V_y. The speed that most efficiently converts power into altitude is also the speed that most efficiently converts power into distance. The Beech Bonanza (for example) has an indicated best rate of climb speed of 96 knots, which at 6,000 feet equals a true airspeed of 105 knots. For comparison, at 45 percent power (the lowest power schedule listed in the Bonanza owner's manual), the true airspeed is 135 knots, and at 75 percent power the TAS is 172 knots. In other words, flying at long-range cruise means giving up as much as 67 knots of TAS, and that is a steep price to pay unless you have no choice.

What are the situations when absolute maximum range is so important? The most obvious situation is when confronted with a long, overwater route to an island airport (Bermuda, Hawaii) with no fuel stops in between. Without any possibility of making an unplanned fuel stop, and with no alternates available, the amount of fuel remaining overhead the destination airport becomes the key factor in determining your ability to compensate for navigational errors, delays, and weather. Long-range cruise maximizes the amount of fuel remaining. In fact, on any long overwater route, regardless of whether alternates are available or not, long-range cruise may be necessary. It's hard to be *too* conservative over blue water.

A less obvious but similar situation occurs when flying a route over land that lacks suitable fuel stops, either because of terrain or weather. For instance, from Boston to Atlanta is about 850 nautical miles, and the most direct route follows a course over the Alleghenys. A Bonanza at 55 percent power has an IFR, no-wind range at 12,000 feet of 860 miles—a little too close for comfort. The problem is, all the logical places to stop are in the mountains, where the weather can be terrible and the approaches are sometimes less than ideal. This leaves you with only two other choices: Fly out of your way, either to the east or west of the mountains to make your stop, or conserve fuel by flying at long-range cruise in order to eliminate the *need* for a stop. (There is a third choice: Go even higher than 12,000—but then you have to breathe oxygen continuously for over six hours.) The advantage in using long-range cruise is that if the winds are better than forecast, or the weather breaks and a fuel stop is no longer a problem, you can always go faster. But once you have flown off the direct route, that time is lost no matter what the winds or weather do.

Another time long-range cruise might make sense is when you see that you can comfortably make a given leg nonstop at normal cruise speeds, but only with the help of a favorable winds aloft forecast. If the winds fail to materialize, you have a problem. A better idea might be to start out at long-range cruise. If the winds are as good or better than forecast, you can then use normal cruise. If the winds are worse than forecast, then long-range cruise will maximize your fuel reserve. You may still have to make a stop if the winds are bad enough, but applying long-range cruise techniques in this situation at least gives you a "look-see" capability.

The key point here is that in each of these cases long-range cruise gives you an alternative to either not going at all, or having to make a fuel stop that is undesirable for one reason or another. It may be slow, but sometimes long-range cruise is the solution to a problem.

True long-range cruise is based on flying at best lift over drag (L/D) speed. Best L/D is the speed where lift is greatest and drag is lowest—or, in plain English, the most efficient speed for the airplane. In practice, long-range cruise schedules incorporate indicated airspeeds just slightly faster than optimum L/D. This reduces maximum range by only one percent (10 miles in a thousand), and ensures that the speed stays on the front side of the power curve. At optimum L/D, even a slight reduction in speed would put you on the back side of the power curve: The slower you go, the more power (and therefore fuel) required, and that's *always* a bad deal.

Unfortunately, best L/D speed, as if it weren't slow enough, gets even slower as the airplane gets lighter. This is because maximum range is really a function of angle of attack, and the only way to maintain this optimum angle of attack in level flight is to slow the airplane as the weight decreases. Therefore, for absolute optimum long-range cruise, the indicated airspeed for best L/D has to be reduced as fuel burns off. (This compensation for weight is what is meant by "cruise control" in the technical sense—the control of indicated cruise airspeed for optimum range.)

The good news is that, as a practical consideration, this only applies to turbine equipment, where the weight difference between full fuel and minimum fuel is usually substantial. The weight of a Falcon 20, for instance, might vary from 27,000 pounds at top of climb, to 20,000 pounds at top of descent—a difference of 35 percent. Long-range cruise speeds for a loaded Falcon 20 at FL350 start out at M.70 (400 knots TAS) and gradually drop, as weight is burned off, to as low as M.62 (355 knots). For an airplane like a Bonanza, where the cruise weight might start at 3400 pounds and drop to 3000 pounds (about a 13 percent difference), cruise control in the technical sense is of negligible value. For most reciprocating engine aircraft, unless extra tanks have been installed, or a distance record is being attempted, the initial long-range cruise airspeed can be held throughout the flight with negligible range penalty. Be grateful for small favors.

Groundspeed is what really counts, and long-range cruise groundspeeds can be reasonable with a decent tailwind. But with a headwind, long-range cruise can be an exercise in frustration. If long-range cruise TAS is 105 knots, and the headwind is 60 knots, the groundspeed will be 45 knots, and at that rate the range is going to be terrible no matter what the fuel flows are. In the extreme case, where the headwind equals the true airspeed, the groundspeed would be zero, and *all* fuel, no matter how low the consumption rate, would be wasted.

The solution is to increase the airspeed a given amount to compensate for the negative effects of the headwind so that a balance is struck between the least amount of time spent penetrating the headwind and the most efficient airspeed. The exact amount to increase is best determined by computer, but Peter Garrison, who has an enormous amount of practical experience in this area, recommends (in his book *Long-Distance Flying*, Doubleday, 1981) that you increase the no-wind, long-range cruise airspeed by 1/4 of the headwind component. In the case of the Bonanza with a 60 knot headwind, that would mean increasing the indicated best L/D speed of 96 knots by 15 knots to 111 knots. (This rule doesn't apply to normal power settings—at those power settings you are already going at least that much faster, and any additional increase will only decrease range.)

The key factor in achieving maximum range with reciprocating engines, without which this entire discussion of optimum long-range cruise techniques is academic, is proper leaning of the engine or engines. The difference in fuel flow between a properly leaned engine and one that hasn't been leaned at all can easily be 50 percent—enough to completely wipe out all the savings in going slowly.

Many pilots are a little afraid of the mixture knob, which is silly, especially at low power settings. Detonation *can* result from an overly lean mixture, causing rapid destruction of the engine, and I don't want to minimize that danger, but detonation is most likely to occur at high power settings—above 75 percent—and even then, only when the engine is running very hot. Some pilots are also afraid of accidentally killing the engine, but an engine has to be lean well beyond the point of initial roughness before it will quit. As long as the manufacturer's recommendations on leaning are followed there is no reason to fear the mixture knob, and without careful leaning, fuel flows are going to be horrible.

Long-range cruise is worth knowing about. I find it interesting in an intellectual sense, but I have to admit that I have seldom used it, even with jets, where it seems like fuel is always a problem. There *are* occasions when long-range cruise solves a problem, but they are infrequent. It's something to keep in mind, though, and maybe experiment with a little when you have the time, so that when you *do* need it you'll have some solid information and a little experience to fall back on. When you have a long way to go and no good way to break it up, long-range cruise may be the answer.

VERY LOW POWER CRUISE

Many of the advantages of long-range cruise can be obtained at very low power settings (something around 45 percent power), but without so many of the disadvantages. The efficiencies that result are *close* to long-range cruise, and using a fixed percent of power eliminates the complexity and super-slow true airspeeds of pure long-range cruise. Most manufacturers provide a *very low power cruise* schedule, which makes for easy flight planning and power management. Speeds will typically be 20 to 30 percent better than long-range, and the range loss will seldom be more than 10 percent. This is a much more practical approach to maximum range, and if you want to call 45 percent power (or something in that area) "long-range cruise," you won't be far wrong.

LOW-POWER CRUISE

Low-power cruise is anything in the area of 50 to 60 percent power. There is no hard-and-fast definition for low power cruise; it's simply the lower end of the normal cruise power region. You may see the label "economy cruise" attached to it, which is as good a name as any—except aviation has been getting along for years without any concern for economy, so I don't see any reason to start now. (Reminds me of the boy who went up to the airplane owner and said, "Man, you must be rich to own an airplane." Airplane owner said, "No, but I *used* to be.")

Low-power cruise *is* economical, especially downwind. With a nice tailwind you can very often make up (over the ground) the airspeed you lose at low power settings. In effect, you're giving up the tailwind in exchange for fuel. But probably the best thing low-power cruise has going for it is that it is quiet and smooth. Even noisy, shaky airplanes usually settle down around 55 percent or so, and that's an important consideration, both in terms of comfort and in terms of safety—noise and vibration create fatigue, and fatigue is one of the enemies of safety. Besides, common sense will tell you that there isn't much point in going fast to save 20 minutes, if in so doing it makes you a nervous wreck and your ears ring and you shake all over. I guess you could always use the extra 20 minutes to rest up, but somehow that doesn't seem like the right way to do it.

So for reasons of comfort and safety alone you may want to use 55 percent power as your standard cruise schedule. In any case, low-power cruise is a good normal cruise downwind—let the wind do more of the work.

NORMAL CRUISE

Most pilots call something in the vicinity of 65 percent power *normal cruise,* and some manufacturers even label it as such. Like most things labeled "normal," it can mean a lot and nothing at the same time. There is certainly nothing *abnormal* about using 65 percent power, but that doesn't make 65 percent power "normal" either—"most normal" maybe, but that's about all. Nonetheless, as long as you understand that 65 percent power is not the only perfectly normal "normal" power setting, we are going to do what everybody else does and call 65 percent power (more or less) "normal cruise."

If you *are* going to use one power schedule all the time, normal cruise power is probably the one to use. It is fairly economical, fairly fast, fairly quiet, and fairly smooth. It is everything all the other cruises are, both the good and the bad, but in lesser amounts. It's your basic compromise. For those who got their flight training at the Rule-of-Thumb School of Aeronautical Wizardry, and who like simplicity above all else, normal cruise is the answer. Using just one power schedule is nearly as easy as a rule of thumb, and is much more accurate. It will be economical downwind, fast enough upwind, and easy to use in any wind.

By using low-power cruise downwind and normal cruise upwind, a conservative *system* of cruise control is created. With this system, fuel economy is good in both directions and groundspeeds will be reasonable and fairly constant. When the wind blows against you, normal cruise compensates for some of the groundspeed loss, and when the wind blows behind you, you back off and save a little fuel with only a slight loss in groundspeed.

The same system can be used by those who like to go fast, only then normal cruise is used *downwind*. Even pulling the power back to 65 percent may be hard for some, but the actual loss in groundspeed will be slight, because the wind is doing part of the work, and the fuel savings will be significant. Then, when you turn around and head back into the wind, you can go back to high-speed cruise if you want. This system gives you the satisfaction of high speeds without having to pay an excessive price in terms of fuel.

In summary, then, normal cruise *is* a good normal cruise for those who like simplicity and ease of use. It is also a good upwind cruise, if optimization of *fuel* within the normal range is the goal, and it is a good downwind cruise, if optimization of *speed* is the goal (again, within the normal range). "Swing cruise" would be a good name for it.

HIGH-SPEED CRUISE

True *high-speed cruise* is about 75 percent power for most reciprocating-engined aircraft. Some pilots use high-speed cruise all the time—they like to go fast, and that's as good as reason as any. After all, there may be a lot of reasons why we fly airplanes, but the only *practical* reason is because flying is generally faster than the alternative. If that's the reason you fly, high-speed cruise will get you there the fastest.

But there are other reasons (and perhaps better ones) for going fast also. A Cessna 150 is a slow airplane, and I think even Cessna would agree. It was designed as a trainer, and cross-country speed is essentially irrelevant in a trainer. But a Cessna 150 (and other airplanes like it) *can* be used for transportation, and as such it probably makes sense to operate it at the highest cruise power possible. Fuel flows, in absolute terms, will still be quite low, and anything slower pretty much negates the advantages of air travel.

In fact, any airplane that is slow for the circumstances it finds itself in can benefit from using high-speed cruise. Pressurized airplanes frequently find themselves mixed up with some pretty high speed company up in the Flight Levels. High-speed cruise can be used to fit in with the flow. This helps avoid vectors off the airway to let everybody else go by. I have seldom seen a Cessna Citation operated at anything less than high-speed cruise. The Citation is a fast airplane, but up in the higher Flight Levels it is still quite a bit slower than most of the traffic around it. High-speed cruise minimizes the difference. If you find that you are regularly having to accept vectors off the airways to let faster aircraft go by, it may make sense to use high-speed cruise.

High-speed cruise is also the one to use whenever the winds are horrendous. What's "horrendous"? I would say that whenever the headwind component (not the headwind itself, but the headwind *component*) reaches 50 percent of the normal true airspeed, it doesn't make any sense to put up with that any longer than you have to and high-speed cruise makes perfect sense. It may even make sense at less than 50 percent—it depends on what you feel "horrendous" means. Once you have a definition of horrendous headwinds that you're comfortable with, you should have no qualms about using high-speed cruise when the winds meet or exceed that definition.

Sometimes the weather can force the use of high-speed cruise. I flew for several years out of an airport located right next to a river. From August to November the airport would fog over about 10:30 almost every night, and would stay that way until about 11 or 12 the next morning. Sometimes the difference between severe clear and zero-zero would be a matter of five minutes—that's how long it would take for the fog to roll up the hill from the river and cover the airport. Obviously, if it looks like a difference of five or ten minutes is going to mean the difference between good VFR versus below minimums (and the same thing could happen with a rapidly diminishing temperature-dewpoint spread), it makes sense to go as fast as you can to try to get there before the airport closes down for the night. Note that I didn't say to hurry up the approach and landing—just the cruise portion. I'm hard pressed to think of anything in aviation more dangerous than a rushed approach.

The longer the trip, the more high-speed cruise makes sense, and the shorter the trip, the less it makes sense. It's only on the longer trips that the difference in speed between high-speed cruise and normal cruise starts to show up: on a trip of 1200 nm increasing the speed from 150 to 160 knots saves 30 minutes; on a trip of 100 miles, the same increase saves two and a half minutes. On a short trip, high-speed cruise is nothing but ". . . sound and fury, signifying nothing." (*Macbeth*, Act V, Scene V.)

There *are* good reasons for at least occasionally using high-speed cruise, even if you normally like to operate at more conservative power settings. In general, the slower the airplane, and the longer the trip, the more sense it makes to use high-speed cruise.

MAXIMUM CRUISE

Maximum cruise is the upper limit for cruise power. For some airplanes, maximum cruise will be "redline." Others have a specific *maximum continuous power limitation*. Still others will have a *maximum normal operating power* which is a recommendation and not, technically, a limitation—it can be exceeded, but normally isn't. Whatever the maximum normal power setting is, that is maximum cruise.

Maximum cruise *could* be called "emergency cruise," because that's really what it is. Maximum cruise isn't something you would normally use as a matter of course, and you wouldn't normally plan a flight using it. (For that reason you will seldom see performance charts printed for maximum cruise.) Maximum cruise means maximum effort, and maximum effort is usually reserved for those times when you don't have any choice.

Maximum cruise is something to consider whenever you have a potentially serious problem that is getting worse. For instance, if all electrical power is lost except for the battery, time is very critical if you are in instrument conditions. Battery capacity varies with battery size and load; if it gives out while still in the clouds, navigation will be reduced to dead reckoning, which is not nearly accurate enough for safe instrument flight. Maximum cruise power will not affect the battery load, and it will minimize the time in the air. In this case, maximum cruise means maximum chance of finding visual conditions before the battery runs down.

Other situations where maximum cruise might be appropriate are: slow fuel leaks, loss of cabin heat, gradual deterioration of attitude or heading gyros (I'd ask for vectors for VFR conditions at the same time), or almost any other serious or potentially serious problem that can't be solved and seems to be getting worse.

I say "almost," because some problems can be made worse if power and airspeed are increased. Engine problems typically fall into this category: Decreasing oil pressure, increasing temperatures, vibrations, propeller overspeeds—all will generally be made worse by increasing power. Maximum cruise is usually not the solution to structural problems either—something like a window cracking, or a flap coming loose. The temptation with these kinds of problems is to get on the ground as fast as possible, but the solution is not maximum cruise in these cases. All of these kinds of things are usually made worse by high speed.

It is obviously impossible to list every situation where maximum cruise is or is not appropriate. That's why airplanes have pilots— to use their heads and make a decision based on the particular situation that arises. The important point here is that maximum cruise may be part of the solution for any problem that is time-critical.

LOWEST COST CRUISE

Lowest cost cruise is an interesting concept. The idea originated with the airlines. When the fuel crunch came in 1973, and jet fuel went from 15¢ and 16¢ to $1.00, the airlines responded in the logical way by flying slower to conserve fuel. The problem was, as they flew slower fuel costs did go down, but maintenance costs, crew expenses, and engine reserves all went *up*. The slower they went, the more time they put on the airplane, and that cost something too. They found that they could only go a certain amount slower and still save money overall—slower than that and the fixed costs exceeded the fuel savings. This point came to be known as lowest cost cruise.

Crew expenses are a very large factor in the lowest cost cruise equation—the slower you go, the longer your crews work and the more you have to pay them. Privately operated aircraft don't have crew expenses, of course, but the other two major factors that determine lowest cost cruise—maintenance and a reserve for overhaul— do apply. Determining what lowest cost cruise is for your airplane is not hard. All it takes is a performance manual, a calculator (a personal computer with spreadsheet software is ideal), and a little bit of time.

The first step is to determine what your hourly fuel costs are for a typical cruise altitude, over a range of power settings. The relationship between power and cost will be essentially constant for all altitudes, so you only need to do this for a single, typical altitude. Determining fuel costs is a simple matter of looking up hourly fuel consumption figures in your performance manual, and multiplying those figures by your average cost for fuel. (If you're using a spreadsheet, put the fuel cost in a separate cell, so you can recompute easily as fuel prices vary.) Table 3-1, line 1 shows how this would look for a typical single-engine aircraft, as power varies from 45 percent to 75 percent.

The next step is to determine the hourly cost for scheduled maintenance. If your airplane gets regular 100-hour inspections, this is also a fairly easy number to come up with. Make your best estimate of what a typical 100-hour inspection costs, and divide that figure by 100—that's your maintenance cost on an hourly basis. (If you only do an annual inspection, scheduled maintenance is not a factor. Presumably the "annual" will cost the same no matter how fast or slow you fly.) Table 3-1 shows this figure for our typical single on line 2. Note that it is a constant figure for each percent of power—a 100-hour inspection should cost essentially the same regardless of the amount of power used during those preceding 100 hours, within the normal range of power settings.

We don't include *unscheduled* maintenance for the simple reason that unscheduled maintenance is only indirectly related to hours in operation—flying faster or slower doesn't affect the "breakage" rate directly or predictably. For purposes of determining lowest cost cruise, the relationship between power and unscheduled maintenance is too vague to be useful.

The last hourly cost figure is a reserve for overhaul. Despite the fact that an allowance for overhaul is not an hourly, "out-of-pocket" cash expense, this chicken will come home to roost sooner or later—if not in an actual cost, then in the form of increased "depreciation" at the time of sale. So we have to account for it if we want a true picture of our hourly costs. Your local mechanic or FBO should be able to give you a figure on what you can expect an overhaul to cost, and he should also know what the recommended time between overhauls (TBO) is. Coming up with an hourly figure is a simple matter of dividing estimated overhaul cost by the TBO. If you're certain your engine won't make it to TBO, use your best guess of how long it will last, but don't count on it going over.

Table 3-1 lists our hourly reserve for overhaul on line 3. It is

Table 3-1. Direct Hourly Costs for a Typical Single Engine Aircraft, from 45 Percent to 75 Percent Maximum Continuous Power.

Percent Power:	45%	55%	65%	75%
1. Fuel @ $2.00/GAL	$19.40	$22.90	$26.60	$30.50
2. Maintenance	$12.00	$12.00	$12.00	$12.00
3. Overhaul	$6.00	$6.00	$6.00	$6.00
4. Total:	$37.40	$40.90	$44.60	$48.50

also a constant figure that does not vary with power. Again, I know it is possible to argue that an engine operated at 55 percent power may be more likely to reach TBO than one operated at 75 percent power, but the relationship is debatable at best—I would use a constant figure.

The sum of these figures, shown in Table 3-1 on line 4, is total hourly cost for fuel, maintenance, and overhaul. As power goes up, the cost goes up. That's pretty obvious. But that's only half the story. The airplane also *goes* faster as the power increases, and therefore covers more miles—we aren't really comparing "apples to apples" if we only look at the hourly figures.

Table 3-2 is the other half of the story—where we look at how much actual work gets done for the fuel expended. Line 1 is just a simple listing of true airspeed (TAS) for each of these power settings, taken straight from the performance section of our typical airplane. Line 2 is a repeat of the total hourly costs from Table 3-1.

Table 3-2. Cost per Nautical Mile. Dividing Cost per Hour by True Airspeed Produces Cost per Nautical Mile. Lowest Cost Cruise is the Per Cent of Power that Results in the Lowest Cost Per Mile: in this Case, 27.6¢ per Mile, or 55 Percent Power.

Percent Power:	45%	55%	65%	75%
1. True Airspeed, 6000 FEET	135	148	161	172
2. Cost Per Hour	$37.40	$40.90	$44.60	$48.50
3. Cents/N.M.	27.7¢	27.6¢	27.7¢	28.2¢
4. Per 100,000 N.M.	$27,703.70	$27,635.14	$27,701.86	$28,197.67
5. Lowest Cost Cruise		=======		
6. Amount Above LCC	$68.57	$0.00	$66.73	$562.54
7. Percent Above LCC	0.2%	0.0%	0.2%	2.0%

Line 3 shows us what each of those miles actually costs, to the nearest tenth of a cent. This was obtained by dividing Line 2 (cost per hour) by Line 1 (true airspeed.) The result is cost per mile (specifically cents per nautical mile).

Reading across Line 3, we see that this particular airplane costs 27.7¢ per mile at 45 percent power, 27.6¢ per mile at 55 percent power, 27.7¢ per mile at 65 percent power, and 28.2¢ per mile at 75 percent power. Fifty five percent power seems to be the cheapest, but the differences, on a per mile basis, are so small as to be virtually meaningless.

To make the differences more meaningful, I carried out the cost per mile to seven places and multiplied it by 100,000 miles. Line 4 shows what the difference would be for 100,000 miles (which may sound like a lot, but at 172 knots that is only 581 hours.) Even here the difference is very slight, but it is easy to see that 55 percent is the cheapest cruise (i.e., lowest cost cruise), that it costs only $66.73 more per 100,000 hours to use 65 percent power (Line 6) and that it costs $68.57 to use 45 percent power—presumably for the privilege of going slower. Stepping up to 75 percent power costs $562.54 more than 55 percent—a 2 percent increase over lowest cost cruise (Line 7). In other words, for all practical purposes the cost is the same to fly this airplane at 65 percent power as it is at 55 percent power, it costs only 2 percent more to fly at 75 percent than it does at 55 percent, and there is no cost advantage at all in flying *slower* than 55 percent.

The only way to determine lowest cost cruise for your airplane is to go through the analysis above. If your airplane is simple to maintain and relatively cheap to overhaul, lowest cost cruise will be biased toward the low power side. On the other hand, a very sophisticated airplane that costs a lot to maintain and has an engine with a low TBO and high overhaul cost will be biased toward the high power end. There is no way to know what your lowest cost cruise is without plugging actual numbers in. The results may surprise you.

It probably goes without saying, but if you rent aircraft by the hour, lowest cost cruise *for you* will almost certainly be high-speed cruise, or as fast as possible. When you're paying by the hour, the faster you go, the less you pay. Even with a "dry" lease (you buy the fuel), the hourly charge will usually be high enough that the time and money you save going fast will more than compensate for the extra fuel you have to buy. I'm not suggesting that you abuse the airplanes you rent to save a little money, but from an economic point of view there is no reason to use anything other than the highest normal power setting. Anything else is a gift from you to the rentor.

None of this is meant to suggest that fuel conservation is not an important consideration on both a moral and a practical level. Oil is a finite resource, and once it's gone, it's gone. But economics is the science of the allocation of scarce resources, and what lowest cost cruise is telling us is that engines and airframes are themselves scarce resources, also worthy of conservation. Lowest cost cruise represents the optimum economic point of balance, which means, in simple terms, that when you operate at the point of lowest cost cruise, you are not only saving yourself a little money, but you are also striking the best balance in terms of total conservation of resources. Even if the financial savings are not great, it's still a move in the right direction.

CONCLUSION

Accurate cruise control is not so difficult or complicated as this fairly detailed discussion might lead you to believe, but neither is it so inconsequential as to not be worth a little thought and analysis. Even the simplest program of cruise control, using a constant percent of power, will pay dividends in terms of more accurate flight planning and more economical operation. Greater returns are available in the form of improved efficiencies, extended ranges, and maximized economies with just a little more effort.

In almost any professional cockpit you will find that the most beat-up book in the airplane is the cruise performance manual. Most captains like to keep it right behind the copilot's seat, where they can easily reach over with their right arm and grab it (unless they have a Flight Engineer to grab it for them). They'll reach over the first time after the airplane has been leveled off in order to set initial cruise power. If there is an altitude change, you'll see the arm go out again to reset the power. Even if they don't change altitudes, you'll usually see the arm go out one or more times to get updates as either the outside temperature changes or fuel is burned off. Cruise control is as normal a part of enroute flying as talking to controllers and tracking VORs.

Good cruise control is one of the signs of a well-run cockpit; but more than that, it indicates a deliberate and thoughtful approach to flying that is one of the marks of a good pilot. It isn't that proper cruise control is so terribly important in and of itself, as much as it is that if this is being done right, everything else probably is, too.

Chapter 4

Approaches

Every time you take an airplane up, you are committed to bringing that airplane down. Remember how you felt on your first solo?—I *know* I can do it, which is good, because I *have* to. If you are regularly using your aircraft for transportation (and regularly filing IFR), then in many cases you are also committed to an instrument approach in order to bring that airplane down.

Most passengers don't like approaches, and I can't blame them. I don't like them when I'm in the back of the airplane either. You can't see anything and you can't tell what's going on; all you know for sure is that you are getting closer and closer to the ground. You just sit back there and hope the person with his hands on the steering wheel knows what he's doing.

The passengers are at the mercy of the pilot, and there isn't anything they can do about it. One of our senior VPs was riding in the back of a chartered Cessna Citation—our own Citation was down for maintenance. It was the middle of winter and the weather was terrible—lots of ice, bumpy, low ceilings—the works. The pilot was shooting an approach to Lebanon, New Hampshire, the corporate flight department base. The "long" runway at Lebanon—the one that is never aligned with the wind—is only 5500 feet, and this particular night it was also covered with ice. Mr. VP hollered up to the pilot;

"Captain, does this Citation have reversers?"

"No, Sir."

A little pause.

"Captain, does this Citation have a drag chute?"

"No, Sir."

A long pause.

"Captain, does this Citation have any more Scotch?"

The passengers are at your mercy. You have a tremendous responsibility to them to do the best possible job you can on every approach. We're going to be talking about all kinds of approaches in this chapter, but not with the intent of trying to teach you how to fly them; that can only be done in an airplane or simulator. Instead, we're going to be talking about some of the little things that can make the difference between a shaky approach and a smooth approach—between an approach that warrants the passengers' trust, and one that doesn't. We're going to start with what is often the most demanding of approaches, the circling approach (when the inbound approach course is not lined up with the landing runway), then we're going to talk about non-precision approaches, both VOR and NDB, and we'll finish up with precision approaches— ILSs and GCAs (Ground Controlled Approaches)—the only approaches truly worthy of the name.

CIRCLING APPROACHES

A circling approach is any approach in which the final approach course and the runway differ by more than 30 degrees; i.e., an approach to a runway that is not more or less straight in and therefore requires "circling" in order to be properly aligned.

Circling approaches are among the most critical maneuvers in aviation. Many corporate flight departments require their pilots to use Category D circling minimums, regardless of the actual category their aircraft fall under. Some flight departments specifically forbid night circling approaches; some forbid circling approaches altogether. Circling approaches can be safe, but only if they are done properly and with scrupulous regard for their limitations. In other words, they're as safe as the pilot or pilots flying them.

Optimum

One of the best circling approaches I've ever seen was flown by a guy named Dave Naylor, ex-Air Force F-102 interceptor pilot. I've seen other pilots shoot a lot of good approaches—approaches to ILS minimums, turbulent approaches, icy approaches, approaches in rain so heavy you had to yell to be heard, and approaches in the simulator with most of the systems out and the rest on fire—but this approach was one of the best.

Well, sure, you say, a former fighter pilot *ought* to able to shoot a good circling approach. You're right, except all I knew about Dave Naylor at this point was that he was one of the least likely "fighter pilot" types I'd ever known. Dave is the kind of guy who thinks it would be really fun to spend two or three hours getting the coffeepot nice and shiny. His idea of a wild and crazy time is to stir his beer until all the bubbles are gone. But that didn't mean Dave couldn't fly an airplane. (It just meant he liked clean coffeepots and flat beer.)

What made this particular approach such a good approach (a circling VOR approach to Hilton Head, South Carolina), was not that the approach itself was that tough—it was a tough approach, circling over the airport right on the deck at circling minimums, but it wasn't *that* tough. What made it so good was that he made it look so easy. It didn't hit me until later what a great job he had done.

Dave was flying (a Hawker-Siddely 125) and I was running the checklist, watching the clock, and occasionally looking outside. I didn't see anything all the way down the final approach segment until we got to the MDA (Minimum Descent Altitude). Just at that point we broke out under a solid overcast with good visibility underneath, but without a foot to spare; up meant back into the clouds, and down meant descending below the MDA. I looked straight down and saw the airport right underneath us. I called it out, just on principle, but assumed Dave would call for the missed approach anyway because we were going by the airport. I thought we were going to ask the controller for another shot at the approach, to see if we couldn't get down to the MDA a little quicker in order to set ourselves up for a right downwind (Fig. 4-1).

But Dave continued more or less straight ahead, still exactly at circling minimums—no missed approach, no climbout, no callouts, just straight-and-level. The clouds were skimming the top of the airplane and the altimeter was glued to the MDA. I thought, "This is great. Dave has decided that if he can't go to Hilton Head he's going to cross the ocean VFR instead, only he doesn't want to tell me yet. It's going to be sort of a surprise. I just hope there aren't any big boats between us and the coast of France."

Finally, after what seemed like about 30 minutes but what was actually only 15 or 20 seconds, Dave started a 25 degree bank to the left, turning downwind, and I realized for the first time that

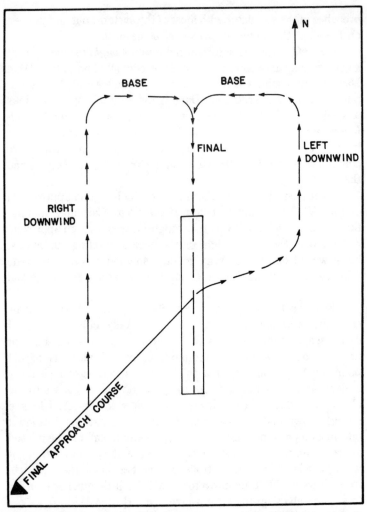

Fig. 4-1. Two possible circling patterns for a runway that lies at an angle to the final approach course.

he was going to circle back to the runway—wherever *that* was now. Dave continued on this heading for about 30 seconds more, banked 30 degrees to the left, and started back around for the airport. As we went through 90 degrees—where the base leg would be—the runway came into view and he called for the gear and flaps and the rest of the landing checklist, lined up on final, slowed to exactly "bug" speed (the reference speed on final), touched down, put the spoilers out, went to lift dump (90 degrees of flaps), applied maximum braking, and taxied off the runway without so much as a word. (The runway at Hilton Head is only 3800 feet long counting the overrun, and there are trees at each end. That's not very much runway for a swept-wing jet with a final approach speed of 130 knots.)

Dave's crew briefing procedures might leave a little bit to be desired (I'm sure one of the nice things about flying fighter interceptors is that you don't have to mess with copilots), but his execution of the approach and landing was flawless. There was no confusion when the runway was first sighted, no diving for the runway, no skimming the treetops or groping around in the murk—just a beautifully done, tricky approach that was so smooth and controlled I suspect the passengers never even thought twice about it.

That, I think, is one of the ironies of aviation: When you do something really well, nobody notices. The smooth, uneventful flight that proceeds exactly as planned, even under difficult circumstances, is boring and unimpressive to the passengers. But that is what you are looking for. Everybody judges pilots on their landings, and I hope you know that the smoothness of a landing doesn't mean a thing. But what *is* hard to take is when they don't even notice when you do everything just right. But that's what you want to look for—"commentless flights." That is really the highest compliment.

Descent to the MDA

I have told you this story partly because I want you to know what I mean by a "good" circling approach, but also because it illustrates so many of the important points about non-precision and circling approaches. First of all, get down to the MDA (the Minimum Descent Altitude) as soon after crossing the final approach fix as you can without dumping or diving the airplane. (If Dave made a mistake it was in not getting down sooner.) The only thing a non-precision approach (any approach without a glideslope) can do is get you out of IFR conditions into VFR conditions, so that a normal, visual landing can be accomplished. You are not going to be able to get any lower than the MDA until you are visual, so you might just as well get on down there. The sooner you do go visual, the more time you have to look for the airport, plan your pattern, and make a normal descent.

Legal Limitations

The legal limitations for circling are: One, you must keep the *airport* in sight at all times, except when losing sight "results only from a normal bank of the aircraft during the circling approach" (FAR 91.116e); two, you cannot leave the MDA unless you have visual reference for the intended runway and a descent to that runway can be made at a normal rate of descent using normal maneuvers. (FAR 91.116c.)

If you lose sight of the airport, you must do a missed approach. Dave and I, in our approach to Hilton Head, could not see the *runway* until on base, but we were over, or could see back to, the airport itself at all times. When the visibility is down, as it usually is whenever a circling approach is required, you want to stay in tight in order to avoid a mandatory missed approach situation.

In the first case we are concerned with keeping the *airport* in sight while circling, and in the second case we are concerned with having visual reference to the *runway* before we can descend below the MDA. What happens if we have the airport but can't find visual reference to the runway? That can happen—you see buildings on the airport, or maybe the tower or rotating beacon, but the visibility is so poor you just can't make out the runways, at least not well enough to know which is which. You can fly over and around the airport, if that helps, but you can't drop below the MDA until you positively have the correct runway in sight and can make a normal descent to it. The minimum descent altitude will keep you above the obstructions on the airport itself, but before you descend below that, the FAA wants you to have a clear shot at the runway without any obstructions.

I have heard pilots say that you can't descend below the MDA until you are within 30 degrees of the runway heading. The reasoning here is that any approach that is aligned within 30 degrees of the runway is considered to be a straight-in approach, so until you are within 30 degrees of the runway heading you can't descend any lower than circling minimums. This makes some sense, but there is no regulation anywhere that says that. The only applicable reg is 91.116c, which allows you to descend below the MDA anytime you have the runway or visual reference in sight and a normal descent can be accomplished. I do think this "rule" makes a very good guideline though—if you can, wait until you are aligned within 30 degrees of the runway before you descend below the MDA.

The regs are vague as to what constitutes a normal rate of descent or a normal maneuver, but if you crack one up I'll bet whatever you did turns out to *not* be normal. The regs are, however, very specific as to what constitutes a visual reference for the intended runway. (This is what can drive you crazy about the regs; sometimes you get one word that can have endless intepretations, like "normal," and the next time you get a list.) There are ten allowable references: the approach light system, the runway threshold, threshold markings, threshold lights, runway end identifier lights (those strobes you sometimes find on each side of the threshold), the VASI, the touchdown zone, touchdown zone lights, the runway itself or runway markings, and the runway lights (FAR 91.116c3.) What the FAA is trying to say is that you have to actually see the runway, or some part of the runway lighting system, to have "visual reference for the intended runway."

If they had just said this in the first place there wouldn't have been any problem, but the reg *used* to say "the runway or the runway environment." That "runway environment" led to all kinds of problems, because pilots were calling the highways and rivers and power lines around the airport the "runway environment," and they were using those references to find their way to the airport with predictably negative results. So the FAA "clarified" what they meant by runway environment and what you get is the list above. Just remember, "runway" means the actual runway and "visual reference" means the runway lights or markings, and you must have one or more in sight to descend below the MDA.

So that keeps us legal, and also keeps us out of a lot of trouble: Lose sight of the airport—missed approach; runway not in sight—don't leave the MDA.

Airspeed Control

What about actually flying a circling approach? What are the main things you want to keep in mind? One of the main things is speed control: not too fast and not too slow. Easy to say, but what does it mean? How do you determine the correct circling speed for your particular aircraft?

To determine the correct circling speed, start with the stalling speed of your airplane in the approach configuration, which probably means one notch of flaps, or 10 to 15 degrees, or the first increment—whatever the Aircraft Flight Manual requires or the manufacturer recommends you use for approaches. The first movement of flaps serves mainly to lower the stalling speed and enable slower minimum speeds; further extensions add drag, which is useful for descent control, but not for speed reduction. We will call this speed V_{s1}.

Having determined V_{s1}, multiply that speed by 1.3 to get your final approach speed—a 30% margin over the stall, just as in a short field landing. (But it won't be *exactly* the same number as you have for a short field landing, because that number is based on 1.3 times the stall in the *landing* configuration—V_{so}.) Then add 10 knots to that number for maneuvering. This will take care of the fact that the stalling speed increases several knots as you bank the aircraft during the circling maneuver. This speed—1.3 times V_{s1} plus 10 knots—is the speed to fly while circling. Any faster than that will widen your turns, taking you that much farther away from the runway. (This is why the circling minimums vary depending on the stalling speed of the airplane. The higher the stall, the greater the circling radius will be. Therefore greater visibility is required to successfully execute the approach.) Any slower than 1.3 times V_{s1} plus 10 knots puts you too close to the stall, and you probably don't need to be told that this is a *bad* place for a stall.

Most pilots are so afraid of stalls that they err on the fast side—which would be my choice too—but the point is to not err. Know your circling speed, know how much power it takes to hold it in level flight, and practice until you can do it. Your goal should be to hold this speed within plus or minus 5 knots. That kind of control will give you a real edge on a circling approach.

Altitude Control

Another important point is altitude control. This is always a big one on checkrides, and rightly so. The minimum altitudes that are allowed on circling approaches are really quite low—much lower than pattern altitudes normally. This puts you quite close to the ground or anything sticking up from the ground; however, as long as you stay within the protected radius for the circling maneuver and do not descend below the MDA, you will be above all obstructions.

The FAA could, of course, make the minimums higher, providing you with a greater margin of clearance, but then you would miss just that many more approaches (and possibly be just that much more tempted to "duck under" minimums). So they let you go as low as they safely can—the rest is up to you. That means absolutely perfect altitude control—not one foot lower than the minimum circling altitude until the runway is in sight.

The "minimum" altitudes on approaches mean exactly that: *minimum*. They are not assigned altitudes, which would imply a plus or minus 100 foot leeway—they are *minimum* altitudes. You can be higher but not lower. The problem with higher is that higher very often means back up into the clouds, in which case you are obligated to do an immediate missed approach. So the importance of accurate altitude control is pretty obvious: not one foot lower than the minimum circling altitude (the MDA) until the runway is in sight, and no higher than the MDA if that will take you back into the clouds. Of course, if you must err, err on the high side. If that puts you back into the clouds, you'll have to do a missed approach. Better luck next time.

One thing Dave had going for him on his approach—and if you have one it can help an enormous amount—was a flight director (FD) with an HSI (Horizontal Situation Indicator). The best way to hold altitude is to use the flight director. Set the heading bug to correspond to whatever heading you need to fly for that segment of the approach, and punch the altitude hold on at the exact moment you reach the minimum circling altitude. Change the heading bug as the circling maneuver requires, and fly the FD command bars. The command bars will tell you the instant you start to vary from the minimum altitude. The command bars are also much easier for your eyeballs to find when you go back to the panel after a glance outside to keep the airport and runway in sight.

It also helps to set up the HSI so that the runway is represented by the OBS needle (Fig. 4-2). Just point the OBS needle to the runway heading—if the runway is 32, put the head of the OBS on 320 degrees. (Don't worry about the middle part going full scale.) The ends of the needle will represent the runway, the heading bug your heading, and you have a picture right in front of you of the circling maneuver. (Naturally, if you are doing a VOR approach, don't reset the OBS until after you break out and don't need the inbound approach guidance anymore.)

Circling Patterns

To use this FD/HSI method you have to have a pretty good idea what kind of circling pattern you intend to fly after you break out, or you won't know what headings to set the heading bug to. But even if you don't have an FD or an HSI, it's important to anticipate what kind of circle you're going to do. If you wait until you break out to figure out how you are going to get to the appropriate runway, you may run into trouble. You need a plan, and the plan will vary with every circling approach. Let's see if we can't break it down into some useful, general principles.

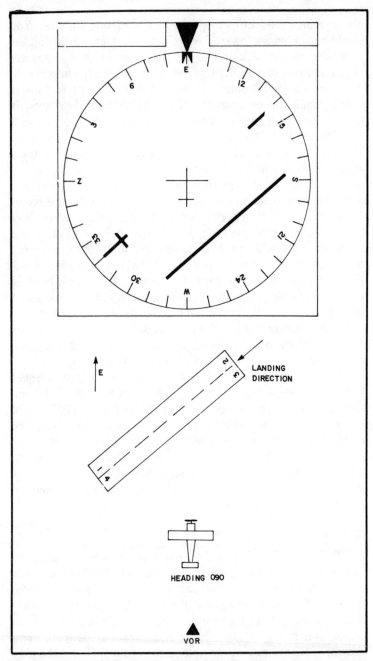

LANDING DIRECTION

HEADING 090

VOR

Fig. 4-2. With the OBS set to the heading for the desired runway, the HSI displays the relationship between the aircraft heading and the landing direction.

If at all possible, you want to get yourself in a position that is familiar to you: i.e., a normal traffic pattern. If you can get yourself onto a downwind, fine. If you can't get downwind easily, but can get onto a base, that's almost as good. But the first choice is to get yourself onto either a right or a left downwind leg, whichever one is closest. You already know how to fly the airplane once you are on downwind, so you really don't have to think through the entire circling maneuver, only the part that gets you to the downwind leg. Figure 4-3 shows several situations where a downwind pattern would be possible, and the best way to maneuver to get downwind. (The approach Dave flew into Hilton Head was a downwind pattern.)

The only part that will seem strange or unfamiliar about the circling downwind pattern will be the pattern altitude: Because circling minimums are usually lower than a normal pattern altitude, you

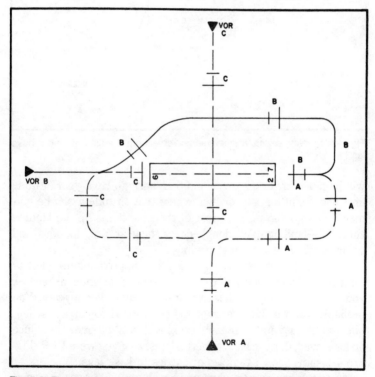

Fig. 4-3. Three different situations where a downwind circling pattern would be appropriate: 1) A left downwind from VOR A to land on runway 27; 2) A right downwind from VOR B to land on runway 27; 3) An overhead, right downwind from VOR C to land on runway 9.

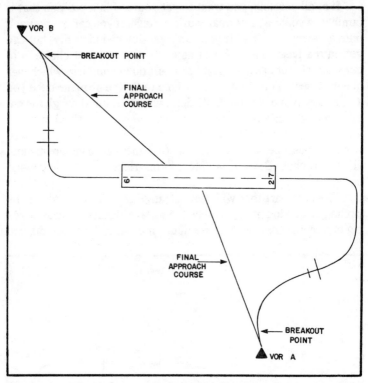

Fig. 4-4. In many cases, a small maneuver will put the aircraft onto a base leg for landing.

will be much lower on downwind than normal. Hold your altitude until that point on base or final where that altitude *would* be normal. Then go through the rest of the final items on the landing checklist—landing flaps, double-check the gear, prop forward, and so on—and make a normal landing.

It is very common to make a circling approach onto a left or right base. The lower altitude won't be such a problem here because you would normally be descending on the base leg anyway. You probably won't be lucky enough to be set up exactly on a base leg, but usually just a little maneuvering will put you onto one. Once on base everything is back to normal, just as if you were VFR. Figure 4-4 shows two examples of entries to base legs.

A tough one comes when you break out right over the point where you want to touch down. Figure 4-5 shows this situation, which is a little like the tennis shot that comes straight at your belt: You just can't seem to twist your racket around the right way to

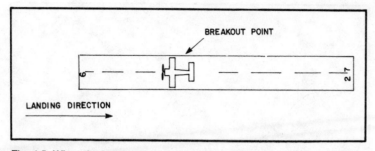

Fig. 4-5. When the breakout point occurs over the desired touchdown point, but with the aircraft going in the opposite direction, a difficult circling situation is created.

hit it. Likewise, in an airplane, you can see the approach end of the runway right underneath you, but can't seem to figure out how to get there—the old "You can't get there from here" syndrome. You need to go somewhere where you *can* get there from there.

My solution to this problem is shown in Fig. 4-6. It certainly means a lot of flying around—puts new meaning into the word "circling"—and if there were low weather or big obstructions behind me, I would use the pattern shown in Fig. 4-7. But the pattern shown in Fig. 4-6 has the enormous advantage of keeping the runway in sight at all times, and it is all familiar pattern flying: first a crosswind leg, then upwind, another crosswind, and finally downwind. The other way works, and is sometimes necessary, but it involves figuring a 45 degree leg at a critical moment, and it means

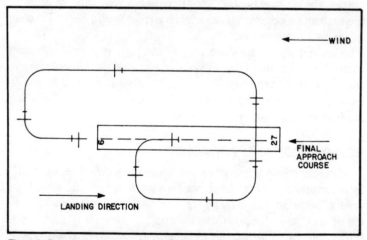

Fig. 4-6. One solution to the problem of getting turned around for landing without losing sight of the airport.

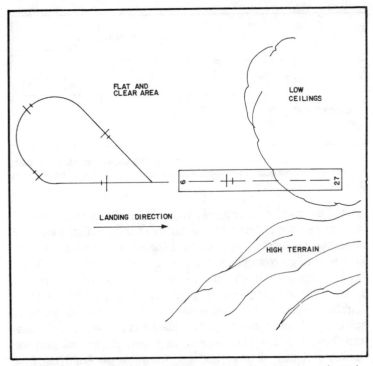

FLAT AND CLEAR AREA

LOW CEILINGS

LANDING DIRECTION

HIGH TERRAIN

Fig. 4-7. This pattern, which is very similar to a procedure turn, is another solution to the problem of getting turned around. It is the preferred pattern when high terrain or low ceilings preclude circling back and around.

putting the runway behind you. (Remember, you can lose sight of the runway as long as you can see the airport itself.) Second choice, as far as I'm concerned.

Circling approaches are tough, and they're worth spending some time thinking about. When one comes up, stay cool, stay in control, expedite the final descent, plan ahead how you intend to maneuver, watch your airspeed, and don't go below circling minimums until committed to land.

NON-PRECISION APPROACHES

Non-precision approaches are sometimes called "let-downs" by older pilots. I think "let-down" is a good name. The word "approach" gets used in so many ways in aviation, it can mean "coming up on," as in *"approaching* the fix;" it can refer to part of the traffic pattern, as in "make short *approach"* or "on final *approach;"* and it can refer to two entirely different kinds of instrument approaches: one, a precision approach capable in its most advanced form of bringing the aircraft all the way down to the runway; the other a non-precision approach whose only real purpose is to get the aircraft out of instrument conditions and into visual conditions in the vicinity of the airport. This is why I like the term "let-down" for non-precision approaches, because that is all they really do: let you down, in a safe area, as close to a runway or at least an airport as possible. If we were to start calling VOR, NDB, and LOC approaches "let-downs," we would eliminate one source of ambiguity with the word "approach."

I am probably not going to start any revolutions in terminology, but if we at least *think* of a non-precision approach as a let-down, I think it clarifies what it can and can't do, and what you as the pilot are trying to accomplish with it. A let-down is a controlled descent. We control *where* we do our descending with either a localizer course, a VOR radial or a course from a radio beacon, and we control *when* we do our descending with various fixes: course intercepts, VORs, non-directional beacons, DME fixes, and crossing radials.

Initial Segment—Vectored

On some non-precison approaches, vectors to the final approach course will be provided—it depends on whether radar is available or not. Normally, when radar is available, an ILS is also available, and that is usually the preferred approach. But that isn't always the case. One of the more common approaches to JFK, for instance, is a VOR approach (VOR to 13L). Also, the smaller airports that lie under the approach control area of a larger airport sometimes only have non-precision approaches, but still have radar coverage. So, while a vectored non-precision approach is not the norm, it is not unheard of, either.

Whenever a vector is provided, an altitude will also be provided. All you have to do is hold that altitude and wait for the inbound course to come in. When it does, you turn inbound and continue the approach on your own. The controller has gotten you started with a vector to intercept the course; the rest is up to you.

Initial Segment—Non-Vectored

Normally, non-precision approaches will not be vectored. This means you have to get *yourself* onto the inbound course. This can be done either from any terminal routing marked "NoPt," which means "No procedure turn" (a radial from another VOR that intercepts the inbound course), or with a procedure turn (a course reversal that intercepts the inbound course). The minimum altitude for either a terminal routing or a procedure turn will be shown on the approach plate. Assuming that you have been cleared for the approach, you may descend to the appropriate altitude for the terminal routing or procedure turn once you are established on the routing or have started the procedure turn. This is the first step in the let-down procedure.

Many pilots think that the reason you have to do a procedure turn is get turned around—which is true, but that's only part of the reason for a procedure turn. The main reason you have to do a procedure turn is that to get established on the inbound course without either a vector or a terminal routing, you have to create your own intercept, and the only sure way to do that is to start from a known point, go away from it, and then turn back around far enough to create an intercept to the inbound course. The known point that you start from is the approach fix itself, either the VOR or the NDB, or in the case of a localizer approach requiring a procedure turn, the beacon. The "going away from it" part is outbound from the fix, and the intercept part is procedure turn inbound. Once established inbound, you are in exactly the same position as if vectors had been provided—you just got there by yourself instead.

Intermediate Segment

The intermediate segment of any approach is that part after the procedure turn (or its equivalent: vectors or terminal routing), but before the final approach fix. The key to this segment is to stay as close to the centerline of the approach course as you can. For a VOR approach, use the approach mode on your flight director if you have one. If you don't have an FD but do have a heading bug on your directional gyro, use the bug to help bracket and track the course. By staying on the centerline of the approach course, you accomplish two things: one, you remain in the safest on-course area for the descent; two, the centerline takes you directly *to* and *over* the VOR or NDB.

Final Segment

It is very important that you get as close to the VOR or NDB as possible. The only point in a non-precision approach where you really know exactly where you are is when you pass directly over the approach fix. Since the most important and critical descent in the approach comes after crossing the VOR or NDB inbound, it is vitally important that that descent be started from as close to the VOR or NDB as possible. If you pass by the final approach fix a half mile off to the side, you won't really know when to start down, because the station passage will be so slow that you won't know with any accuracy when you have gone by it. You also won't know exactly where you are, except that you are off to the side of the desired course "somewhere." This is one of the ways accidents happen—low, off course, in the clouds, groping.

If you do get yourself in a mess like this you are *much* better off doing a missed approach. You can always go back and try to do a better job the next time. Or you can go to your alternate, which, if you have picked it carefully and conservatively, should have better weather or better approaches or both.

Just as most bad landings have their origins with something done poorly further back in the traffic pattern, most bad approaches have their origins with something that wasn't done properly back in the initial stages of the approach—a procedure turn that wasn't carried out far enough, or a poor intercept of the inbound course, or an altitude that was allowed to slip. To keep things from getting out of hand, don't ever let them start. Remember the principle of multiple small corrections: It is much easier to fix lots of small things than it is to fix one big one.

NDB APPROACHES

It is especially important that you go directly over the beacon on an NDB approach. Going directly over the beacon on an NDB approach is the only way to add any real accuracy to what is, if the truth be told, a very imprecise type of approach.

I'm going to tell you how most professional pilots fly NDBs, but don't tell them I told you because they don't like this stuff getting out. First, do the best job you can of tracking inbound to the beacon, just like you always have. (See any good instrument manual for a review of tracking techniques.) Make sure you go directly over the beacon, even if you have to "home" to it the last little bit. You're looking for a good, clean station passage—no slow, sliding-by stuff. Then, once you have passed the beacon, concentrate on flying the heading for the final approach course—don't worry about perfect tracking at this point. If there is no crosswind, the heading and the approach course will be the same anyway. If there *is* a crosswind, the airplane may drift slightly off the final approach course, but it will still be parallel to it.

The key to an accurate NDB approach is not tracking. The key is starting the final segment from directly over the beacon—the final approach fix. The distance from the final approach fix to the missed approach point is usually no more than three or four miles. At this point you are already pretty close to the airport, and the heading for the final approach will point you directly at it. Tracking is nice, but it's not essential—you just aren't going to drift that much in three or four or even five miles. It is also very easy to get it wrong, and turning the wrong way will take you much further away from the correct course than any wind can. Here is a little quiz to illustrate my point:

Question #1: You have passed the beacon and are final approach inbound. The point of the needle is to the right of the tail and moving towards the bottom. In order to correct you turn (a) right; (b) left; (c) wait a while and see if it gets any worse; (d) experiment; (e) I'm not sure you need to correct—isn't it supposed to be at the bottom?; (f) not enough information; (g) too much information; (h) do a missed approach and resolve to go directly over the beacon the next time.

Question #2: Something tells me one is enough.

ᵀf you go directly over the beacon and then fly the heading that corresponds with the final approach course, you won't have problems with interpretation, and you'll know that any needle movement is caused by wind drift and nothing else.

An NDB is a *let-down* approach. Its purpose is to get you down and out of the clouds in the vicinity of the airport. At the NDB itself you are no more than five miles from the airport. The final approach course heading will point you directly at the airport, and your clock will tell you fairly accurately when you are overhead. That's all an NDB approach can do. Don't expect any more of it, and don't try to make it any more complicated than that. Flown properly, with careful attention to altitude, course intercept, station passage, heading, and time, if the weather is above minimums, the airport should be there.

ILS APPROACHES

I remember reading an editorial several years ago in one of the general aviation magazines in which the writer was complaining that the airline types were trying to hog all the federal airway money in order to have ILSs at all the airports served by the airlines. The editorial said the airline pilots considered any airport without an ILS to be inadequately equipped, and the editor disagreed with that. In fact, he implied that the airline types were a bunch of featherbedding sissies. I agreed with the editorial at the time. I figured it wouldn't hurt these guys to have to do an NDB or a VOR approach now and then.

Now I think I see what the airline types were getting at. I think, in a perfect world, all airports *should* have ILSs (or MLSs—Microwave Landing Systems, the next generation). An ILS is the safest approach we have at the present time. Any other approach is less safe—not *unsafe*, just *less* safe. Safety is not an absolute, it is a continuum that stretches from wildly reckless at one end to paralyzingly conservative at the other. There is a large area in the middle which is "safe," but some parts of the middle are more safe than others. An ILS approach is much safer than an NDB or VOR approach, and I put a much higher priority on ILSs now than I used to.

An ILS is an integral part of the instrument system. (Why do you think they call it an "Instrument Landing System"?) It isn't something tacked on to the end of the enroute part of the airway system, and it isn't just a way to get down out of the clouds. An ILS is a precision *approach* to the threshold of a runway (and here I think the word "approach" is exactly right). Instead of being just a "let-down" into what you hope are visual conditions, an ILS is a three-dimensional course aimed directly at the approach end of the runway. If flying a VOR approach is like following an electronic highway to the airport, then an ILS approach is an electronic tunnel to the end of the runway. As long as you stay in the tunnel formed by the localizer course (for the sides) and the glideslope (for the top and bottom), the light at the end of the tunnel is the approach end of the runway.

I'm not going to give you a rehash of how to chase ILS needles down the localizer-glideslope. If you are having trouble shooting good ILSs, get an instructor and do some practicing. An instructor can help you hone your techniques for your particular airplane and instrument configuration, and after that it is just a matter of practice. But I do want to mention a couple of important points.

You are seldom alone on an ILS. At a busy airport like DCA (Washington National) you can assume there is an airplane three miles in front of you and another three miles behind you. Even at less busy airports you can assume there are aircraft somewhere behind and in front of you. The only way to maintain separation is with speed control. If the controller tells you to do 160 knots to the marker, it isn't because he gets his break as soon as you get down, it's because someone behind you is doing 160 knots and will run you down if you don't. So do it—or if you can't go that fast, tell him so. He will then have to slow the traffic behind you, and the guy behind him and so on—which he can do, but it takes time. Whatever you do, don't say you will do 160 knots and then *not* do it.

If the ILS has a beacon—and most do—this can be a tremendous help in staying oriented while being vectored around for the ILS. The needle always points to the beacon. Flying vectors for an ILS is just like flying a big traffic pattern: dowr·vind, base and final (although sometimes you will enter on a base leg, and other times straight in; Fig.4-8). On downwind vectors, you'll know when you are abeam the beacon when the needle is 90 degrees off the nose. The further downwind you get, the closer to the tail the needle will get. On base, the information is harder to interpret, but it still points to the beacon, giving you at least a rough idea where on the approach you are. Once on the localizer, it will point more or less straight ahead outside the beacon, and more or less straight back past the beacon.

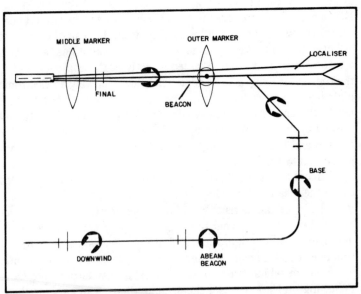

Fig. 4-8. An ILS has a downwind, base, and final leg, just like a VFR traffic pattern. The ADF needle always points to the beacon—a useful aid in orientation.

Since most beacons are co-located with the outer marker, this can be a good backup check on the marker. If you wonder or forget whether you went by the marker, just look at the beacon. If it is straight up, you haven't; straight back, you did.

ILSs are the bread-and-butter of the instrument system. They are accurate, reliable, and can safely handle large numbers of aircraft. It is hard to imagine our present airway system without them. They provide for a very nice flow from the higher speeds and altitudes of normal flight to the slower speeds and lower altitudes of the approach and landing. The transitions are logical, smooth, and consistent. That, I think, is the key point the airline types were trying to make: An ILS approach is consistent. Every VOR approach is different, but by and large all ILSs are alike. The consistency and inherent accuracy of an ILS approach is what makes an otherwise critical maneuver—a blind descent to within 200 feet of the ground—a routine event.

GCA APPROACHES

A GCA is a precision approach, meaning it has a glideslope, just like an ILS, but unlike an ILS, a GCA is controlled from the ground, rather than from the air. It is only found at military or joint-use (combined military and civilian) airports. The GCA approach is a radar approach, and it is the most accurate approach there is—more accurate than an ILS.

The pilot's part is easy: All you have to do is keep quiet and follow orders. The controller will give you a missed approach procedure and instruct you to do the missed approach if communications are lost for a certain number of seconds, and to discontinue acknowledging all further transmissions. He will then assign headings, within one degree of accuracy, to capture and track the localizer, and will tell you to increase or decrease your descent rate to capture and track the glideslope. He will be talking almost continuously so that positive communication is maintained; when he is not issuing a correction he will advise you of your position on the localizer and glideslope, as in "On the localizer, slightly above glideslope, correcting nicely." It is all very reassuring, easy to do, and, most important of all, a GCA can take you right down to the centerline of the runway. The controller can even issue headings to make sure the rollout is on the runway. With a GCA you can complete approaches where the fog is so thick you can't taxi in once you stop—they have to send a "Follow Me" car out to find you.

So what's the point of all this, besides being a lot of fun to practice? (You can only practice them to decision height—the military normally won't let you land out of it except in an emergency.) The point is, if both your destination and your alternate and every other airport in range go below minimums, as they could if dense fog were to overspread an entire area, you have only two choices. One is to go to an airport with an ILS to 200 and 1/2, declare an emergency, and hope you can shoot a perfect approach right down to the runway. The other is to go to a military field with a GCA. Everything else being equal, the GCA is better.

An ILS *can* be used down to the deck and *is* used for that in a CAT III ILS, but a CAT III ILS requires the use of a flight director plus a complete autopilot including autothrottles—a completely automatic landing. Not only is the Captain not expected to be able to hand-fly the airplane to the ground, he is not even *allowed* to. (The Captain's role in a CAT III ILS is to monitor the aircraft and be ready to take over and do a missed approach if anything goes wrong.) Without this extra equipment and training the GCA is simply the better approach when it comes to emergency approach conditions.

A GCA is *meant* to be hand-flown and it doesn't require any extra equipment or certification to be safe. It is a good idea to always have, filed away in the back of your head somewhere, the location of the nearest major military or joint-use airport: "any safe port in storm." It goes without saying that if you haven't ever done a GCA, you should hire a knowledgeable instructor and practice a couple. You don't want the first one you do to be the first one you *have* to do.

SAFETY VERSUS THE MISSION

I haven't tried to teach you how to fly instrument approaches in this chapter (that's a job for your flight instructor), nor have I dwelt on the basic terminology or procedures (that's a job for textbook writers). I hope I have been able to give you some pointers gleaned from the real world of instrument flying, and emphasize to you the importance of safety over mission accomplishment. Approaches are critical because they are done "low and slow," the most dangerous situation for an airplane. They are high in workload, and unforgiving of serious errors. Conservatism, practice, and attention to detail are the pilot's ways of showing respect for the most demanding but also the most rewarding part of instrument flying—

the instrument approach. If you always keep your priorities straight—safety first, the mission second—you won't have anything to be afraid of.

Chapter 5

Aircraft Limits

Pilots tend to accept the limitations of their aircraft with reluctance. They want their airplanes to be able to go anywhere, at anytime, even though they know that isn't possible. All airplanes have limits: A fighter, stressed to 9Gs, can come apart in a severe thunderstorm, and freezing rain will still keep an airliner on the ground. Power and sophistication extend capabilities, but all aircraft are limited to one degree or another.

Failure to know and observe whatever limitations exist is a fool's paradise: Paradise, because ignorance is bliss; foolish, because it's a game of chance. If, for instance, a pilot flies a single engine airplane across a body of water in the wintertime, and does not even contemplate the possibility of engine failure, then he is an ignorant but happy pilot; if the chances are one in 5,000 that the engine will fail during that time that he is out of reach of land, and if his survival time in the water is not long enough to be rescued, then he is also a foolish pilot, playing Russian Roulette with a one-in-5,000 chance of losing. Pilots who are not aware of the limitations of their aircraft are unknowingly taking these kinds of chances, both with themselves and with their passengers.

Up to a certain point, it doesn't make much difference what the odds are—whether the chance of engine failure, for instance, is one in 5,000 or one in 10,000. I say "up to a certain point" because at some point, when the odds reach something like one in a million, they approach the infinitely small and can be disregarded. But the chance of engine failure with current technology is much greater than one in a million and must be considered a real possibility. If it *can* happen, it *will* happen—maybe not to you, maybe not today, but it *will*.

CONTINGENCIES AND BACKUPS

One of the keys to safe flying is accepting and dealing with unlikely contingencies—the unlikely "what ifs." *If*, for instance, an engine quits right now, what will I do? If you find there is no good answer to that question, then you have discovered one of the limitations for that aircraft. There very often *are* good answers, but they also very often involve some inconvenience or additional expense the pilot would like to avoid. In the example above (flying single engine over icy water), an answer involving some inconvenience would be to fly around the body of water, and an answer involving an additional expense would be to invest in a raft. The wise pilot doesn't gamble. He always has a backup. If there is no backup, he doesn't do it.

People who don't fly seem to think that the only difference between a pilot's license and a driver's license is that the pilot's license is a little bit harder to get, but once you have it you can start flying everywhere instead of driving. You can drive a car in almost any kind of weather, assuming you have good equipment (snow tires, good wipers, fog lights, etc.) and drive slowly. But that's not true of airplanes. It doesn't take too long for even the new student pilot to figure out that he can't just replace his car with an airplane. The advantage of extra speed is balanced by the disadvantage of more limited utility.

Airplanes have limitations. We're going to start with the simplest and most basic airplane, and see what it can and can't be expected to do safely. Then we'll look at what additional capabilities can do to reduce the limitations of the basic single-engine aircraft. The idea in this chapter is not to give you a hard and fast list of limitations for your particular aircraft type, but to get you thinking about airplanes, their capabilities, and their limitations. I hope when we are done that you will have a pretty good idea of what you can expect from the airplane you fly, and you will also have a pretty good idea of what money can do to make an airplane more useful—not that you don't know that already, but it never hurts to dream a little.

BASIC LIMITATIONS

The first airplane I ever tried to buy was about as basic as an airplane gets—an Aeronca Champion, otherwise known as an "Airknocker Champ." I was a Second Lieutenant in the Armor Corps, Fort Knox, Kentucky, and a student pilot. There was a town just south of Ft. Knox called Elizabethtown ("E-town" in GI lingo), and this town had a little airport with one semi-paved runway and a bunch of little airplanes that spent most of their time sitting in the sun. One of these airplanes was a little Airknocker with a blue fuselage and white wings and a "For Sale" sign on it. The wings had been recently re-covered, which is why the paint didn't match, but I still thought it was great.

The two old boys who owned it, E-town natives, made it pretty clear without saying much that they were happy to take a Lootenant's money but weren't going to waste too much time getting to know him. They wanted $1900 for their treasure—which, in 1968, on a Lootenant's salary, was more than I thought I ought to spend. (My increasingly incredulous new bride, who was just beginning to realize that she had not been given all the information she was entitled to prior to entering into the marital contract, may have unintentionally influenced me also.) So I found a partner. Unfortunately, at the last minute my partner remembered that he was due to get out of the Army in a few months, and I was expecting orders to Viet Nam, and somehow reason prevailed and we decided finally that maybe it wasn't such a great time to become aircraft owners.

I've regretted it ever since. It would have been a bag of worms, and it would have ended up costing us a lot more than $1900 before we got it the way we wanted it, and I would have ended up having to buy him out, but then I could have cruised around the countryside in my own airplane whenever I felt like it.

I really do wish I had bought that Champ, because even though it was very limited in utility, all I wanted and needed was a fun machine. After all, I was in the Army. Where was I going to go? I had no illusions about using it for transportation. If the Kentucky murk cleared to six or seven miles visibility, I could have built some time and confidence following roads and rivers for an hour or so. If the engine, quit there were lots of fields to put it down in, and if I picked the wrong field it landed at about 3 miles an hour, so I could hardly get hurt. I couldn't have gone far enough to really get in trouble with the weather, because it only flew for about two hours and max cruise downhill was maybe 80 mph. It would have been great. I may buy one still.

It's important to remember, though, that that airplane was originally designed and sold as *transportation*. When that airplane was built, people thought there was going to be an airplane in every garage. It is easy to see now that as transportation that Champ had about as much utility as a glider, but they didn't think so when it was made. Keep that point in mind as you think about what people expect of their airplanes today.

ENGINE RELIABILITY

I did buy an airplane eventually, a Cherokee Warrior, "fully IFR:" two coms, two navs, an ADF, full gyro panel, and pitot heat. The salesmen told me I'd be able to fly in any kind of weather I wanted with that airplane. It was a neat little airplane, and I did get my instrument rating in it, and I did fly it in instrument conditions right down to minimums. Crazy.

It wasn't that I didn't think about the risks in flying single-engine IFR either, or that I didn't have some plans worked out for various contingencies. If the belt to the alternator broke, I would tell ATC right away before the battery ran down. If I lost an engine in the clouds I would declare an emergency, descend on instruments (I still had a battery and maybe even a windmilling engine) and when I broke out I would make an emergency landing just like always. And I would try, as much as possible, to avoid mountainous and over-water routes. I really thought those constituted contingency plans. It was actually just wishful thinking. The simple, hard truth is that I assumed the engine would never quit.

The engine never did quit. (I knew all along it wouldn't.) I cheated the limitations of that aircraft for as long as I owned it, which wasn't too long. There *is* utility in an instrument-equipped single-engine airplane, if you think about it and develop *real* contingency plans, but that doesn't mean you can safely fly a single-engine airplane in any weather, or over any terrain.

I think one of the real problems with single-engine airplanes is the fact that the engines *are* so incredibly reliable. I don't mean I wish they weren't reliable, but reliability does lead to complacency and a denial of the risks. Pilots usually have all kinds of explanations ready for non-fliers whenever the subject of single-engine reliability comes up. Does this sound familiar?:

"Aircraft engines just don't quit. If your car were built and maintained and inspected and treated the way an airplane engine is, it would never break down and would last 500,000 miles. Besides, an automobile has so many more parts than an airplane: water pumps, clutches, transmissions—there just aren't nearly as many things to go wrong on an airplane. Airplanes are inspected by highly trained and licensed mechanics, and then an additional preflight inspection is done before every flight by the pilot. The odds of anything slipping by are pretty remote." And so on.

"I know," they say, "but what happens even so if it *does* quit?"

"Nothing happens," you say, "You just glide down. It flies fine without the motor and you can land it in any field—there are plenty of places you can safely land it in. Really."

"What about over water," they say, "or in the mountains, or if you're in the clouds and can't see any fields, or at night? What do you do then?"

Well, what *do* you do then? Time to replay the tape: "Aircraft engines just don't quit. If your car . . ."

Let's take it from the top.

OVERWATER

A single engine, *fixed gear* aircraft should normally not be flown overwater out of gliding distance of land. A fixed-gear aircraft is very difficult to ditch successfully. The instant the wheels hit the water, no matter how gently they are set down, they stop, but the rest of the airplane continues forward. The airplane usually ends up flipping over onto its back. It can be survived, if all the belts are tight and shoulder harnesses are worn, but then you have the problem of getting out of an airplane while hanging upside-down from your seatbelt as it sinks. Flying single-engine, fixed gear aircraft overwater, out of gliding range of land, is very risky business, even with a raft on board.

To stay within gliding distance of shore you have to have a good idea of the gliding range of your aircraft for any given altitude. As a general rule, most single-engine, fixed gear aircraft have glide ratios of about 8 to 1: one mile of altitude (about 5,000 feet AGL) will allow you to glide 8 miles, in a no-wind situation. If your manual doesn't tell you what this ratio is for your aircraft, or does not provide a gliding distance verses altitude chart, then you should find out what it is. To do this, on a good day with light winds climb to 7,000 or 8,000 feet above the terrain, accelerate to cruise speed, and over a known landmark bring the power back to idle and glide into the wind, at best glide speed, until you have descended a total of 5280 feet. (If you don't know what best glide speed is for your airplane, use best rate of climb speed. This will be very close to best glide speed.) Don't forget the carb heat, if applicable, and clear the engine frequently. Note where you are, measure the distance traveled in statute miles on the Sectional, subtract one mile for the slight boost from the idling engine, and you will have a good, conservative idea of the glide ratio.

If we assume a glide ratio of 8:1, and we assume that the highest altitude we want to file for is 11,000 feet or about 2 miles high, then the widest body of water we ever want to cross is 32 miles: $2 \times 8 = 16$ miles to the no-wind midpoint. That will get you across Long Island sound at the widest point, but none of the Great Lakes at their widest points.

You don't have to avoid the water entirely, though; just climb to 11,000 feet and stay within 16 miles of the shore—a little closer if you have to penetrate into a headwind to reach the shore. To be really safe I would stay a little closer yet, because you want to have a little altitude "in your pocket" when you get to the shore in order to set up a pattern of some sort; you don't really want to get to the shore at the exact moment you run out of altitude.

I don't think this requires much of a sacrifice. You may have to climb higher than you otherwise would to cross a given body of water, and you might have to go a little bit out of your way crossing any of the Great Lakes, but the inconvenience is minor compared to the peace of mind. Remember, being an excellent swimmer or being in continuous radio contact with ATC isn't going to help you much if you are trapped inside a semi-submerged airplane, hanging upside-down from your seatbelt. Fixed-gear aircraft cannot be reliably ditched—you might get lucky, but you can't count on it. That is one of their limitations.

Retractable-gear aircraft *can* be ditched, but the success of the outcome varies in direct proportion to the calmness of the seas. Assuming you have an adequate life raft, and assuming it is in a place where it can be gotten to quickly and that you have a rope attached to it so that when you throw it out the door it doesn't leave port all by itself, being able to fly out of gliding range of the shore becomes a possibility, even for single engine airplanes. Ditching is still not a pleasant thought, nor is it a desirable outcome, but at least you have a plan—a backup. *If* the engine quits out of gliding range of land, you will ditch with the gear up (remembering to override any automatic gear extension provisions your aircraft might have), and get into the raft.

If you don't want to risk losing your airplane, or you don't want to buy a raft or just don't ever want to have to use one, fine; I didn't say you *had* to. Just stay within gliding distance of the shore. No pilot likes to go out of his way, but you're already going quite a bit faster than cars go and the cars have to go all the way around the lakes in any case, so going around is a fairly small price to pay to avoid possibly having to ditch.

With a multiengine airplane, flying overwater really isn't a limitation. Being able to do this sort of thing is one of the reasons you buy a multiengine airplane. If an engine quits, the remaining engine will take you to an airport. It is still a good idea to have life vests, a floating ELT, and a raft with flares and lights for any flight over 100 miles from land, and this is in fact a requirement for large and turbine aircraft flying overwater. (Once the first engine has stopped, you revert to being a single-engine airplane.)

Even in a multiengine airplane there are still risks; I flew from West Palm Beach to San Juan one dark night in a Citation, and found out the next day that a Beech Queen Air had gone down in the same area that night, while we were flying, and that when the Navy got to them the only thing left was an oil slick and a lot of sharks. Nobody ever knew what went wrong, but it's pretty clear that *something* did. Overwater flying does involve an additional element of risk, but I think the risks, with proper precautions, are acceptable in a multiengine aircraft.

For very long, max range overwater legs you would also want to check the single engine range, which is usually shorter than multiengine range. You would want to be sure that you could lose an engine at any point and still be able to reach land, either by turning back or continuing on. The point where it is closer to continue on is the famous "point of no return;" this is not the same as the halfway point, unless there is no wind. (If you were to fly with a tailwind away from land until exactly half your fuel was gone, and then turn around and head back on the remaining half, you would run out of fuel trying to get back; the tailwind that took you out is a headwind coming back.) The computation of the exact point of no return is complicated, but as long as you avoid the maximum effort overwater legs it is a fairly straightforward process to ensure that you can complete the leg from any point on one engine. There may be a short section in the middle where it is not obvious whether it is closer (considering the winds) to turn around or go forward, but if you have determined that you can make it at that point no matter which way you turn, you have satisfied the most important requirement.

INHOSPITABLE TERRAIN

"Inhospitable terrain" is an area that lacks suitable emergency landing sites—wilderness, mountains, rough seas, some large urban areas. A single-engine aircraft should never be out of gliding distance of a suitable emergency landing site. I used to fly in single-engine aircraft over mountainous terrain, and over urban areas at low but still legal altitudes (1000 feet), but I don't anymore. There aren't any "outs." If the engine quits, the landing will be a crash. I am willing to accept some damage in an emergency landing and expect to be possibly "shaken up" a little; the potential emergency landing site doesn't have to be perfect. But I want to be able to walk away from any landing following an engine failure, and you can't count on doing that if you crash land in the mountains or on city streets.

This doesn't eliminate flying over inhospitable terrain altogether. From 10,000 or 11,000 feet the gliding distance for most single-engine aircraft is in the 16 to 18 statute mile range, which may well be enough to enable you to get across a small mountain range or to stay within gliding distance of an airport. (If you look at *all* the airports, including private strips, you will find that there are a lot of airports, even in the mountains.) But it does limit your selection of routes in many cases. In the big, high mountain ranges such as the Rockies or the Sierra Nevadas there may not be any acceptable routes. If you have a turbocharger, and oxygen or pressurization, you will be able to climb much higher than 11,000 feet, which will allow you to glide much further and make available more routes. But as a general rule, the high mountains are no place for non pressurized single-engine airplanes.

Terrain is a consideration for multiengine airplanes in the higher elevations where single-engine ceiling is a factor. Single-engine ceilings for non-turbocharged twins are typically in the 6,000 to 8,000 foot range. (Turbocharging adds several thousand feet to single-engine ceilings.) This is fine for most of the country, but not for the high country in the West. You want to pick your routes very carefully out there. If it meant flying several hundred miles out of my way, I would do that before I would file a route with an MOCA (Minimum Obstruction Clearance Altitude) higher than my single-engine service ceiling.

If you do lose an engine on a multiengine airplane, you can trade airspeed for altitude by slowing to best single-engine rate of climb speed; this is the speed that will give you the slowest "drift down" and the highest single engine altitude—a little more time and altitude to help clear the high terrain. But don't count on too much. If you do lose an engine, it is best to assume that you will descend to the single-engine ceiling almost immediately, and plan accordingly. As long as you are careful about only filing routes you can handle on one engine if you have to, terrain should not be a problem. Being able to fly over most mountainous terrain is another one of the very good reasons people invest in multiengine airplanes.

URBAN AREAS

For single engine aircraft, being low and out of gliding range of any suitable landing site is sometimes completely unavoidable over cities—and, in fact, the regulations allow for this on takeoff and landing. FAR 91.79 *Minimum safe altitudes; general,* says "Except when necessary for takeoff and landing, no person may operate an aircraft below . . . an altitude allowing, if a power unit fails, an emergency landing without undue hazard to persons or property on the surface." This is an unavoidable risk which you must accept if you want to fly single-engine aircraft from an urban airport. This risk is one of the reasons single-engine aircraft are completely prohibited under Part 121, the regulations covering the major scheduled airlines. The FAA just does not want the public to fly on a single-engine airliner. As long as you and your passengers understand and accept the risk inherent in using airports that are surrounded by built-up areas, that is your business and the business of the people whose backyard you land in, but making it legal doesn't necessarily make it a good idea. You have to accept the consequences if something goes wrong on takeoff or landing, including the fact that there probably isn't a jury in the world who will see *your* side of it.

Flying over cities is not a problem if you're up high, because there are always lots of airports within gliding distance. But it *is* a problem down low. The problem most often arises when pilots try to avoid flying over or through a TCA (Terminal Control Area) by going low, under the edges. It is always densely populated under TCAs, and low enough to get under the TCA usually means 3500 feet AGL or lower, which is only about a five or six mile gliding range at the most. Sneaking along single engine under a TCA may be expedient, but it isn't very smart and it is usually illegal. Thirty five hundred feet or lower over an urban area is seldom "an altitude allowing, if a power unit fails, an emergency landing without undue hazard to persons or property on the surface." You should be IFR anyway, but if you insist on waiving the advantages of IFR and do go VFR on a route that takes you over a large urban area, go high and stay out from under the TCAs, except as necessary for takeoff and landing.

SINGLE-ENGINE IFR

Single-engine IFR is a tough one. If you plan on using your single-engine aircraft for transportation, you are going to be filing IFR, and that inevitably means you are going to find yourself in the clouds. If the engine quits, and the clouds go all the way to the ground, you have a problem.

Single-engine aircraft *can* be safely flown in the clouds, and can and should be operated IFR in any case, but one important limitation should be observed. That limitation is to fly only when the ceiling is high enough that if the engine fails, you will still be able to pick out and glide to an emergency landing site after descending through the bases. You need, in other words, some "clear air" between the ground and the bottom of the bases—the ceiling.

The height of the ceiling required will vary with the terrain. In the Midwest, where the terrain is flat and there are fields everywhere, 1,000 feet might be enough—all you really need is enough altitude to fly a pattern. Over hilly, semi-cleared terrain such as you might find in parts of the South or Mid-Atlantic states, you would probably want 3,000 or 4,000 feet—there are lots of fields, but there might not be one right underneath you when you break out. Over areas that are sparsely cleared and settled, like parts of Maine, Michigan, or Minnesota, 8,000 or 9,000 feet might be more like it. These are just guidelines. You will have to use your best judgement on this. Any area less suitable for an emergency landing than that is "inhospitable terrain" and should be avoided.

You may have figured out that this limits single engine IFR to situations where you could have gone VFR anyway—at least 1,000 foot ceiling, and three or four miles visibility—but that still leaves a lot of utility. Being able to operate single engine aircraft within the instrument system protects you from the vagaries of scud-running and deteriorating or unexpected weather, and provides you with the same protection and assistance available to every other aircraft operating in the instrument system.

You don't *have* to observe this ceiling requirement (unless you want to operate for hire). Part 91 does not specifically limit single engine IFR to situations where sufficient VFR exists beneath the clouds to make a safe emergency landing, but it doesn't specifically allow it, either. If the engine quits, the burden of proof will be on you to show that your emergency landing was not unduly hazardous to persons or property on the surface (FAR 91.79), and that your operation with ceilings less than that necessary to find a suitable landing site was not careless and reckless (the great catch-all, FAR 91.9). In any case, you should think twice before you assume risks the FAA has found unacceptable for paying passengers.

SINGLE-ENGINE NIGHT FLYING

The last major limitation of single engine airplanes involves night flying. The inherent safety of single-engine aircraft is predicated on being able to make safe emergency landings. Darkness severely limits your ability to do this. The only time you can really see the ground adequately at night is when the sky is clear and the moon is full or almost full. (It also helps if the ground is covered with snow.) The rest of the time, all you can really see are lighted areas and dark areas. That doesn't give you much to go by. A dark area could be a field or it could be woods; it could be flat or hilly, smooth or rocky. Whether a particular dark area is suitable as an emergency landing site is purely a matter of luck. At night it is also almost impossible to see obstructions such as trees and towers, and it *is* impossible to see power lines.

The only good solution to the limitations of single-engine night flying is to stay within gliding range of lighted airports at all times. It is usually possible to pick a route that keeps you within gliding distance of a lighted airport at all times, although you may have to zigzag some and you may have to go higher than you would have otherwise. Naturally, the more altitude capability your aircraft has, the greater the gliding range and the more likely it is that you will be able to find a route within range of lighted airports. If having to zigzag or fly higher than you would like to is the difference between taking a chance on the engine not quiting that night and not taking a chance, that seems like a small price to pay. The need to stay within gliding range of a lighted airport is an unavoidable limitation of flying single engine aircraft at night.

MULTIENGINE AIRCRAFT: TAKEOFF PERFORMANCE

Weather, terrain, and time of day are major limiting factors affecting the utility of single-engine airplanes. Freedom from the requirement to have a suitable emergency landing site—and therefore the freedom to operate with low ceilings, over nearly any terrain, day or night—is the single best reason for the additional expense and complexity of the multiengine airplane.

The next best reason is power itself: In practical terms, it is very difficult to get more than about 400 hp out of an engine without going to a radial or turbine design, each of which has disadvantages of its own—small turbines are very expensive, and radials are heavy and bulky. Therefore, if an aircraft requires more than 400 hp for adequate performance, the simplest and least expensive solution is to use two smaller reciprocating engines, the sum of which equals the required horsepower. Having two engines adds to the expense of the airplane, but it is the only practical way to power aircraft with a loaded weight over 4,500 pounds. But this is also why multiengine airplanes don't fly so well on one engine—to a very large extent, they have two engines because they *need* two engines.

The most serious limitation for multiengine aircraft is in takeoff perfomance. For non-jet airplanes grossing less than 12,500 pounds, there is no requirement to be able to clear obstacles or even to be able to climb to a specific altitude in the event of an engine failure after takeoff. The only requirement is that the aircraft be able to achieve a positive rate of climb, at sea level, in the takeoff configuration. Most piston twins can climb—eventually—to 6,000 or 7,000 feet above sea level, if the airplane is clean and the prop on the inoperable engine is feathered. But being able to eventually climb to 6,000 or 7,000 feet is a lot different from having an assured takeoff and initial climbout capability.

If you lose an engine on a multiengine airplane on the ground, during the takeoff roll, you really have a handful of airplane on your hands. Instructors don't like to cut engines on the takeoff roll unless the speed is very slow; the resulting swerve is instantaneous and dramatic—sometimes too dramatic. At the higher speeds there is no way one little nosewheel can keep a multiengine airplane tracking straight down the runway with one engine pulling full power and the other windmilling and creating a lot of drag. To keep it on the runway, the power has to come back on the good engine, and it has to be done *right now*.

This is the reason "zero-zero" takeoffs are so dangerous in multiengine airplanes. Without visual clues, you will almost certainly find yourself off the runway before you can cut the good engine and regain control. Having two engines cannot make minimum visibility takeoffs (less than 1/4 mile) safe; in fact, it probably makes them even *more* dangerous.

If you have never had any training in takeoff aborts, which is what this is, you should find a mature, experienced multiengine instructor and the widest, longest runway around, and practice them, starting first with an engine failure just at the start of the takeoff roll, and work your way up to whatever speed the instructor feels both you and he can handle. (*Don't* try this with a hood on. The lesson will be sufficiently impressive with everything going for you that there is no reason to take unnecessary chances.)

If nothing else, you will learn firsthand how quickly you must react to keep the airplane on the runway, and how important training in aborted takeoffs is. I have noticed in Falcon and Citation simulator training that about one in every three aborted takeoffs on minimum-length runways ends up going off the end. The problem with jets is getting them stopped. The problem with piston twins is control. You have to be able to see several runway centerline stripes to have control, which means that piston twins are limited to better than 1/4 mile visibility for takeoff.

Once the airplane is airborne, but before the gear comes up, climb capability on one engine will be marginal to nil for most piston twins. If you have a lot of runway ahead of you, the best thing to do is pull the power levers back and land straight ahead. (This applies only to Part 23 airplanes; Part 25 airplanes are committed to continue the takeoff at this point.) If you don't have enough runway, you have a real challenge ahead of you: You must nurse the airplane along in the air while attempting to accelerate to at least V_{xse} (best single engine angle of climb), then attempt to achieve a positive rate of climb so the gear can be retracted. But one of the main sources of drag preventing the airplane from accelerating and then climbing is the gear hanging down—a real "Catch-22." If you've got the strength to hold the rudder in there as long as it takes, and you hold V_{xse} perfectly, and the density altitude isn't too high, it should eventually start to climb, enabling you to get the gear up.

Once the gear is up, the *real* tricky part is over. (After that, it's just *merely* tricky.) If you can't get it to climb . . . well, that's why it's nice to have enough runway to put it back on when an engine quits. Your indiscretion and bad luck will have conspired, in that case, to help you find out how good your insurance is.

If you lose an engine on a multiengine airplane after the gear is up, the success of the outcome will depend on pilot proficiency, the weather, and the terrain. If you can get the engine feathered without losing control, and if the airplane is not overloaded or operating out of a very high airport, it should continue to climb at this point. If the terrain is flat and without obstructions, you should be able to climb to a 400 foot pattern altitude and return to the field. If the weather is below pattern altitude, precluding an immediate return to the field, you should be able to climb high enough to do an approach if the airport is above landing minimums. If it is below landing minimums, then you have to continue the climb and go to your takeoff alternate.

TAKEOFF ALTERNATES

If you didn't think about a takeoff alternate, this is a good time to do so. Anytime you take off in a multiengine airplane from an airport where the weather is lower than 400 feet, you want to know where the nearest airport is that is above minimums, in case you do have a serious problem on takeoff. Otherwise, what are you going to do? You can't circle back—the ceiling is too low. If the departure airport is below minimums you are going to have to go somewhere and shoot an approach. A good guideline is that a takeoff alternate should be within 30 minutes of the departure airport at single engine airspeeds. In the absence of a decent takeoff alternate, multiengine airplanes should be limited to ceilings of at least 400 feet for takeoff.

ENGINE-OUT CLIMB GRADIENTS

If the terrain isn't flat, then the single-engine climb gradient— the ratio of altitude gained verses distance traveled—becomes the key factor. All piston-engine airplanes suffer from marginal single engine climb characteristics. Some are better than others, but even the best will only climb about 400 feet per minute under ideal circumstances. Since for most multiengine airplanes the best single engine rate of climb speed is around 120 mph, or two miles per minute, this means the best climb *gradient* you can hope for is 200 feet per mile. Our star performer would have to go five miles out, straight ahead, just to climb 1000 feet, and that's about the most that can be expected.

Therefore, for all practical purposes, if there are hills or obstructions around, you have to be able to see them to avoid them, because you almost certainly are *not* going to be able to outclimb them. One of the scariest things I can think of is to be sitting in an airplane with an engine out, in the clouds, climbing for all you're worth, wondering whether you will clear the hills or not. The only way to avoid that feeling for sure is to wait for the weather to lift enough so you can see a way through and around the hills if you do lose one and have to nurse it along.

The back of the Jepp plate sometimes has takeoff minimums for Part 135 and 121 operators. These takeoff minimums allow for marginal single-engine climb capability and take into account the surrounding terrain, and are well worth observing. If a SID is available, it will sometimes describe required climb gradients, in feet per nautical mile. It would be nicer if these restrictions were given in feet per minute, but it is fairly easy to convert: If your multiengine airplane climbs on one engine at 100 knots, divide that by 60 to get nautical miles per minute—1.66 in this case. Divide your expected single-engine climb rate by that number to get gradient in feet per mile. For example, if you expect a single-engine rate of climb of 250 fpm at 100 knots, dividing 250 by 1.66 results in a gradient of 150 feet/mile. If the SID requires a climb gradient greater than that, don't go until the weather clears.

I think it would be great if the FAA were to publish a "reverse" approach for each airport; that is, if the approach plate shows you the safe way down and into the airport, the reverse approach plate (most likely it would be called a "departure plate") would show you the safe way up and out for a given minimum rate of climb off a given runway. But they don't. Some pilots like to use an ILS "backwards" on climbout for just this reason—what is safe going down must be safe going up. The only problem with that is that very few non-jet airplanes have enough power to climb on one engine up a 3 degree glideslope. So in the absence of an official instrument route around the obstructions, you are going to have to rely on your eyeballs, and that means waiting until the ridges are not obscured.

When it comes to multiengine airplanes, the simple fact is this: For all the utility they give you once you are in the air and on your way, there is no guarantee they will always *get* you into the air and on your way. Multiengine airplanes do a pretty good job of maintaining level flight on one engine, but when it comes to takeoff and climb, they very often need both engines.

This is still a big improvement over the single-engine airplane. In a single engine airplane the entire flight is limited by the terrain and the ceiling. In a multiengine airplane, normally only the initial part is limited—the takeoff roll, liftoff, and initial climbout until clear of the surrounding terrain. But it is still a limitation. You still have to ask the question, "*If* I lose an engine here, or here, or *here*, what will I do?" If the weather or the terrain, or a combination of both, precludes a satisfactory answer, then you must confront this limitation. *All* airplanes have limitations—no matter how much money you spend you will never completely eliminate them. If you want to operate airplanes safely, you just have to live with them.

You hear a lot of talk about how multiengine airplanes are really more dangerous than single engine airplanes—that their accident rates are much higher; that having two engines gives you two chances to lose an engine; that all the remaining engine is good for is to take you to the scene of the accident, and so on. I don't believe it. If people really believed that, they would provide for some sort of automatic shutdown of the good engine in the event of engine failure. Then the multiengine airplane would be just as "safe" as the single—you wouldn't have to worry about single-engine control problems because there wouldn't be any—just emergency landing problems.

Clearly, flown properly, the multiengine airplane *is* safer than the single-engine airplane—why else would the FAA *require* all airliners to have at least two engines? But this talk does point to where the problem lies with multiengine airplanes: It's not that multiengine airplanes aren't safe on one engine, but that for them to be safe, a very high premium is placed on pilot skill and proficiency, and they are very unforgiving when that skill and proficiency is lacking.

It isn't multiengine *airplanes* that are sometimes more dangerous than single-engine airplanes, it's multiengine *pilots*. We will talk more about this in the chapter on Personal Limits, but in a way, it is helpful to think of this requirement for skill and proficiency as a limitation of the airplane: Multiengine aircraft are limited to being flown by skilled and proficient pilots. If that limitation is not observed, then the multiengine airplane *is* more dangerous than the single engine airplane.

TURBOPROPS

A turboprop is a turbine engine in which the exhaust gases drive (via a turbine, hence the name) a propeller. (If the turbine drives a fan, the engine becomes a turbofan; if the turbine drives only a compressor, the engine is a turbojet.) Turbine engines have many advantages over reciprocating engines—and several disadvantages. Turbine engines are small (relative to power), light (relative to power), easy to start, tolerate a wide range of operating temperatures, are reliable, easy to maintain, and go a long time between overhauls. They are, however, expensive (even relative to power), not as fuel-efficient as reciprocating engines (given current technology), and not quite as responsive as reciprocating engines—they are slower to "spool up" when power is called for. Despite these disadvantages, the advantages are so great that turbine engines of one kind or another are generally the engine of choice for aircraft requiring more than 800 horsepower for adequate performance.

For aircraft with max gross takeoff weights between 8,000 and 12,500 pounds, turboprop engines are the norm. For aircraft grossing more than 12,500 pounds ("large aircraft," by FAA definition) the turbofan is the more common engine type, although, because of their improved fuel specifics relative to turbofans, turboprops are becoming more common on larger commuter aircraft. The pure jet engine (the turbojet engine) is virtually obsolete, although it still has some limited military, very high altitude, and supersonic applications.

Most turboprops gross out at or under 12,500 and are certified under Part 23, just like piston twins. Heavier aircraft, regardless of engine type, are normally certified under Part 25, which is a much more demanding set of certification standards. But there isn't any magic to a Part 25 airplane—performance is performance, no matter how an airplane is certified. The main difference between a Part 25 aircraft and a Part 23 aircraft is that the Part 25 aircraft has had its performance tested and measured in a way that assures a safe takeoff in the event of engine failure. Performance charts tell the pilot how much runway he will need for a given ambient temperature, airport pressure altitude, takeoff weight, runway slope, and wind. With this information, the pilot then knows that, given an engine failure anywhere on takeoff, he will be able to stop the aircraft or, beyond a certain speed, continue the takeoff (meaning, achieve a positive rate of climb, retract the gear, raise the flaps, and continue the climbout at a climb gradient of at least 24 feet per 1000). A Part 23 aircraft may well be able to successfully complete a takeoff through climbout also, but the information necessary to assure it in advance may not be available.

Regardless of how an airplane is certified—and, to a large extent, regardless of whether the turbine drives a prop or a fan—turbine engines provide large amounts of power, and power is what enables a multiengine airplane to fly on one engine. Whether you use that performance wisely depends on whether you voluntarily observe the same limits that you would be required to observe if small turboprops *were* certified under Part 25. The power is there, but the limits have to be self-imposed. Since the performance of the Part 23 airplane has not, in most cases, been documented as thoroughly as the Part 25 airplane, the limits usually have to be estimated.

There is a minimum safe takeoff distance for any given set of conditions, and that minimum safe distance is most affected by single-engine performance. If, for instance, it takes two engines to clear the trees at the end of a field, what's going to happen if one engine quits just at liftoff? If it just cleared the trees with two engines, how is it going to clear them with one? It won't. The alternative is to abort the takeoff, but at this late date there can't be much runway remaining—probably not enough to get stopped. There is no "out" to this situation; you lose no matter what you do.

You can't very well make the runway longer, or make the engines suddenly more powerful, but there is something you can do to make the aircraft performance fit the runway available.

One of my favorite stories is about a truck which got completely stuck under a bridge—couldn't go forward, couldn't go backwards. The experts were called in and after much mumbling and figuring and nodding of heads they determined that it was going to cost a billion dollars or so to raise the bridge enough to get the truck out. A little kid watching said it might be easier to lower the truck than to raise the bridge. "How are we going to do that?" asked all the experts. "Let some air out of the tires," said the kid. In the case of a short field takeoff, "letting some air out of the tires" means taking some weight off—people, baggage, or fuel—whatever is easier, and that usually is the fuel.

There are other variables that affect takeoff distance—ambient temperature and wind—but weight is the only variable that can be easily changed. (Sometimes you can't take any weight off. Then your only choice is to wait for the air temperature to drop, or the wind to pickup.) All a Part 25 airplane does that a turboprop doesn't *have* to do is match its takeoff weight to the conditions that exist at the time of takeoff. You can't "bump up" the performance by boosting the power of your engines, but you can do the same thing by limiting the weight of the airplane. The lighter the airplane, the less runway is needed to accelerate to liftoff speed, abort, and stop on the remaining runway. Reducing the fuel load in order to make the accelerate-stop distance equal the runway length may force you to make a fuel stop, but at least if an engine quits on the takeoff roll (or even acts like it's going to quit), you should be able to get the airplane stopped on the remaining runway—which is a lot better place to stop than the Burger King parking lot across the street from the airport.

Ideally, you are also looking for enough runway to be able to continue the takeoff after an engine failure at liftoff, with a climb rate after gear retraction and prop feathering of about 250 fpm. This would be the equivalent, for all practical purposes, of a Part 25 airplane. I say "ideally," because, after all, a small turboprop is not a Part 25 aircraft. Only the Part 25 airplane can *guarantee* a successful single engine takeoff, and then only if the appropriate weight limitation is observed. But a turboprop, operated with a careful eye to its weight, eliminates *most* of the takeoff performance limitation of the piston twin.

JETS

The pilot of a Part 25 airplane (which basically means jets) has no choice but to observe the weight limitations dictated in the Flight Manual. If he does, and an engine quits, he knows that up to V_1 (decision speed) he will have enough runway to stop the airplane, and past V_1 he will be able to keep going. He still has to ensure terrain and obstacle clearance—there is no guarantee a Part 25 airplane can outclimb the hills or jump over tall buildings, only that it can achieve a climb gradient of at least 2.4 percent. (That translates into a climb rate of about 250 fpm for most business jets.) But at least the problem is limited to the climbout segment—you don't have to worry whether or not it will *fly*.

The irony is that jets are easier than either piston or turbine twins to fly on one engine; all you have to do is set the correct pitch on the attitude indicator for single-engine climb, and center the ball with the rudder—there's no prop to feather. Once you reach at least 400 feet and the obstacles are clear, you push it over a little to accelerate to flap retraction speed, call for the appropriate checklist, and fly away. Jets are great. I think the government ought to buy us each one. The government's got *lots* of money.

I'm not trying to rub it in that you don't have a jet. I don't have one either. I just get paid to fly one once in a while. I *do* want to remind you of what I said in the Introduction: The non-professional pilot has the hardest job in aviation, and this is just another example. As easy as engine failures are to handle in jets, and as experienced, proficient and thoroughly trained as most professional jet pilots are, mistakes still happen—which means you just can't be too careful.

WEATHER LIMITATIONS

The way in which an airplane is equipped for weather also determines its limits. Without radar or other storm detection equipment, an aircraft's ability to avoid thunderstorms is very limited, and without de-icing (or anti-icing) equipment, real cold weather instrument flying is virtually impossible. But these are as much weather problems as they are aircraft problems, and are covered in Chapter 6, Weather Strategy. Just remember that the airplane doesn't know anything about chapters. If the airplane won't fly anymore because it's covered with ice, it really doesn't matter whether we say the pilot exceeded the limits of his aircraft, or the pilot showed bad judgement concerning the weather. The result is the same. An aircraft's ability to deal with thunderstorms and ice is a major limiting factor in its operation.

COMMON SENSE

"Know and observe the limitations of your aircraft" is just another way of saying "Use common sense." But if I had said that at the beginning of this chapter, you wouldn't have known what I meant. We all would have nodded wisely and acted like we all understood, when in fact, all by itself that statement is just another meaningless, gold-plated platitude. I hope it's clearer now. Common sense tells you you can't expect the engine in a single-engine airplane to never quit. Common sense tells you you can't expect 200 hp to drag an airplane through the air as well as 400 hp can, especially if that 200 hp is stuck out on one wing and is dragging the other 200 hp along with it. Common sense tells you not to put yourself in a position where the answer is "I really don't know" when the question is "What are you going to do?" All airplanes have limitations, and being a good pilot means living with them.

That's just common sense.

Chapter 6

Personal Limits

"Know your limits and do not exceed them." I have been hearing that since I was a student pilot. It didn't mean very much to me then and it doesn't mean very much to me now. It's sounds good, but that's about all. Its easy to say things like that, and it's easy to nod your head in agreement, and there's probably no harm done in either. But *simply* saying it doesn't increase the overall safety level one iota.

Our limitations as pilots are a direct function of our level of experience and training. There is nothing mysterious about it, and there is no reason to make it any more difficult to understand than it needs to be. What I want to do in this chapter is avoid beating you over the head with platitudes, and try to give you instead a clear and specific idea of what is meant by "knowing your limits." I want to give you something concrete you can hang on to—something you can use when you look at a situation so you can say either, "Yes, I can handle this," or, "No, I can't handle this—not for sure, not yet, but I am working on it and I will be able to soon." The reason I want to do this is because nobody ever did it for me, and I spent years trying to "know my limits" without anything to go by except that dumb phrase.

Every time you go to fly, you are presented with a different situation, and in the beginning each situation is a new one. How do you know what you can handle and what you can't, and how do you safely go about getting the experience you need so all these situations aren't new all the time?

PRIVILEGES AND LIMITS

As a student pilot your limits are prescribed by your flight instructor. You can only do what he or she allows you to do. This is in recognition of the fact that the student pilot doesn't have enough experience or training to determine his own limits. After you get your license, though, you are supposed to be able to determine your own limits. A Private Pilot's license has very few limitations—a brand-new Private Pilot can legally fly from JFK to LAX, at night, with passengers, as long as he observes VFR ceiling and visibility minimums (which can be as low as one mile visibility and "clear of clouds"). But that doesn't mean he *should*. The privileges granted to a Private Pilot are enormous, which puts a tremendous premium on self-discipline.

INSTINCT

Too often, pilots react to "knowing your limits" by relying on instinct or intuition—their "gut" reaction. They look at the sky, or the weather report, or the airplane, and they try to get a "feel" for whether going is the right thing to do or not.

The problem with this is that we are all cut out differently. Some people look at a new and potentially threatening situation—one they have no experience with—and just shrug their shoulders, and off they go. Others are *too* cautious. They stick to the same routine: touch-and-goes, sightseeing, a short hop to get a hamburger at the one airport they are familiar with. They don't seem to be able to find enough confidence to try anything any harder. Their "gut" reaction is an unreasonable fear.

If you do feel real anxiety about a trip—anxiety that seems to go beyond "butterflies"—you should not ignore those feelings; you are probably taking on too much. Likewise, just because you *don't* have any feelings of anxiety or fear doesn't necessarily mean you must be foolhardly. But if we rely strictly on these "feelings" (or lack of them), we will never know what our real limitations are. Our real limitations can only be derived rationally.

A SYSTEMATIC APPROACH

When I was a kid, we used to move around a lot—my father

was in the Army. Moving all the time was "normal" for me, and since it very often meant living with other Army kids, it was normal for most of my friends, too. When you move all the time, you tend to develop a system for mapping out the territory and getting your bearings in a new place. (As kids, we didn't know we were doing this, of course—it is only in retrospect that I can see that we had, in fact, a regular system for getting settled.) Our "system" was based on starting from a known point. We then expanded our base outward from that point.

Specifically, if you were a new kid, you went outside and hung around the yard, and sooner or later some kids would come over to check you out, and that would lead to going over to their house, and the next day you would meet some other kids, and so on. Within a week or so you knew the whole neighborhood, and within a couple of weeks you even knew all the "secret" places.

So what's this got to do with aviation? The reason I bring it up is because the process of knowing and observing your limits as a pilot is exactly analogous to getting settled in a new area as a kid. As a pilot, you start from a known base—your home airport—and you then extend your limits outwards. But this base is more than just a geographical base; it is also a base of skills, and it starts with those skills you learned as a student pilot.

This is the opposite of what having a Private Pilot's license implies. The license itself allows you to do almost anything—it gives you the world, and tells you to *restrict* that world as discretion and judgement dictates. I think that's the wrong way to go about it. I think starting from a known base and *extending* your world is the way to do it.

You've probably figured out by now that this problem of limitations *is* a problem only because your license allows you so much freedom. It would be much easier if your first license restricted you in some way, telling you just exactly how far away from home base you could fly, and what the weather had to be, and what kind of airplane you were allowed to fly, and so forth. You wouldn't have to worry about limitations because you would always be bumping up against the restrictions if your license.

But each time you wanted to extend your privileges you would have to take a test to prove you were capable of exceeding your previous limitation. That would be a real nuisance, and it would be expensive, and it isn't the way we have traditionally done things in private aviation in this country. But it *would* get rid of that vague feeling in the pit of the stomach, standing on the ramp, wondering whether to go or not.

So let's figure out first what a typical new Private Pilot can do. Then let's take a look at what he probably ultimately wants to be able to do, and try to devise a rational plan for achieving those goals. Somewhere along the way you should find the spot where you come in.

NEW PRIVATE PILOTS

A brand-new Private Pilot is really limited to the specific skills he learned for his checkride: fairly short cross-countries in good weather, some basic airwork, and takeoffs and landings. Those are really the only things within his limits at that point. I'm not trying to demean those accomplishments. I know those skills don't come easily and any new Private Pilot has a right to be proud of them. But you know and I know that just because you have a Private Pilot's license doesn't mean you know everything you need to know to safely exercise the full privileges of your "ticket."

Generally, the two best tricks in the new Private Pilot's bag are takeoffs and landings. He (or she) has worked hard at them, done a lot of them, and generally enjoys doing them. They're his showpieces. He may not be able to do a soft or short field takeoff or landing very well, and he may still have a little trouble getting oriented in the traffic pattern at an unfamiliar airport, but he can do regular takeoffs and landings consistently well and safely. The new Private Pilot can also do some basic airwork fairly well—simple stalls, steep turns, ground reference maneuvers; he can plan a cross-country quite well, but is generally uncomfortable setting off on routes he either didn't cover as a student or that lack prominent landmarks such as major rivers or four-lane highways; he can keep the airplane upright on instruments fairly well, and can usually manage turns to headings and controlled descents solely by reference to instruments. All in all, a pretty good start.

What do these skills translate into in practical terms? In practical terms it means the new Private Pilot has a lot of room to have fun, but very little capability for transportation. He can go sightseeing with a friend, he can do touch-and-goes, he can extract himself from certain emergency situations such as approaches to stalls and inadvertent instrument flight, but if he wants to actually *go* somewhere, he has to limit himself to the same kinds of days and the same kinds of trips his flight instructor limited him to as a student—namely, short day trips out and back when the weather is good.

The typical new Private Pilot wants to get out of his trainer and into something with a little more "performance," and he wants something with four seats—nobody has just one friend when he's a new Private Pilot. So the first thing he usually does is to get checked out in the next bigger and more powerful airplane up from his trainer. Unfortunately, "checked out" often means 30 minutes of dual, most of that in the pattern—and takeoffs and landings are what he does best and needs the *least* practice with.

So what happens is that the new Private Pilot gives up 40 or more hours of experience in one airplane for a quick familiarization in another. He gives up a good part of his limited competence because he wants to go just a little bit faster and carry two extra people. It's hard to build on a known base when you give a good part of it away.

What should he do? What he *should* do is get a lot more comfortable with the airplane he knows—particularly with the airwork, but also with adding precision and smoothness to his flying in short forays away from his home base. That's what he *should* do. But what he is *going* to do anyway is get checked-out in the bigger airplane—which is okay, but only if he is willing to spend five or six hours in it getting some dual instruction in all the maneuvers, just like he did for his Private. Then he will be as competent in the bigger airplane as he was in the trainer.

At this point the new Private Pilot can go sightseeing with his friends and make short cross-countries out and back. But what he *really* wants to do is what brought him down to the airport in the first place—that is, he wants to go places that are far enough away to make the use of an airplane worthwhile, and he probably doesn't want to have to come right straight back. And that's when he starts running into trouble.

INSTRUMENT TRAINING

The only way to consistently, safely, and routinely use an airplane for transportation is to file IFR, which means that the next step for the new Private Pilot who wants to use an airplane for travel is an instrument rating. Regardless of whether you are a new Private Pilot or have had your license for a while, if your goal is to use an airplane for regular transportation, and you don't have an instrument rating, you should start working on it.

Don't worry if you don't have 200 total hours yet (the minimum to take the instrument checkride.) Go ahead and start anyway. The necessary hours will take care of themselves. You probably have 50 or 60 hours already, even as a brand new pilot, and the rating takes at least 40 hours, so you are already close to the halfway mark with the minimum training alone. You will probably do some fun flying at the same time you are working on your rating, and you will find, in any case, that once you have started your instrument training, your confidence will have increased so much that you will want to do a lot of flying, and the remaining hours will most likely take care of themselves. If you do finish your instrument training before getting the necessary total amount of time, you will know exactly how many more hours are needed, and you will have the *benefit* of the instrument training for *all* those hours, even if you can't actually file IFR yet.

By the time you have finished your instrument training you should have gotten over your shyness about talking on the radio, and you probably will have discovered the secret for handling busy airports: Go IFR. When you file IFR, you are "in the system" to start with, and while things may get busier as you approach the "aerodrome," if you're already IFR there won't be that terrible sense of getting picked up and thrown into the middle of a maelstrom that there is when you attempt to enter busy airspace VFR. Two of the biggest problems for the new pilot—shyness with the radio, and dealing with busy airports—are well on their way to being solved the day you begin your instrument training.

DAY TRIPPING

In the meantime, before you complete the instrument rating, you can still have fun and extend your capabilities a little bit with easy cross-countries. You might, for instance, want to pick a spot that interests you and your family or friends to fly to for a short day trip—a resort airport, or an airport near a lake or the ocean, or maybe one that has a specialty such as gliders or antique aircraft. Treat it strictly as fun, but plan it as carefully as if your instructor were looking over your shoulder. In fact, don't hesitate to ask an instructor to check you out or offer advice; I have yet to meet an instructor who wasn't happy and even flattered to be asked to help out new pilots.

If the weather is nice, go. If it rains that day, so what? You wouldn't want to go to a place like that on a lousy day anyway.

Plan on staying only a short time. That way the weather won't have a chance to catch you. (But, of course, check the weather with Flight Service before heading home anyway.) This is the way a new Private Pilot can use his license in a safe way that recognizes his limitations, and gain a lot of confidence in the airplane and himself, which is the first step toward eliminating further limitations.

EXTENDED CROSS-COUNTRY FLYING

Once you have your instrument rating, a new world is available to you—the world of true cross-country flying. Until you have that rating, there really isn't any point in even trying to use your airplane for reliable transportation, or worry about going to busier airports, or flying at night, or trying to divine in some obscure way when the weather is "too bad" to go, or whether you can handle a cross-country requiring several stops—you shouldn't be doing any of these things anyway. They all involve a high probability that instrument skills will be required, and without those skills and the rating that goes with them, you aren't left with any good choices. (Neither "scud-running" nor sitting in the motel waiting for the weather to clear are what I would call good choices.)

Until you have an instrument rating, real cross-country flying exceeds your limitations. You may disagree with me, of course, especially if you live in an area of the country that generally has VFR weather, but my guess is that your likelihood of agreeing with me will be directly proportional to the number of times you have embarrassed or scared yourself trying to prove me wrong.

You may be expecting me to say that after 200 or 300 hours you should be able to handle most VFR conditions, and after 500 or 600 hours you should have the experience and judgement to handle even low VFR conditions, but I'm not going to. You can certainly become accomplished at flying in marginal VFR weather, but that's not the point. The point is that flying for transportation always involves certain elements outside of your control, and the instrument system is the only reliable system for dealing with those contingencies.

LIMITATIONS OF VISUAL FLIGHT RULES

Actually, the instrument system is also the *only* system—Visual Flight Rules really aren't a "system" as such. For all practical purposes, VFR means "As long as you observe the hemispherical rule and stay out of the clouds themselves, you can do just about anything you want—but watch out for yourself." Visual Flight Rules don't provide you with any separation, or any protection against deteriorating weather, and your access to assistance is several steps removed from simply picking up the mike and asking for it—you have to look up an FSS or ATC frequency, try to raise them, possibly climb to establish contact, and then explain your situation. When you fly VFR you are literally "winging it." I think your time and your money are infinitely better spent getting an instrument rating than in trying to extract some marginal cross-country utility out of Visual Flight Rules.

BENEFITS OF INSTRUMENT FLIGHT RULES

The immediate benefits of an instrument rating—beyond the obvious benefit of being able to fly in the clouds—are numerous. Filing IFR is one of the best things you can do to make night flying safe. It's hard to get very far away from an airport on an instrument flight plan; the Victor airways tend to stay close to airports because so many of the VORs are located on or near airports. In addition, you have immediate assistance available if you need it—the controllers know their sectors extremely well, and if the engine does quit, they can steer you toward an airport, or at least toward the most suitable terrain. By planning your routes so as to optimize the availability of lighted airports, and by filing IFR, you have gone a long way toward making single-engine night flying safe. Since you are operating on instruments anyway, the physical fact of flying at night is fairly irrelevant—the only real difference is that the windows are white in the daytime and black in the nighttime.

With the instrument rating, long stayovers are no longer a problem, nor are long trips. The main reason long stayovers or long trips are a problem for VFR pilots is that the weather changes over time and distance—stay anywhere long enough and the weather is sure to get worse, and fly far enough and you are bound to fly into some marginal weather. Having a rating doesn't eliminate weather as a factor, but it does provide you with a very valuable tool for dealing with it.

Another big problem VFR pilots have that IFR pilots don't is getting lost—or, if not actually lost, the closest thing to it, which is not being able to find the destination airport. Instrument rated pilots certainly have to be careful when they fly to areas that are new to them—the VORs have unfamiliar names, the approaches have significant differences, and the airport layout may be confusing. But when all is said and done, an airway is an airway, an ILS is an ILS, and a runway is a runway. The pilot on an instrument flight plan doesn't have to worry about getting lost over unfamiliar terrain, or not being able to find an airport, or landing on the wrong runway—at least he doesn't have to worry nearly to the same extent the VFR pilot does. If he follows his instrument procedures carefully, he can't help landing on the right runway at the right airport.

I once thought I had proved this rule wrong. I had a flight from Northampton, Massachusetts to Allentown, Pennsylvania (ABE), in a Piper Arrow. I had just gotten my flight instructor's license (including Instrument Instructor), so I had had quite a bit of instrument training, but not a lot of experience, and in particular I had never flown to ABE before, nor had I ever had a flight that kept me in the clouds for the entire trip. (This was all done back when I trusted engines completely and didn't worry about flying single-engine IFR with low ceilings.) The flight went very uneventfully and routinely, I shot a nice (I thought) ILS approach to minimums, and I broke out at decision height with the runway right in front of me. So far so good. I made a normal landing, called Ground Control, and Ground Control cleared me to the ramp.

As I turned the corner and headed for the FBO, my heart almost stopped—the sign on the hangar said "Reading Aviation Service." (Reading, PA is just down the road from Allentown.) I *knew* I couldn't have shot an approach to the wrong airport—the frequencies wouldn't have worked out right (I had checked the ILS ident for the approach to Allentown and had gotten the correct ident), and the runway had the right number on it—and, anyway, I was in radar contact the whole way. The controllers *couldn't* have let me make such a gross error.

But there it was, right in front of me: "Reading Aviation Service." I taxied in to the ramp, completely confused, and tried to find something to confirm or deny that sign. I couldn't find anything, so I had to 'fess up to the lineman that I really wasn't sure where I was. He laughed and said, "That sign gets a lot of people. You're at Allentown, all right—Reading Aviation has several locations; this is just one of them."

I was relieved, but not amused. It illustrates the point I'm trying to make, though: It is pretty hard to fly the *right* approach to the *wrong* airport. The reason even experienced pilots still sometimes land at the wrong airport is because they cancel IFR and "go visual" too soon in marginal conditions. (I could tell you a story about that, too, but I'm sworn to secrecy.) Landing at the wrong airport is a real *faux pas*—the "ultimate embarrassment" is the way a good pilot I know described it. Going IFR and *staying* IFR is the best way to avoid it.

NEW INSTRUMENT-RATED PILOTS

So, to a large extent, the VFR pilot solves a lot of his problems the day he gets his instrument rating. But the new instrument pilot still has limitations. Most of these limitations are related to inexperience with actual instrument conditions, and not knowing how to operate smoothly within the system. If every new instrument rated pilot were to fly for a while with a series of different Captains, he would very quickly get the experience he needed to fully and competently operate within the system. But he can't, so he needs to know what his limitations are, as a new instrument pilot, so he can safely use his ticket while he acquires the knowledge and experience necessary to extend his limits.

The new instrument pilot generally knows how to fly the airplane on instruments pretty well. He can follow the airways, and he has a pretty good idea of what it takes to shoot a good approach. In addition, after flying around with an instructor for 40 plus hours, he is pretty comfortable with his airplane under normal circumstances.

What he probably *hasn't* had much experience with is flying in real clouds—most if not all of his instrument experience will have been under the plastic cloud, the "hood." In addition to not having much "actual" time, the brand new instrument pilot has no experience flying instruments solo, and he probably hasn't had to deal with any emergencies or abnormalities while on an instrument flight plan. In other words, the new instrument pilot tends to be fairly well trained, but he lacks experience with the reality of instrument flight. This isn't his fault, but he should be aware of it in order to acquire that experience in a safe way.

THE NEW CAPTAIN PRINCIPLE

The best way for him to do this, I think, is to impose certain limits on himself, in a very formal way, so he can "get his feet wet" gradually and safely. A new airline captain must increase his personal approach minimums by 100 feet on the ceiling and 1/2 mile on the visibility for his first 100 hours as PIC (50 hours if previously checked out in another type). In addition, the regulations for all commercial service, from air taxi on up to the major airlines, prohibit even *starting* an approach when the reported visibility is below minimums. This means, when the "New Captain" looks at the approach plate, that he adds 100 feet to the decision height (DH) or minimum descent altitude (MDA), and 1/2 mile to the required visibility for the approach. If the reported visibility is below minimums, then he doesn't even try the approach (he can't), but proceeds instead to his alternate; however, if the visibility is *above* minimums, he shoots the approach, but observes a 100 foot increase in the DH or MDA (even though the approach itself is perfectly safe for another 100 feet).

Part 91 does not have these restrictions, but if they're good enough for airline Captains, I think they're good enough for newly rated instrument pilots. In fact, as both a "New Captain" *and* a newly rated instrument pilot, I think a better idea would be to initially increase your personal minimums by 200 and a mile. This will still give you lots of opportunities to complete instrument approaches—after all, increasing the minimums by 200 and a mile still allows a normal ILS to 400 feet and 1 1/2 miles visibility, which is well below VFR minimums. This gives you an extra 200 feet between you and the ground, and the extra mile of visibility virtually assures you of being able to find the airport when you break out.

After 100 hours of instrument PIC time, and at least 25 approaches, you can start thinking about increasing your personal minimums to the "New Captain" level of plus 100 feet and 1/2 mile; after another 100 hours you should be sure enough of your ability to shoot an accurate approach to be able to use published minimums. At some point you have to get out there in the real world and do some flying in actual weather, but you want to do it safely and you want to test yourself gradually. Increasing your personal minimums is one way of doing that when you no longer have an instructor watching you.

ANXIETY

Probably the biggest problem for new instrument pilots is nervousness. Anything you can do to eliminate anxiety will allow you to do a better job of the task at hand. Fuel, for instance, is one thing you don't want to have to worry about. This doesn't mean you should always just "fill it up," but it does mean planning a good, fat reserve, and it means very careful and conservative flight planning with a cómplete flight log for every flight—even the short ones.

Freedom from nervousness also comes from having "solid gold" alternates: Initially, I think it is a good idea to increase your personal minimums for an alternate to 1000 and 3 (as opposed to 600 and 2, the normal legal minimums for an alternate). It is awfully nice to know, when you launch on one of your first solo, actual-instrument flights, that if things really go badly you can proceed to VFR conditions somewhere. You probably won't have to resort to it, but having a VFR alternate takes the pressure off knowing you *have* to complete an instrument approach prior to running out of gas. I'm not going to give you a rule for reducing your alternate minimums to the legal minimum; it doesn't take very long to get over nervousness about *having* to shoot approaches. But as long as you are at all concerned with the anticipated approach segment of the flight, plan and fuel for a VFR alternate.

You also don't want to have to worry about the airplane itself. If you have any misgivings about the condition of the airplane, don't go. If you do have misgivings, they will grow like monsters in the dark as soon as you enter the clouds. If the airplane has a history of even minor radio or gyro or engine problems, for instance—little ones such as a gyro that is a little slow to spin up, or an engine that has started to burn slightly more oil, or a slight drop in the aux fuel pressure—and those problems cannot be resolved or satisfactorily explained, don't go. That gyro or engine or fuel pump is going to preoccupy you as the flight goes on, and that's a setup for making mistakes.

UPGRADING

After 40 hours of dual in your instrument trainer, you should be pretty comfortable with that airplane, so stick with it. Don't upgrade to a more sophisticated airplane until you are completely comfortable in the instrument system. Not only will the unfamiliarity of the more sophisticated airplane distract you from the job at hand, but its systems will require more attention and are more likely to malfunction. So stick to the airplane you know for a while before you take on something new. You've still got a lot to learn. Take it one step at a time.

What you want to do, as a newly instrument rated pilot, is not so much learn how to handle the weather as learn how to deal with the instrument *system*. You want to get out there and learn how to flight plan, how to talk on the radio, how to fly the airways and shoot approaches, how to handle the little glitches that inevitably come up enroute—and you want to be comfortable with the airplane itself. You want to accomplish these goals, if you can, before you take on any "real" weather, even though being able to operate in the clouds is ostensibly what an instrument ticket is all about.

An instrument rating isn't so much a license to fly in the clouds as it is an admissions ticket to the ATC system. The "system" is the important part, and that part you can learn when the weather is good. But to do that you have to file IFR and you should do this for every single flight, regardless of the weather. If you always file IFR, the actual weather part will take care of itself.

LOW CEILINGS AND VISIBILITIES

For serious weather flying, where the ceilings are low and visibilities are reduced, you need a multiengine airplane. (See Chapter 5 again, Aircraft Limits.) This level of flying is reserved for experienced pilots who have already spent quite a bit of time learning, first, to fly on instruments, second, getting completely comfortable with the instrument system, and third, mastering at least one type of complex, single-engine airplane. To "put a pencil to it," this means 400 to 500 hours of flying time: 200 to get the rating, and at least another 200 getting comfortable with the system and the airplane. When you have done that (however many hours it takes—the actual number of hours doesn't make any more difference here than it did when you soloed or got your first license), then you are ready to take on multiengine flying.

The two most important factors in flying a multiengine airplane IFR are pilot proficiency and the weather. Each of these factors is the subject of subsequent chapters—that's how important they are. But the process of knowing and observing your limits as a newly rated multiengine pilot is the same as it is for new Private Pilots or newly rated instrument pilots: Start from a known base and go from there.

The "known base" in this case is the skill you obtained in getting your multiengine rating—specifically, your single-engine skills. The newly rated multiengine pilot generally can do a pretty good job of handling the airplane on one engine. The trick is maintaining that proficiency. There is no point in trying to expand the base if you fail to maintain your original proficiency.

Single-engine work gets all the attention in multiengine training, but it is also very important to maintain your proficiency with the aircraft systems—electrical, hydraulic, gear, fuel, anti-ice, and so on. This is a very important part of the "known base," because you can't safely deal with weather that goes right down to the ground until you fully understand how your aircraft works. Flying in this kind of weather is going to be demanding enough; you don't need the distraction of systems you haven't completely mastered.

Mastering the systems is what a checkride for a type rating is all about. The examiner assumes by the time a pilot gets to the point where he is ready to take a checkride for a type rating, that he knows how to fly instruments. (They sometimes find out differently, but that's the assumption.) What an examiner looks for on a type rating ride is the ability to handle the aircraft systems, including abnormal and emergency situations, while operating within the instrument system. As the PIC of a non-jet aircraft with a max gross not over 12,500 pounds, you don't have to take a checkride or get a type rating, but since you are going to be the PIC of a complex multiengine aircraft just the same, you want to start from the same level of competence as if you *were* going to take a checkride for that airplane.

I think it is a good idea for new multiengine pilots to also raise their personal approach minimums by 200 feet and a mile for the first 100 hours, and then 100 and 1/2 for another 100 hours. The extra margin of error that this provides takes a lot of the pressure off a "New Multiengine Captain." If the newly rated multiengine pilot plans his fuel loads carefully and conservatively, and stays away from ice and thunderstorms, he shouldn't have any trouble learning to use his airplane for what it was intended: going places.

Flying a multiengine airplane under a variety of different and varying weather conditions is the ultimate extension of your personal limits. When you reach this stage you are basically doing the job of a professional pilot and your success or failure will be determined by the same factors that determine his: proficiency, experience, maturity, and judgement.

CONCLUSION

All pilots have limits. What separates the capable pilot from the rest is an honest awareness of his limits. That awareness begins with a known base of technical competence upon which additional capabilities are built. The point of this chapter is to help you find where on the continuum from student pilot to experienced, instrument rated, multiengine pilot your "known base" is, and to give you concrete guidelines to follow in extending your base beyond its present limits. I hope I have succeeded, because the only alternative (other than further FAA regulation and control) is for you to scare the daylights out of yourself a bunch of times trying to figure it out by trial and error, and that's really not a good way to do it. I can assure you of that.

Chapter 7

The Weather

I'm not a weatherman; I'm a pilot. I'm not going to try to make you into a weatherman, either. You probably know as much about the weather as I do anyway.

Weathermen—meteorologists—are scientists who have been trained to apply their knowledge and experience (and computers) to the task of measuring, recording, and predicting the weather. I think they do a great job and I'm happy to let them practice their craft in peace. But, as Bob Dylan said, "You don't need a weatherman to know which way the wind blows."

Between the theory of forecasting and the reality of the elements sits the pilot. I can't teach you to be a weatherman, and I can't fly your trips for you, but I can give you a *strategy* for dealing with the weather—a practical link between the theory of weather forecasting and the reality of flight.

THEORY AND PRACTICE

I have enormous respect for weathermen and I am fascinated by their subject. But weathermen deal in *generalizations and probabilities*. I have yet to actually *see* weather that was as simple and straightforward as that shown on the weather charts: The highs don't come with big Hs on them outdoors, and the cold fronts (the real ones) are a lot harder to find without the little pointed arrows. To understand the weather—and to describe it—we are forced into pushing and pulling it into boxes with labels and lines and arrows. Weather charts are intentional simplifications—necessary generalizations. They reduce the weather to its lowest common denominator—which is helpful, but you won't always find the lowest common denominator on the other side of the windshield.

We can take pictures of real weather from space, which is great because a picture helps us relate the charts to what is actually out there—but by the time you see the picture it is already ancient history. We can feed 50 years of figures into a computer, and the computer will tell us what the weather did for the last 50 years—but the computer can't guarantee that the weather will do the same thing for the next 50 years. We can build an airplane that can withstand a gust factor of 50 feet per second—but the weather won't always agree to limit itself to gusts of 50 fps.

And so it goes. The real weather won't stand still, it won't organize itself into neat highs and lows with fronts that start and stop right where the line is, and it won't be intimidated by computers or pilots. The weather we fly in and the weather on the charts is not always the same thing.

Nonetheless, I think you should know all you can about the weather from a theoretical point of view. Without an understanding of the theory behind the forecasts, you have no basis for dealing with the weather that does exist. A good place to start is with *Aviation Weather,* an FAA publication. This book is particularly good at explaining and illustrating the basic concepts of weather theory. If it seems a little tough going, remember, weather is applied physics: There is no way to make it easy and still get beyond "High pressure means good weather, and low pressure means bad weather." It's worth the effort, though.

I also recommend Bob Buck's *Weather Flying* (Macmillan, 1970), a classic for pilots. There are, of course, numerous others, and I can't think of any that aren't valuable, each in its own way. Each one has a little different angle and that's what you need to deal safely with the weather—the angles—because nobody has all the answers and the weather itself is not going to make it easy.

I have an angle, too. My angle is this: Leave the weather to the weathermen. *Optimize* their abilities to *minimize* your risks. Learn all you can about the weather, but don't try to outguess the guys who do it for a living. The experts make mistakes often enough; how well do *you* expect to do?

I've been playing this game of amateur weatherman for years—trying to predict the weather myself from the charts and maps. I know all about jet streams and upper level troughs and steepness of pressure gradients, and I still miss *all* the time. I could throw darts and do better—a trained monkey could do better than I do.

In fact, *I* used to do better when I just looked at my barometer—if it said "Change," it usually changed. I'm thinking of getting one of those cute doll houses with the little people that come out with umbrellas if it's going to rain. I'm going to set myself up as a consultant. I'll have an 800 number, and pilots will call me from all over the world, and if the little people are out there with their umbrellas, I'll say, "*Don't go.* Looks like it's gonna rain." I'm going to focus my advertising on all the people who don't believe in weathermen. I'm gonna make a million bucks.

FORECASTING

What I mean by "leave the weather to the weathermen" is leave the weather *forecasting* to the professionals. Obviously, I think Bob Buck's book is great, or I wouldn't have recommended it, but Capt. Buck and I may disagree a little on this issue of forecasting. The way I read *Weather Flying,* Buck seems to be saying that if you read enough books on the weather, and you fly in enough weather, that eventually you start to have enough knowledge and experience to be able to "read between the lines" of the forecasts—to fine-tune and improve upon the official forecasts. Probably Bob Buck can. Probably he can look at a forecast and a surface chart and put the two together into a something that is better than the two parts, but *I* can't—not with any consistency—and frankly I don't think *you* can either.

We all play that game, of course: We stand there looking at all the charts and we say, "I know the forecast says it's going to be 400 indefinite, 3/4 miles visibility with light rain and fog, but I think that low is going to push on out of here tonight—400 and 3/4 is still above minimums at any rate, but I don't think it's going to be that bad."

And often we're right. The problem is those are the only times we remember; we forget the times we were wrong, so we end up with a distorted view of our value as forecasters. Forecasting the weather is and always will be a matter of playing the odds; nobody is right all the time. There is nothing wrong with playing the game and comparing results, and there certainly is nothing wrong with learning all you can about the theory behind the forecasts, especially if you use that knowledge to make the official forecasts more conservative (e.g., "I *don't* think that low is going to move as fast as they think; I think I'll throw on 30 minutes more fuel for weather delays"). But if you can't pick your days, I think you have to go with a winner, and the guys with the best record are the professional meteorologists. I don't want to try to do their job; I want to use what they can give me to optimize my strategy for dealing with the weather.

TIME ELEMENT

You can't talk about the weather without talking about *time*. The weather won't stand still. It is slightly different this moment from the moment before and will change yet again in the next moment. On a second-by-second basis we are not aware of the changes, but the changes are taking place just the same. I think it is important to always ask yourself the question, anytime you are dealing with any aspect of the weather, "What is the time factor here?" It is very important to have straight in your head whether you are looking at past history, a present fact, or a future expectation. If you don't, it is too easy to go into a Flight Service Station and look at all the charts and read all the reports, and forget that some are history, some are current, and some are speculation.

If you confuse the time element, you are likely to see the picture as static, and it is not. The past doesn't exist anymore and the present won't for long. The past serves to give you an idea why the present is what it is, and that is helpful, especially to the forecaster. But it doesn't help much with the planning process—the weather strategy. That strategy has to come from present, short-term fact (mainly the current sequence reports), and future, longer-term speculation (mainly the terminal and area forecasts).

THE STRATEGY

To deal with the weather you need a strategy—a plan—something that takes the available information and applies it in such a way that you are no longer vulnerable to whatever the weather throws at you. The strategy I have developed has five parts; they are listed below. The highlighted letters form a memory aid: IBFAH. (I know it doesn't mean anything, but what does "GUMP" mean?) The rest of the chapter will deal with these five points in detail.

☐ I—Always file *I*FR.
☐ B—Ask for a complete weather *B*riefing.

☐ F—*F*light plan thoroughly.
☐ A—Always have an *A*lternate.
☐ H—Stay away from *H*azardous weather.

FILING IFR

In filing IFR you eliminate in one stroke all concern with "ordinary" weather: clouds, rain, haze, smoke—all the common restrictions to visibility that plague VFR pilots. (If you don't have your instrument rating yet, refer back to Chapter 6, Personal Limits.) There are a lot of good reasons for filing IFR in any case, but the best one is the most obvious one: If you already *are* IFR, you don't have to worry about inadvertently *becoming* IFR. If you don't think that doesn't solve a whole bunch of problems in one easy shot, then you either haven't tried to do much VFR cross-country flying, or you haven't read many accident reports, or both.

THE BRIEFING

The key element in this system is the weather briefing. The weather briefing forms the basis for the flight planning, the identification of alternates, and the avoidance of hazardous weather. It's really a very simple system, but it does take a little bit of work. You can't just blow into the Flight Service Station, take a quick glance at the destination sequence and forecast, and go.

When it comes to getting weather briefings, professional pilots are no different than anyone else: what they *say* they do and what they *actually* do are very often two different things. If you ask most professional pilots how they go about dealing with the weather prior to a flight, they will tell you that they go in and study, at length and in detail, the surface progs and the synopses and 300 and 500 mb charts and everything else hanging on the wall, and then they take a look at the sequences and forecasts.

The fact is, I've watched a lot of professional pilots brief themselves on the weather, and the first thing they usually look at is the current weather, and the second is the forecast, and the third is the winds aloft, and after they have gotten that information for as many stations as they can think of, they may glance at the charts on the walls on the way out.

That's not the way to do it, but there are several reasons they get away with it:

1. They are going to file IFR in any case, so they don't need to look at the VFR possibilities along the entire route of flight.

2. They are probably flying an airplane with two or more engines, full de-ice/anti-ice capability, and top-of-the-line radar, so they can already handle 90 percent of the weather that is out there.

3. They learned long ago to always have an alternate—all they have to do is pick one.

4. They are alert to the signs for the 10 percent of the hazardous weather they can't handle.

Briefing yourself like this is not an example to follow, but in a non-systematic way, they do end up covering all the important points of the weather strategy:

1. I—They always file IFR.

2. B—They do get a weather briefing, even if it isn't always a complete briefing.

3. F—They use the weather information to flight plan thoroughly.

4. A—They have an alternate.

5. H—They are aware of the hazardous weather and have flight planned around it.

The only thing that I *really* think is wrong with this is that you shouldn't try to brief yourself on the weather, no matter who you are or how much experience you have. If you want a complete weather briefing, ask for it. ("I know it's a long shot, but it's so crazy it just might work.") Both National Weather Service and Flight Service Station personnel are trained to give weather briefings. They know the format, they know where to get the information, and they can get you a hard copy to take with you.

Pilots often let their egos get in the way of a good briefing. They don't want anyone to think they don't know what they're doing, so they brief themselves on the weather. Very few briefers will fight them; the more work the pilot does, the less they have to do. But briefers can and should do the briefing. That's their job. If a briefer hands you a clipboard of sequences, explain to him that when he has a chance, you would like a complete weather briefing. Self-briefings are dumb. It's just too easy to miss important information.

Asking specifically for a weather briefing also forces the briefer to concentrate on the facts. Remember, a Flight Service Specialists is not a weatherman—a meteorologist. He is a trained weather briefer, but he is not trained or qualified to analyze or forecast the weather—nor are you. In asking for a briefing you show that you are interested in facts, not opinions. Don't expect, or let, a briefer make your go/no go decisions for you. That's *not* his job—that's yours.

The military has a pretty good system for handling weather briefings: You *will* have a weather briefing, you *will* receive a hard copy of the briefing, both you and the weather briefer *will* sign off on it, and a copy *will* be retained in case there is a need to refer back to it. In the military, you can't *not* get a complete weather briefing; if you don't have your signed copy of the briefing, your aircraft will not be dispatched. The military can be hardnosed, but the system works, and you would be wise to copy it.

Having asked for our complete weather briefing, what can we expect? A weather briefing can be broken down into three basic parts (don't write all this stuff down; it won't be on the test): the background, the specifics, and the hazardous weather.

BACKGROUND INFORMATION

The briefer should start by asking you pertinent questions about your route of flight, altitude, equipment, and filing intentions, if you haven't given him that information already. This helps him (or her) focus the scope of the briefing. Then he should take you through a summary of the Big Picture; this is where you go to the wall and look at all the charts. This is all "good-to-know" stuff, and will help you understand why the actual and forecast weather is what it is. You want to make mental notes here of things to look for later on in the briefing if the charts hint at turbulence, thunderstorm activity, low ceilings, ice, snow—any potentially hazardous weather.

DEPARTURE WEATHER

With this background information in mind, he then looks at the departure weather, both the current sequence and the forecast, for your expected departure time. If the departure weather is below landing minimums, he should include a takeoff alternate in his briefing. If he doesn't (and he may not if he knows you are operating Part 91 and aren't required to have one), then ask about one. You want to know where the nearest airport is that has landing minimums in case there is a major problem such as a fire, a fuel leak, a rough engine, structural failure—anything requiring immediate action—right after takeoff.

WEATHER ENROUTE

After taking care of the departure weather he will take a look at the enroute weather. The exact content of this part of the briefing will vary depending on your equipment and how high you intend to go. The guy down low in the single, with no ice capability or radar, wants to know a lot more about the stations enroute than the guy with the loaded, pressurized twin does; the more limited the capability, the more likely a precautionary landing is.

The guy flying the single will also want to know what the ceilings are along the entire route of flight in order to ensure adequate visual gliding range for an emergency landing. A good briefer will supplement the enroute sequences and forecasts by going back to the surface progs in order to get an overall idea of the weather along the route of flight.

DESTINATION WEATHER

The briefer will then go on to the destination weather. He will give you their current weather and the forecast. Make sure he gives you the *whole* forecast—everything he's got. You want to know what the weather was, is, and is expected to be for as far ahead as the weather wizards are guessing.

It is particularly important to compare the current sequence to the forecast for that period. If it is better than forecast, fine; that's money in the bank, but base your planning on the forecast anyway. The forecast may be too pessimistic, or a little off on the timing, but go with it anyway. A little bit of conservatism goes a long way. If the current sequence is worse than forecast, be on the alert for an amended forecast. If it stays worse than forecast, an amended forecast will be issued; check back just prior to takeoff.

If the weather is *below* minimums at your destination, and forecast to *stay* below minimums, it doesn't make any sense to me to flight plan for that airport anyway, but it's a free country and Part 91 says you can go try. If the airport is below minimums and forecast to stay that way, there is usually no mystery as to what's causing it. It takes either a big weather system or something obvious like coastal fog to create that kind of situation and both are hard to hide. About one time in five or six the weather will come up for you prior to attempting your approach, but most of the time you are just wasting your time and money. I think you're better off planning on another airport from the beginning, and using the time you will probably save in not having to do a missed approach and diversion to drive the extra distance.

If the destination is forecast to be *above* minimums, but at the time of the last report was actually *below* minimums, it may be worth a try, but again, check just prior to takeoff for an amended forecast. If you decide to have a try, make sure you have a solid gold alternate because, despite the forecast, it may still be below minimums when you get there. (My definition of a "solid gold alternate" is an airport with an ILS to 200 and 1/2 and a forecast of 1000 and 3 or better: VFR.) The chances are good enough that it will be above minimums to head that way, but if, as you get closer, you check and it's still down, just tell ATC you want to go straight to your alternate. The "try" up to that point doesn't cost much.

If (this is the last one) the airport is forecast to be *below* minimums, but the actual weather is *above* minimums, then you probably have a case of an overly pessimistic forecast. But don't count on it. We're going to leave the weather to the weathermen, remember? You still have to believe the forecast and plan accordingly with a solid alternate. But if in fact the airport is currently reporting conditions above minimums, the chances are fairly good it will stay that way. If it goes back down again, then that just proves that the forecast was right after all and that you were smart to believe it and plan accordingly.

In each of these last two cases, where there is a discrepancy between the sequence and the forecast and one or the other is below minimums, you have to plan for the worst-case situation, which means a solid gold alternate. The reason for the "solid gold" alternate is very simple: The chances are fairly good you're going to need it, and you want it to be extra conservative since the discrepancy has already shown that something is going on that isn't reflected in the forecasts.

ALTERNATES

In any case, after the briefer has given you the sequences and forecasts for the destination, he will attempt to determine whether you require an alternate or not. You *do*, no matter how great the weather is. Always having an alternate is part of the strategy for staying out of trouble. Tell him what your alternate requirements are (normally 600 and 2 for airports with full ILSs, but if you want to use higher minimums, as discussed in Chapter 6, tell him), and he will attempt to find the nearest suitable alternate—and ideally, a couple of others, too.

This is one area where the FSS system could use modern computers. As things stand now, you and the briefer have to pore over bunches of yellow paper looking for the closest airport to your destination with a forecast, in most cases, no worse than 600 and 2. It is tedious and error-prone, and a computer could do it in about three nanoseconds.

Too often this process of finding an alternate is an afterthought, and it shouldn't be. This is your ace in the hole, after all. I wouldn't even consider using an airport for an alternate that doesn't have a precision approach (ILS). (Airports without precision approaches can be used for alternates, but then the minimum forecast weather has to be at least 800 and 2, in some cases higher, verses 600 and 2 for an ILS equipped alternate. If in doubt about the exact forecast minimums for use as an alternate, check the back of the first Jepp plate for the proposed alternate—NOSs list them in a separate section.) I want my alternate to have an ILS. If worse comes to worst I know I can—in an emergency—get on the ground with an ILS, no matter how bad the weather is, but I don't have that same "ultimate" assurance with a non-precision approach. This is your fallback position—your "pre-vent de-fense"—don't send in the second string.

As you flip through forecasts looking for an alternate, be careful to read the entire forecast all the way through. The fine print will be listed at the end for each time period. This is where the "chance of," "variable," and "occasional" conditions will be listed. They count also. Even if there is just a "chance of" (for instance) conditions less than 600 and 2 at your expected time of arrival at the alternate, this eliminates it as a legal alternate, because the forecast no longer says it "will be" 600 and 2 or better—it says, in fact, there is a chance it *won't* be.

WINDS ALOFT

Another place a computer would be nice is in analyzing winds aloft. The briefer will go to the winds aloft forecast for the appropriate time period, and give you whatever altitudes and locations you need to figure your winds. This means, if you want accurate winds aloft information, that you still have to take this raw data and interpolate between them for your intended cruising altitude, unless you happen to be planning on going at one of the altitudes listed—3, 6, 9, 12, 18, 24, 30, 34, (why 30 and 34 is a mystery known only to those in the Weather Bureaucracy—those aren't even usable altitudes except over the ocean) and 39. In these days of computers there is no reason why the winds aloft couldn't be listed for every altitude, but work with what you've got.

When the briefer checks the winds aloft, don't forget to look at the temperatures—they are the last figure listed on the winds aloft report: "222711" means from 220 (true) at 27 knots, 11 degrees centrigrade." Other than to get an idea of the freezing level, the actual temperature isn't as important as is its variance from ISA—International Standard Atmosphere. ISA means "normal" in this case; ISA plus so many degrees means warmer than normal, and ISA minus so many degrees means colder than normal.

It's not a bad idea to keep a list of standard temperatures for each altitude handy (Table 7-1). A quickie method is to double the altitude, subtract 15, and reverse the sign; i.e., if 9(000) is the altitude, doubling it equals 18, minus 15 is 3; *negative* 3 degrees is ISA for 9000 feet. At the lower altitudes it's easier to use a chart. For the Flight Levels, the quickie method works fine.

If the winds aloft indicate it will be warmer than standard (ISA plus something) then the aircraft will perform as if it were at a higher altitude—the air is thinner—and of course colder than standard equals a lower altitude. You may want to consider filing a little higher for ISA − 5 or colder, and a little lower for ISA + 5 or warmer.

Table 7-1. International Standard Atmosphere (ISA), Temperatures from Sea Level to 17,000 feet. For Flight Level 180 and Above it is Easier to Use the Rule-of-Thumb: Double the Altitude (in Thousands), Subtract 15, and Multiply by −1. Example: For FL 250, 25 × 2 = 50, Less 15 = 35, Times −1 = −35. ISA for FL 250 is −35 degrees C.

Altitude	Degrees Centrigrade
Sea Level	15
1000	13
2000	11
3000	9
4000	7
5000	5
6000	3
7000	1
8000	− 1
9000	− 3
10000	− 5
11000	− 7
12000	− 9
13000	− 11
14000	− 13
15000	− 15
16000	− 17
17000	− 19

HAZARDOUS WEATHER

That takes care of the second main part of the briefing, the specifics. You now have the Big Picture and you have specific information about your route of flight from takeoff to alternate. The last part is the hazardous weather, if any. While the hazardous conditions could be included with the background information and the forecasts, it is an important area that gets its own separate treatment. The main areas of hazardous weather are thunderstorms, icing, freezing rain, snow, and turbulence.

Thunderstorms

As far as the weather briefing part goes, don't expect to get too much information on thunderstorm activity. Thunderstorms are the ultimate "real time" events, and real time is what the weather gathering and distribution system has the most trouble with. (Even sequences, which we call present information, are at least 15 minutes old by the time you see them on the screen or teletype.) A thunderstorm can come and go in 30 minutes, so unless the information is real time, it is fairly useless. The real time radar repeaters which some Flight Service Stations have now (some of which even work) cover such a large area that what you are looking at are not necessarily individual thunderstorms, but more likely an *area* of thunderstorms. This is good information, but unfortunately it isn't detailed enough to use for an area penetration.

The simple, sad fact is that if you don't have airborne radar (or possibly a lightning detecting system, but I have no experience with those), you have no business around thunderstorms of any sort, even the isolated airmass types. The airlines aren't allowed to dispatch an airplane without a working radar unless there is no chance of thunderstorm activity along the entire route of flight. If you don't have radar, the purpose of this part of the briefing is simply to tell you what route you must take to avoid all areas of possible or known thunderstorm activity.

If you do have airborne radar, then you must take the information you can get from the briefing on the size and type of thunderstorms forecast, compare it with the capability of your equipment, and make a decision. All radars are not equally capable. This is not a reflection on the product; it is a simple fact of physics. A radar's ability to see ahead—and its accuracy and detail in displaying the information it receives—is a direct function of its power, the size and type of its antenna, and the sophistication of its circuitry.

I'm not going to try to tell you how to use your radar in this book. There are several very good ground schools you can attend on radar, and a lot has been written already on the subject. But I can say that the smaller and simpler radars can only help you avoid *areas* of thunderstorm activity. They don't have the power to see far enough ahead to give you a reliable path *through* an area of thunderstorms.

I wish I could tell you more about thunderstorms and radar. I'd like to be able to tell you when you can go with thunderstorms in the forecast and when you can't, when you can trust a "hole" to be safe and when you can't, how much power it takes to "see" embedded thunderstorms in a bunch of rain, and so on. In short, I wish I could give you a system for dealing with thunderstorms, but I can't. There are just too many variables, and, at any rate, neither radar nor lightning detectors tell you directly what you want to know—which is "Where is the turbulence?" They can point to it by inference; where there is heavy rain and/or lightning there often is severe turbulence, but they can't see it directly.

The only device that detects turbulence directly is Doppler radar. The Doppler Principle says that raindrops moving away will appear to reflect energy of a lower wavelength than raindrops moving forward. Since turbulence is just air that is going in all kinds of directions at rapidly changing rates, applying the Doppler Principle to radar reflections (via a computer, of course) gives a picture not just of raindrops, but of the turbulence itself. (It can't see clear air turbulence. It's still radar and it needs moisture to work.) Doppler radar technology is just now (late 1984) becoming available at the airline level. I think it is the biggest advance in thunderstorm avoidance since radar itself. It may be a while before it is available and affordable for general aviation, but it should be worth waiting for.

In the meantime, if you don't have any radar capability, stay *completely away* from thunderstorms. If you have some radar capability, use it to fly around *areas* of thunderstorm activity; if you have a lot of radar capability, use it to stay *10 miles* away from small cells and *20 miles* away from big cells. A normal airplane has about as much business inside a thunderstorm as a butterfly does in a wind tunnel.

Icing

Information on icing conditions is a lot more plentiful and useful than thunderstorm information, and the time factor is not nearly so critical. The briefer should tell you where the icing level is, what type of icing is forecast (clear, rime, or mixed) and the amount expected (trace, light, moderate, or severe). He should pass on any pilot reports of actual icing, and make note of any stations reporting freezing precipitation of any kind.

If your aircraft is prohibited from operating in known icing conditions, then any pilot or station report of actual icing conditions precludes you from operating in that area. This is a real gray area as far as legality is concerned, though, with holes big enough to fly a 747 through. How old is the information? When is the information old enough you can disregard it? How big is an "area?"

But, of course, the idea isn't to find loopholes in the law. The idea is use the briefing to avoid icing conditions if your aircraft is not approved for flight in icing conditions, and to minimize your exposure to ice if it is approved. Whether icing is reported or simply forecast is an academic question. The purpose of the weather briefing is to give you information for flight planning purposes, and for planning purposes you have to assume that the forecast is correct.

How do you use icing information then for planning purposes? Do you have to automatically cancel every time someone says "Ice?" No, of course not. The purpose of the briefing is to help you find a way the flight *can* be safely accomplished. There usually is a way, although, as with any other limiting factor, it may involve some inconvenience or expense.

If you can safely fly below the icing level, the solution is obvious—stay below the icing level. If your aircraft is approved for flight in known icing conditions, you can often climb on top, or at least high enough that it is so cold that ice is not a problem. (Generally, colder is better when it comes to avoiding ice—doesn't make a lot of obvious sense, but that's the way the mechanics of ice formation work.) Frequently, by flight planning around a mountainous area or by avoiding the lee side of a large body of water, the icing area can be avoided.

With approval for flight in known icing you have the option of flight planning into areas of light or moderate icing. This really isn't as reckless as it might seem *if* you have provided for an "escape route." It is pretty much standard operating procedure to include the possibility of light to moderate rime icing in all winter forecasts, just to be on the safe side, and in fact you usually *can* find a little ice at one altitude or another if you try hard enough. But it usually isn't anything you can't handle with normal deicing equipment.

But every now and then, for various unpredictable reasons, light to moderate icing becomes severe—well beyond the capability of the airplane to shed or carry it—and when it happens it usually happens very quickly and without too much warning.

When that happens you must have an "out"—an alternate course of action. The most common "out" is a known area of above-freezing air nearby. Sometimes this "warm" air will be *behind* you, sometimes it will be *below* you. Occasionally, when the tops are low, or the temperature is unusually cold, or there is an inversion of temperatures (warm air *above*), your "out" will be to climb. Your last choice is a lateral move *away* from the icing area. This works only when the icing is a relatively local phenomenon, such as around a lake, in the mountains, or flying east-west along the southern edge of an icing area. Trying to fly away from an icing area is risky; you sometimes have to fly a long way to escape to non-icing conditions.

This is why the weather briefing is so important—you want to know ahead of time what your best move is if the light to moderate icing turns out to be severe. Any time you elect to test the capability of your aircraft to handle known or forecast icing conditions, you must find out in the briefing where the closest ice-free air is. If there isn't any—the cold air goes all the way to the ground, or the tops are too high to outclimb, or the nearest area not forecasting ice is hundreds of miles away—if, in other words, you don't have any "outs," you had best plan on going another day.

In any case, you should plan your route of flight so that you fly over a series of good airports, all well above minimums. Then, if you make your move up or down and it doesn't solve the problem, you have an "out" for the "out." This is important, because you can never be absolutely sure that you will be able to find ice-free air. As long as you have good airports to "shoot into" at any point, and as long as you do not hesitate to *do* so when the ice appears to be accumulating beyond the capability of the aircraft to shed it, you should be able to get on the ground before the accumulation becomes a problem.

With any ice on the wing at all, carry 10 knots extra airspeed all the way through the approach and landing. With a significant amount of ice (an inch or more), 20 or even 30 knots extra is not out of the question. This will, of course, add significantly to the landing roll, so you want to pick an extra-long runway if you can. But even if you can't find a long runway, don't skimp on the airspeed with ice on the wing; it's better to run off the end than to stall turning final.

Freezing Rain

One situation that is an automatic "no go" is freezing rain (or its cousin, ice pellets—what you and I call "sleet"). As soon as you see, hear, or feel freezing rain outside, or as soon as the briefer says anything about freezing rain at your destination, just put your stuff away—you can ask him on the way out what the outlook is for the next day.

Wherever there is freezing rain, there is warm air above. (The reason you get frozen rain—and not snow—is because frozen rain starts out in warm, above-freezing air aloft, but falls into colder air below where it freezes. Snow starts out in cold air.) The question is, how do you get to it? Freezing rain can coat an airplane in just a few seconds, adding many pounds to the weight of the aircraft, increasing the stalling speed well beyond climb and approach speeds, and enormously increasing the aerodynamic drag.

Power isn't always the answer here; if the wing is covered with ice and is no longer capable of generating any lift, no amount of power short of Saturn booster rockets is going to get it into the air.

Even if the ice is light and the airplane does manage to get into the air, this may be the day one of the engines quits—trying to ingest a bunch of half-frozen moisture is a good way to provoke it. If it will barely fly on two engines, losing one is going to present you with a "challenging" situation. If you only *have* one engine, and *it* quits, the descent rate under these circumstances is likely to be of major accident proportions. Freezing rain at either end is an easy one: You picked a bad day to want to go somewhere.

Freezing rain enroute is also to be avoided at all costs, and fortunately that usually isn't too hard to do. The trick is to get above the freezing level before you get to the area where the freezing rain begins, and make sure that you can overfly the area of freezing rain before starting your descent.

If you should inadvertently enter an area of freezing rain, you may be able to climb into the warmer air above—*if* you have a lot of climb power available, and *if* you make your move at the first sign of freezing rain. (Normally the first sign will be clear, frozen water on the windshield.) Tell the controller you are experiencing freezing rain and *require* a higher altitude. Usually the warm air will be just a couple of thousand feet above you. If he can't give you higher, ask for a 180 back to non-freezing rain conditions. If he can't give you that, ask for an approach to the nearest airport. If he can't give you that, declare an emergency and do whatever you have to to get out of the ice or get on the ground—because if you persist in flying in freezing rain, you're going to be on the ground shortly *whether you plan it or not.*

If you don't have much climb capability left, your only choice is the 180. A quick way to tell how much climb capability you do have is to apply climb power, wait a second for the airplane to accelerate, and then compare your indicated cruise speed to the best rate of climb speed—V_y. That difference represents excess power available for climbing. If there isn't a pretty good margin between the two—30 or 40 knots—don't try to outclimb the freezing rain. You won't get very far, and getting stuck in freezing rain at high angles of attack will just result in the underside of the wing getting coated with ice, too.

Just as with unexpected severe icing, encountering freezing rain enroute is usually an easily solvable problem if you do something about it *right away,* but don't fool around waiting for it to get better. The idea, obviously, is to avoid getting into conditions of freezing rain in the first place, and this is another area where the weather briefing plays a key role in planning your weather strategy.

But if you do get into it, *do* something about it—don't just sit there.

Snow

Snow is sneaky—it can get you in so many different ways, and some of the time it doesn't bother you at all. Generally, the colder it is, the less of a problem snow is. Cold snow is dry snow, which means it blows around a lot, sometimes causing visibility problems. But it won't stick to the airplane as you fly through it, and it won't stick to the airplane on the ground if the metal is below freezing. (This means cold-soaking the airframe prior to bringing it out of the hangar. If you bring a warm airplane out of the hangar into the snow, the snow will melt on contact, and then freeze, and you have will have to take it back inside and start over again.) So cold is generally good, but the sneaky part is that it is usually also windy and gusty whenever it is that cold, which can whip up the snow to the point where the visibility on the ground is just about zero.

I had a trip to Oklahoma City a few winters back. For those of you from the East who think Oklahoma is some kind of perpetually hot desert populated by kids with pickup trucks, it may come as a surprise to find out that winters in Oklahoma can be cold, windy, and snowy, and that only about half the kids have trucks. Actually, "cold, windy, and snowy" is an understatement. An Oklahoma blizzard can make Minnesota look like the South Pacific. On this particular trip, we got caught in one of those blizzards.

The wind was blowing 30 knots, gusting to 50, the drifts were 10 to 15 feet high, and snow covered everything in sight—taxiway markings, lights, signs—but it didn't matter much because you couldn't see anything through the blowing snow anyway. The airport itself was a huge maze—most of the taxiways were blocked by aircraft with frozen brakes. The wind was blowing so hard that you had to use a lot of brake to keep the taxi speed under control going downwind. This caused the brakes to heat up, which melted the blowing snow, which in turn froze as the brakes cooled, locking the wheels, often one side at a time. Airplanes were doing pirouettes and glissades all over the taxiways and ramps. A 727 locked one side up, got his sails sideways to the wind, forgot to put his centerboard down, and was blown into a huge snowbank. If Boeing made a four-wheel drive airplane they could have sold a couple that day. It was just a real bad day.

In order to avoid having to stop and use the brakes at all, we got a takeoff clearance while still at the ramp. We mapped out a route that didn't run into any deadends due to stuck airplanes, and we taxied on one engine to keep the taxi speed down without braking. It worked, but calling in sick probably would have been a better idea. Once we got in the air, though, our problems were over. We broke out on top in a matter of seconds—bright sunshine. A pilot flying overhead never would have known there was any kind of problem on the ground at all.

I'm telling you this mainly because it's one of my better war stories; if it helps you remember that cold snow is usually blowing snow, and that brakes will generate heat, melt the blowing snow, and then freeze, that's all right, too.

If the snow isn't dry enough to blow off by the time you get to the takeoff lineup point, it probably isn't going to come off. Here's a little review of advanced aerodynamics: The reason an airplane can fly is because it has a wing. What makes a wing a wing, and not just a big place to put fuel, is its shape. If you change the shape in any way—such as by putting snow all over it—you no longer have a wing, and without a wing the airplane won't fly.

So if you get to the runway and there is snow on the wing, you're going to have to go back and remove the snow, and then you're going to have to de-ice the airplane to prevent the same thing from happening again. (Technically, this is "anti-icing"—the *prevention* of ice formation; "de-icing" means the *removal* of ice, but everyone calls it "de-icing" anyway.) Don't ever assume that the airflow on takeoff will blow the snow off. Some of the snow may be blown off—maybe the top inch or so, and some of the snow along parts of the fuselage—but the snow close to the wing won't come off. I know that doesn't seem to make sense; you would think that at 100 knots or more, anything would blow off, but it's not true. The air in the layer right next to the wing is actually still—it doesn't move. (That's why dust and dirt don't blow off the wing either.) Therefore, if there is any snow left on the wing prior to takeoff, you have no choice but to go back and remove it.

The right way to de-ice an airplane is to use heated, full-strength glycol. Even a good soaking with hot glycol will only keep heavy snow off for 10 or 15 minutes, and anything less—cold glycol, or a diluted solution—will reduce that interval even less. Hot glycol is expensive, but this is not the place to compromise on materials.

While the airplane is being de-iced, work on a plan to get from the hangar to the runway as quickly as possible. If the airport isn't busy, you can call the tower and tell them you want to stay in the hangar until released by ATC. Get everyone in the airplane, do as much of the pre-takeoff checklist as you can, and as soon as you get your release, have somebody tow you out, unhook and remove the tow bar (at least one airplane has gotten airborne, briefly, with a tow bar attached), complete the checklist, and move smartly to the end of the runway. If all goes well you should only be out in the open for a few minutes prior to takeoff and the wings should stay snow-free.

If not, you have lost your gamble and are going to have to go back to the hangar; nice try, though. If the tower can't approve waiting in the hangar for your release, you can still try, but the chances of success go down. At a busy airport with a long line waiting to go, you probably aren't going to be able to get any consideration. If it's snowing hard I would save my money and wait for another day. Life's too short as it is. Go find yourself a nice fireplace and a good book, and enjoy the storm.

During the winter months the briefer may have some information on runway and taxiway conditions in the NOTAMS, but the best and most current information can only come from calling ahead—talk to the people actually on the scene. Ask how the plowing's going, what percentage of the runway surface is bare, how high the snowbanks are, whether the runway is sanded, whether the sand was put on hot and is sticking or was put on cold and is rapidly blowing away, what the ramp looks like, and so on. If refueling is a factor, ask about the fuel truck or pumps—they love to break down in snow storms. These are all important factors that in all likelihood can only be determined by a direct phone call, but the briefing is your starting point—you may find out right there that the airport is closed and that's that.

One last word about this snowstorm business: When a major snowstorm is forecast, it very often is forecast to start during the night and continue all the next day; expected accumulations of 4 to 12 inches are typical. What usually happens is everybody involved in the trip talks it over the night before and decides there's no harm in going on out to the airport in the morning "to take a look at it." In the morning, 8 inches of snow have fallen and there is no end in sight. Somehow everybody manages to straggle in to the hangar. The airport is closed, of course, but the plows are out trying to make a dent in it. The airport crew thinks they can have one runway open in a couple of hours. Everybody talks it over again and decides it's worth waiting it out. You start making arrangements to glycol the airplane, shovel the ramp, and get the rest of the weather in case you ever do get in the air. The passengers start making their phone calls to the other end. The snow keeps coming down, the plowing continues, and it doesn't take a couple of hours to get one runway open, it takes all day. The net result is that everybody ends up wasting most of a day trying to do something they should have postponed the night before.

I have found that most people will *always* think whatever it is they have to do is important enough to be worth at least "giving it a try"—and pilots, especially if they're getting paid, will generally be reluctant to tell them otherwise. If you live in the snow-belt regions, you're going to lose a couple of days to snowstorms every winter. There's nothing you can do about that. If people want to pay me to run around trying to make snow go away, I'm happy to play the game. There's no real harm done; as long as the airport stays closed, nobody's going anywhere. But if it were *my* company, I'd give my chief pilot the authority to cancel flights the night before, and I would promise him, in writing, that I would never say a word if the 12 inches turns out to be a light dusting—no second-guessing. Once the decision is made, that's it, and you don't look back. If it *is* your company, and you *are* the chief pilot, consider the wisdom of giving yourself the same authority.

Turbulence

Turbulence is normally included in the hazardous weather part of the briefing. When turbulence is a function of either thunderstorm activity, clear air turbulence, or rotor turbulence under a standing wave, it can definitely be hazardous. But by and large, turbulence isn't truly "hazardous," just something to be avoided if at all possible. In your briefing you want to find out not only where the *areas* of turbulence are (in case these areas can be avoided), but also how *high* the turbulence is forecast to go, in case you can climb above it. If the turbulence can't be avoided, you should think about slowing down to maneuvering speed. This will be a little bit more comfortable and much easier on the airplane.

AIRMETs for "moderate to occasionally severe turbulence, below 8000 feet, particularly in mountainous areas" are so common in parts of the country from October to April that they tend to be ignored. I ignored one once, flying a Twin Comanche near Mt. Greylock, in western Massachusetts. I hit the ceiling so hard I thought I had broken my neck. On inspection the stabilator was found to be loose enough to require a teardown and replacement of all the bushings.

Turbulence isn't normally hazardous, but it *can* be.

NOTICES TO AIRMEN

Notices to Airmen—NOTAMS—are not literally part of a weather briefing, but since they come off the teletype with the hourly sequence reports, this is the best time and place to get them. If the briefer didn't go over the NOTAMS when he went over the sequences for the destination and alternate, make sure you go back and get them before you leave.

A lot of pilots skip this part, figuring nothing of any real importance is ever in a NOTAM—and frequently they are right. You can, however, avoid an awful lot of embarrassment (or worse) if you check them. An "embarrassment" would be to inform approach control that you had a "flag" on the glideslope, only to be told the glideslope had been "NOTAMed out" since last week. "Worse" would be finding out, on your way to the alternate, that the ILS there had also been "NOTAMED out" since last week, and the field was below non-precision minimums. You can skip checking the NOTAMS and get away with it many times, but if you fly often enough or long enough, sooner or later there will come a time when you will wish you had checked them.

TELEPHONE BRIEFINGS

You don't have to appear in person to get a weather briefing, but it sure helps. Sometimes, of course, it just can't be helped and you have to use the phone, but just because there is a phone to Flight Service in the pilot's lounge doesn't mean you have to use it. Sometimes the FSS is right next door. Too often a pilot will walk into an FBO, see a phone to FSS, and pick it up. He never even asks if there is a Flight Service Station on the field or not. (But if he's hungry, and he sees a bunch of vending machines, he usually remembers to ask if there aren't any restaurants nearby. Funny thing.)

You *can* get a good briefing over the phone, but it takes time. You have to make the briefer go slowly (so you can write it all down), and you have to write neatly so you can read it later. If an FSS or Weather Bureau office is anywhere nearby, make the effort to go there for your briefing. You'll get a lot more information, the hard copy they can give you is much easier to work with, and you'll be able to see the wall charts firsthand.

CONCLUSION

It has been my unscientific observation that pilots get in trouble with the weather not so much because they look at a given situation and then make a bad decision—although that sometimes does happen—but because they don't get the information they need to make an intelligent and very often fairly obvious decision. Getting enough information means getting a thorough weather briefing, and the best way to get one is to ask for it.

With a good briefing you have the information you need to make intelligent decisions about the weather. If you make intelligent decisions, you aren't likely to get into situations with the weather that you can't handle. As you fly and gain in experience, you will almost certainly improve your ability to fly on instruments, you will probably become more conservative and careful with your flight planning as you learn from the hard lessons of experience, and you will increase your awareness of the enormous variety of weather you have to deal with flying airplanes.

All of which is fine. Experience is great, especially weather experience, but it's hard to come by. It takes *time* to get experience, and it takes *experience* to get experience—you can't safely take on icy runways until you have some experience with wet runways, for instance. There isn't any easy way to obtain experience.

But regardless of your experience level, the strategy for dealing with the weather is the always the same: File IFR, get a complete weather briefing, flight plan thoroughly, always designate and fuel for an alternate airport, and stay away from hazardous weather—whatever that means for your particular aircraft, its systems, and your capabilities.

If there *is* an easy way to obtain experience, this is it.

Chapter 8

Radio Procedures

Most things we do in an airplane are private—nobody else really knows what's going on or what we're doing. Even in a jet, we share our decision-making and flying abilities with at most two other people: a copilot and a flight engineer. But when we pick up a mike to talk on the radio, everybody on the frequency gets a chance to observe our performance.

Student pilots know this instinctively. That's why they have such terrible "mike fright." They memorize perfectly what their instructor has told them to say—"Moosechip Ground, this is Waco 32 Xray, Shade Tree flight line, taxi for takeoff"—they pick up the mike, position it 19 different ways in their sweaty palms (none of them right), and then they say, "Ah, Ah, flight control for takeoff. Permission." They don't really know who is listening, but they assume that whoever it is knows how to do it, and they don't.

You can do all kinds of things wrong when you fly around by yourself and most of the time no one will notice. No one is there to tell you you ought to do *this* or try *that* or whatever. When you fly by yourself you can usually keep your mistakes to yourself— private *faux pas*. But everybody hears you talk on the radio.

The problem is, doing it badly is like having bad breath— nobody will tell you. You never see an experienced pilot go over to a less experienced pilot and say, "Hey buddy, I heard you talkin' on the radio back there, and I hate to tell you this, but you got a problem." If you were to fly with a seasoned Captain, though, and your only real job was to talk on the radio and you couldn't even do that right, you'd hear about it. It's his flight, his "airplane," his "ticket on the line," and you work for him, so you're going to do it *his* way or you're going to find yourself sweeping hangars again.

I happen to know for a fact that this is true. My first copilot position was on a Cessna 421. I had a couple thousand hours instructing and flying single-pilot charter, but this was my first job flying with somebody else. The Captain on my very first flight was a senior, gray-haired type—former military and airline pilot. At the time he was the Director of Training for the company that had just hired me, and had a reputation as a nitpicker. I had my work cut out for me, but I wasn't really worried—I had talked on the radio lots of times without any problems, and I didn't see how this could be any different.

I got the clearance and taxi instructions without incident. The tower told us to hold short of such-and-such runway for landing traffic and I said "Roger." That was a *big* mistake. Captain Grayhair wheeled around and let go:

"You don't say 'Roger' to something like that. The guy in the tower has a plane on short final and he doesn't have any idea what you're going to do now; he doesn't even know if you heard him right. Maybe *you* think he said 'Expedite crossing the runway for landing traffic' and you just said 'Roger' and are now about to cross right in front of his traffic and even if you *did* hear it right he still doesn't really know what you're going to do because all you said was 'Roger.' In fact, he doesn't even know for sure *who* said 'Roger,' does he? You didn't identify yourself."

Well, *excuuse me.* I mean, the guy said "Hold short" and I said "Roger." What could be clearer than that? But I kept my mouth shut.

There were other incidents, all of which my memory has graciously allowed me to forget in the intervening years, but needless to say, the flight did not go well. He went to the Chief Pilot and told him I needed a lot of work and that he was getting a little tired of having to teach copilots who were supposed to know what they were doing how to talk on the radio. It was just a wonderful way to start a new job.

Anyway, as I thought about it, I was gradually able to admit to myself that he was right. I had, over the years, invented my own radio language, and nobody had ever pointed out to me the deficiencies in it. I think, in retrospect, that this particular captain probably came loaded for bear when all he needed was a .22, but nonetheless the lesson has never escaped me. Using radio as a way of communicating absolutely essential and critical instructions is a not a great idea to start with, but the alternatives—at least in any practical form—don't exist. It is therefore absolutely imperative that you learn to use the system in a way that minimizes as much as possible the opportunities for confusion and error.

POINT OF VIEW

I think the most important thing I learned from this mistake and subsequent "correction" was that I learned to think about the situation from the controller's point of view. He (or she) has to make a bunch of unwieldy airplanes do certain things in order to keep them from running into each other, and the only form of control he has over them is to issue instructions over a radio to the people driving them.

The job is tough enough to begin with. The airplanes are in constant motion, they operate at different speeds and altitudes, and the instructions they can respond to are basic and primitive: Go faster, go slower, go up, go down, go here, go there. As simple as these instructions are, there is still a lag in the response time and a limit to how much faster or slower they can go. What is worse, having issued these instructions, there is no guarantee that the person driving the airplane will do what he is told. A controller with one plane on the runway and one on short final, for instance, can issue an instruction to the airplane on the runway to "expedite clearing the runway" (i.e., "go faster"), but there's nothing the controller can do if the pilot doesn't expedite except to tell the other airplane to go around—and hope he does.

LIMITATIONS OF RADIO COMMUNICATIONS

What really makes his job hard is that at various times the radio will: quit working, make noises, garble words, fade, receive but not transmit, and transmit but not receive. Even when the radio does work properly, there may be as many as 20 aircraft on the same frequency, and only one person can talk at a time. If anyone else is talking it completely ties up the frequency, preventing the controller from issuing his instructions, and there isn't anything he can do about it but sit there and go crazy.

But probably the single most frustrating characteristic of using a radio for communication, from the controller's point of view, is that there is almost no way to tell who is talking unless that person identifies himself. When I said "Roger," the controller didn't even know (for sure) who said it.

With all these problems, aren't you glad you're a pilot and not a controller? I think if you always try to keep in mind what the controller is trying to accomplish—i.e., think from his point of view—and if you keep in mind the limitations inherent in trying to do that with a radio, you'll have no trouble understanding why proper radio technique is so important.

DATALINKS

Someday airplanes will have datalinks. You won't use the radio at all except as a backup. When the controller wants you to do something he will punch it into some kind of keyboard and it will be transmitted to your aircraft and displayed on a screen. A bell or light will go off directing your attention to the message. You'll push a button acknowledging receipt of that particular message, which will go back to the controller's panel. If there is any discrepancy between what he sent and what you acknowledge, the controller will be alerted. The communication will be positive, clear, and verified both ways. Because it can be transmitted without modulation (voice communication must be modulated, which takes a lot of power), it will carry further and penetrate interference better.

It will be a better system, but I will miss the human contact between controller and pilot, and I will also miss not hearing what is transmitted to the other aircraft. The more you fly, the better you get at visualizing the Big Picture from what you hear going to the other airplanes, and once in a great while you even catch a possible mistake. These problems will have to be "addressed," as the politicians say, and I'm sure they will be. It will be a better system. I wish I could get more excited about it.

COMMUNICATION PROBLEMS

Problems with radio communications usually fall into one of two large categories—either a lack of clarity or a failure to verify the transmission. No matter how good radios get, a lack of clarity—communication in the literal sense—will be a problem from time to time. Even in normal speech we sometimes don't hear or understand what is being said properly, and radios only make the problem worse. Since communication is so crucial to aircraft control, and since radios are less than perfect communication devices, there has to be some way to verify that what you actually heard and what you were supposed to hear are the same thing.

If the controller says "Hold short for landing traffic," but you think he said "Expedite crossing for landing traffic," *that's* a problem of clarity. If you respond with "Roger" to what you think is an instruction to cross the runway, the controller assumes you are responding to his actual instruction to hold short, and won't know anything is wrong until he sees you crossing in front of his traffic. *That* is a problem in verification. Throughout this chapter we will be emphasizing, in various specific ways, these two main points of radio communication: *clarity*, to avoid confusion and repetition, and *verification*, to catch the inevitable misunderstandings that happen anyway.

CLARITY

This same Captain I was talking about (we eventually got along fine, by the way, and I still see him from time to time) used to talk so slowly, and enunciate so carefully, I was embarrassed for him. He talked on the radio as if he were talking to a foreigner. I sure wasn't going to say anything to him, but I thought he had a lot of nerve criticizing me for the way I talked on the radio when *he* sounded like a 45 being played at 33 1/3. But a couple of weeks later, I was flying in another airplane and heard him on the frequency and he sounded great. His transmissions were clear and distinct, and while he did talk slower than almost everybody else on the frequency, it didn't seem too slow at all. In fact, it was a pleasure being able to understand someone so well. I figured somebody with more nerve than I had must have talked to him. But the next time I flew with him he was back to that baby-talk again. And the next time I heard him talking on the radio from another airplane he sounded good again.

You got the picture, right? (Probably quicker than I did.) To be understood over the radio, you have to speak extra clearly and probably much slower than you normally would. It may seem strange in the airplane, but it doesn't over the air. If you don't think so, make a point of *really* listening the next time you fly. The fast talkers take a lot of work to understand, especially if they also don't speak extra clearly. (And of course, the faster you talk, the harder it is to speak clearly.) The guys who really come across well are the guys who are actually speaking slower than normal—it ends up sounding normal over the air.

Probably the most common mistake pilots make with the radio is to talk too loudly. This causes their voice to rise in pitch, and the result is a high-pitched, distorted sound that is hard to understand, annoying, and one that unmistakably stamps the pilot as an amateur. I think I know why they do it, though. Student pilots are always a little afraid of the radio, and their instructors are always telling them to speak up:"Hold the mike close to your mouth and speak up!" Eventually it becomes a bad habit. (Also, the radios they put in trainers are almost always bottom-of-the-line, and shouting, in a vain attempt to compensate, is the inevitable result.) Holding the mike close to your mouth is correct (in order mainly to take advantage of the noise-cancelling properties of the microphone, not to increase the volume), but speaking up doesn't mean shouting. Radios need vocal energy to create radio energy, so to a certain extent you *can* increase the power of your radio by increasing the volume of your voice—but only up to a point. After that point, all you get is distortion. If you *have* to shout for the other guy to receive you at all, you need to have your radio looked at.

SIDE-TONES

There really is only one way to learn to use the radio properly, and that is to hear what you sound like. Once you hear yourself, you'll know exactly what's wrong and what to do. The way you hear yourself speak is with a side-tone. A side-tone is an "echo" of the actual transmission that is routed through the speaker or earphones so you can hear what you actually sound like as you say it.

A side-tone is essential if you use earphones, because while we are not aware of it, we need to hear our own voices to speak properly—it is very hard to speak if you can't hear yourself. (This is one of the reasons people who lose their hearing are hard to understand—they still remember how to talk, but they don't get any feedback on what they're saying.) Since the earphones cover up your ears, it is very hard to hear yourself speaking with them on, so a side-tone is provided. While a side-tone is not essential when you are using a speaker, it is still very desirable in order to monitor the actual sound of your transmissions.

Using a side-tone takes a little getting used to, but once you learn to listen to what you sound like without being distracted by it (which comes very easily, actually), you will have no problem making your transmissions clear, readable, and properly pitched. The whining, semi-hysterical sound of the amateur will go away.

This is why "airline captains" all seem to affect that low-pitched, command presence-type growl over the radio. You *can* carry it too far, of course, but the airline types have learned, mainly by listening to themselves, what it takes to make their voice as clear and readable as possible. Talking like an airline pilot may sound like an affectation at first, but it isn't—it's the right way to talk on the radio.

If you don't have a headset (an earphone/boom mike combination, which I will assume has a side-tone built in), talk to your radio shop about getting a side-tone wired into your speaker system. It may take a new audio panel, which can be expensive, so the headset route may be the better one. A headset with a push-to-talk switch is probably the way to go in a single-pilot operation anyway. It is easier to hear the transmissions with earphones, and you don't have to reach for a mike.

THE LANGUAGE

That should take care of the physical aspects of clarity: speak slowly, carefully, and listen to yourself so you can adjust your tone and pitch to what "sounds right." But there is another aspect of clarity, and that is using the language in a consistent and predictable way. No matter what you may tell your friends and companions when they say, "I just don't know how you understand a *thing* they're saying on that little bitty radio," the fact is it *is* hard to understand what's being said sometimes. The more predictable and consistent the language is, the easier it is to understand.

If you've ever tried to learn Morse Code, you know that you can learn to decode as fast as 10 words per minute just by memorizing the dots and dashes that go with each letter. But you can't get any faster than that without breaking The Barrier. The Barrier is the translation process—you hear a pattern of dots and dashes, and you remember just as fast as you can what letter goes with that pattern, write it down, and hope you did it fast enough not to miss hearing the next letter. For most people, the fastest they can go through this process is about 10 wpm. The only way to go faster is to learn to recognize the letter from the sound of the dots and dashes themselves—you hear the code and know the letter without stopping to remember what it is. Once you can do that, you can quickly move up to 20 wpm or more. (So they say. I can't even remember all the letters anymore.)

The same thing happens in speech. When someone says

something unexpected, you have to pause for a second to reconfigure your brain to what was actually said, instead of the pattern you expected. This slows things down and leads to misunderstanding and error. This is what a writer often tries to do on purpose: He rearranges words in unexpected patterns, and in so doing causes us to realize new meanings.

But talking to ATC isn't poetry. In fact it is the opposite of poetry. This is communication in the most basic and literal sense. You can't play games with words here.

Radio talk really is a language of its own. It is very similar to English (thank goodness for that—imagine having to pass a French or Spanish test before you could learn to fly), and it has a very simple grammar and vocabulary, but it is still a language of its own—and you have to learn it, just like you have to learn any other language. When controllers train to become controllers, this is one of the most important parts of their training, and using nonstandard terminology is a serious error. In fact, you can usually spot a trainee controller by his fumbling with the language. He isn't "fluent" yet. It is disconcerting to hear a controller say something "nonstandard." It makes you wonder if that's the only thing he has messed up, and it causes you to doubt whether you really understand what he means even though you think you do. On the other hand, the controller who uses standard, predictable terminology has an air about him of control and assurance. You have to assume that controllers react the same way to pilots.

The best way to learn standard terminology is to listen to the pilots who do it right, and to avoid slang and shortcuts. Don't get cute. You may not like saying "Affirmative" or "Negative," and people who talk like that in everyday speech usually are a little offensive, but that's the way you talk on the radio. Not only is it clear and unmistakable—"Affirmative" doesn't sound like anything else—but it is predictable. It won't cause the controller to have to mentally stop for a microsecond to translate what you really said into what he expects—"Affirmative" is "Affirmative." "Sure" is something *like* "Affirmative," after translation, but it isn't "Affirmative."

To learn the language of radio communications you have to listen, imitate, and practice—just like kids learn to talk, or the way you would learn to speak a foreign language. Listen to the guys who seem to know what they're doing, who act like they are in charge of the situation, and who get respect and cooperation from the controllers. This is one area where you don't have to actually fly with the old guys to learn from them. You can listen to other transmissions on your radio and learn by example.

Also listen to the controllers. They *have* to use standard terminology, so they are the models for "radiospeak." (Of course they do deviate from standard from time to time, just as Arnold Palmer sometimes holds the club the "wrong" way. But you have to know how to do it right before you can get away with doing it "wrong.")

KEY WORDS

To help you get started, here is a short list of the most useful words, with some comments on how to use them:

Roger: Might as well take the hardest one first. "Roger" does have its place, but only in nonessential communications. It basically means "Yah, that's right" or "Okay." If a ground controller asked you if you could move up a little closer to the aircraft in front of you, "Roger" would be an acceptable reply. Or if he said, "You can take it to the end" (but you don't have to), you could say "Roger." "Roger" should never be used in place of "Affirmative" or "Wilco" in essential communications, nor should it be a short-cut for not repeating a clearance. (The proper reply to "32 Xray, taxi up and hold short" is "32 Xray, taxi up and hold short.") Using "Roger" is like calling the boss by his first name—if you don't know for sure that it's okay, you better call him "Mr."

Stand by: This is a very useful term. It gives you back some of the control over the communications. If you are busy, or don't know the answer right at that moment, just say "Stand by." If his request is critical and can't wait, he'll let you know. Nine times out of ten it won't be and a later, well thought out, accurate answer is much better than a quick, hasty one. Occasionally a controller or Flight Service Station Specialist will ask you something inconsequential right after liftoff. You're busy flying the airplane and don't want to be distracted right at that moment, but you know if you don't say anything he's going to bug you again. A quick "Stand by" usually gets him off your back and gets the message across too—"Don't talk to me when I'm busy trying to fly, unless it's important."

Once in a great while someone will even call you with something nonessential while rolling. This is just unforgivable, because your first reaction should be to abort as soon as you hear your call sign on a takeoff roll; normally no one calls you on the takeoff roll unless they see something very wrong, and the sooner you start stopping the better. I saw this happen once to an Eastern 727 at Washington National. Eastern was in position and had been cleared to go, but was slow in rolling—a serious offense at DCA or any other busy airport. Just after he did start to roll, though, the controller said, "Eastern 123 (not the real numbers), you *are* cleared for takeoff, you know." I could see the 727 aborting as he said it—the Captain heard "Eastern 123" and that's all he needed to hear to abort. The tower said again, "I repeat—Eastern 123 is cleared for takeoff."

All the Captain said was, "Too late now."

This was more of a screw-up than anything else—I suspect the tower controller didn't see him start to go—but it illustrates the point. If a controller calls you on the takeoff roll, assume it is a critical communication and act accordingly. This is not the place for "Stand by." Whatever you do at this point, talking on the radio is not part of it. If it turns out that the call was *not* essential, a telephone call later to the tower may be in order. We are all human and controllers make mistakes too, and a reasonable explanation of the problem you have when someone calls you on the takeoff roll would not be out of line.

Unable: This little, short word can cover a lot of ground. It takes the place of a bunch of words in "We're not going to be able to use the short runway" ("Unable the short runway"), or "I couldn't raise anybody on 32.5—you got another frequency?" ("Unable 32.5"), or "Cherokee 8 Fox Lima is a little too heavy for Flight Level 350 today" ("Unable Flight Level 350"), and so on. Save the full text for the war stories later.

Over: To be used rarely. The only purpose of the word "Over" is to signal the end of your transmission, and the end is usually very obvious and does not need this embellishment. Your call sign works much better and provides positive identification at the same time. For instance, "32 Xray, climb and maintain niner thousand." "Out of eight for nine, 32 Xray." About the only time you might need to use "Over" would be after a long pilot report or at the end of a flight plan or maybe a long request—just to make sure the person at the other end knew you were through. But these times will be rare. If you're using "Over" a lot, you've probably picked up a bad habit.

VERIFICATION

All of this has to do with clarity—making yourself understood. Speak slowly and clearly; don't shout; use standard terminology.

The other half of the picture is making *sure* everybody understands everybody, because the things that have to be said over the radio are too important to leave to assumption. (In the Army we used to say, "Assumption is the mother of all mistakes." Actually, we didn't say "mistakes." We said something else.)

All clearances should be verified. (A "clearance" isn't just the IFR route clearance you get on the ramp prior to takeoff. That's the initial clearance. Any instruction you receive from ATC is, technically, an amendment to the initial clearance and must also be verified.) Verification means reading the clearance back. The regulations do not specifically require a readback, but you *are* required to "request clarification" if the meaning of a clearance is uncertain (FAR 91.75 (a)), and to operate IFR you must "receive" an appropriate clearance (FAR 91.115 (b)). I'm not exactly sure what constitutes "receiving" a clearance, but as long as you read all clearances back I think you're covered.

It is all right to abbreviate the readback somewhat, as long as the essential words are included. (But if in doubt, it's always better to err on the side of reading back too much—and there is nothing wrong with reading it back word for word.) Thus, if ground control says "32 Xray, taxi to runway 19," you might read back: "Taxi to 19. 32 Xray." But if he says "32 Xray, call holding short of Golf taxiway," you should reply: "Call holding short of Golf. 32 Xray." There's only one word in that clearance that isn't essential and that does not need to be verified, and that is "taxiway." The controller must have a reason for not wanting you to go any further than Golf, or he would have cleared you to the runway, and he has some reason for wanting to know when you get there, and he wants to make sure 32 Xray and not somebody else gets the message. So the only proper readback in this case is: "Call holding short of Golf. 32 Xray."

Once you're "on tower," you will most likely get one of the following clearances: "Taxi up to but hold short of the active runway;" "Taxi into position and hold;" or "Cleared for takeoff." The standard answers are, in order: "32 Xray, up to and hold short;" "32 Xray, position and hold;" and "32 Xray, cleared to go." (This last one isn't technically proper of course—you really should say "Cleared for takeoff"—but it is so common that it is completely acceptable.) The aircraft ident can go at the beginning or the end of each of these transmissions: i.e., either "32 Xray, cleared to go," or "Cleared to go, 32 Xray", but it's got to be there somewhere.

At some point on climbout the tower will tell you to contact

Departure Control. He usually will not give you the departure frequency, since you normally get it with your clearance, either directly, or as part of a SID (Standard Instrument Departure). Sometimes it will be on the ATIS (Automatic Terminal Information Service). If you don't have it, ask. If you don't come up on departure, the Departure Controller can call the tower on the landline and tell the tower to rattle your cage, but it's better to do it right in the first place. Assuming you do have the frequency, when he says "32 Xray, contact Departure," just say: "32 Xray; good day," and go on over.

Once enroute, most clearances will be for either altitudes or headings. The custom on altitudes—going back to the days when control was based entirely on aircraft reports—is to report leaving your old altitude for the new altitude, but to omit the report reaching it—he assumes you get there sooner or later. If he really needs to know when you get there he will ask you to tell him. Thus, when the controller says "32 Xray, climb and maintain four thousand and report reaching," you say: "32 Xray, out of three for four—call reaching." When you write it down, put a circle around it, or something like that, to remind yourself to call him reaching.

Any time you get a heading change, read it back—these are just as important as altitude changes. If he says "32 Xray, left heading 270," you read back: "Left 270, 32 Xray." If he says "32 Xray, turn 30 degrees to the left," you say: "Hey, why me? Make the other guy go around. I'm in a big hurry and you always give the airlines preference." Let the guy know he's dealing with a real professional who isn't going to be pushed around! *No, seriously*, you say: "32 Xray, 30 degrees left." And that's all. If you like picking fights, take up drinking or hockey. Or tell your wife you think she's giving too much to the church and it's cutting into your flying. But keep it out of the cockpit.

After a while, when you get used to reading back all the essential numbers and words, it almost becomes a litany: He says this, you say that. It becomes automatic. This is not to say you just blindly repeat everything he says; obviously you have to know what he means and you have to comply with it. But there is a sense of assurance and confidence in the system that comes with knowing how to use the language properly. Listen to the airline types. Try to sound like they do. Listen to the corporates and charter guys, too. You hear good and bad here, depending on company policy and flight department "personality." Try to see why some guys seem to communicate easily, and others, while being possibly entertaining and original, seem to interfere with the basic job at hand.

Above all, avoid slang and don't get cute. You may be a really wild and crazy guy, and that's just the way you are and the way you like to be, but when all is said and done, this isn't playtime, this is work. This is the job of getting yourself from one place to another using a form of transportation known as an airplane, and there is a right way to do that job and a wrong way. Before you go breaking the rules, make sure you know them. When you've got a couple of thousand hours of instrument cross-country time, maybe you can take the liberty to chit-chat and break a rule once in a while, but I'll bet it will be pretty rare even then. In fact, I'll bet the more you fly, the less fooling around you do.

FREQUENCY MANAGEMENT

Some notes on management of your radios: I'm going to assume you have two com radios, even though you can legally operate with just one. (Radio communication is too important, and radios themselves fail too often, to even *think* about operating IFR with only one radio.) The ideal arrangement is to have one radio with a frequency preselect feature. This allows you to do two things. On the ground, you can "lead" your frequencies by one, since you know what the next frequency will be. (They're written on the approach plates.) If you are talking to ground, the next frequency up will be tower; by putting that frequency in the preselect window, all you have to do is throw the switch when the time comes to go over. Likewise, once on tower, put the Departure frequency in the preselect window.

After departure, though, the rest of the frequencies will be assigned, so you can't anticipate them. In this case you use the preselect window for storage of the old frequency. When the controller says "32 Xray, contact Kansas City Center on 132.7," you say "Thirty two seven. 32 Xray." You then take what is now the "old" frequency and transfer it to the preselect window, and dial up the new frequency, 132.7, in the active window. If you don't get any response on 132.7 (after trying three times with at least 30 seconds between each try), all you have to do is switch to the preselect window, the frequency you *were* using, and tell him "32 Xray, unable 132.7." This saves having to write down and cross out frequencies as you use them.

While we're on this subject, if you ever need to go back to your old frequency, and discover to your chagrin that you either forgot to write it down or somehow messed up storing it, don't panic. There are two things you can do. The first is to look on the low altitude chart for the appropriate Center frequency for the area you are operating in, or at least an active frequency nearby. As long as you can get a hold of someone in that Center's area, he can put you on the right frequency. (These guys are all sitting in a big room together—all they have to do is holler down the row for whoever was working 32 X.) The other way is to call Flight Service and tell them your location and your problem. They have direct land-lines to Center and can give Center a call and straighten it out. It happens to everybody once in a while, but if it happens a lot—like more than once a year—you're doing something wrong.

What do you do with the second radio aside from having it as a backup? This is an area of personal preference, but common practice is to use the second radio for non-ATC functions: Flight Service, Unicom, or company frequency. In the more remote parts of the world it is common to tune the number two com to 121.5, and overwater it is mandatory. I set 121.5 in sometimes anyway, just for kicks; once in a while you can help someone, and you hear some interesting transmissions. It is a good idea to segregate the uses, though: number one radio for ATC, number two for everything else. That way you always know which radio is for what.

I think this is a much better method than trying to switch back and forth from number one to number two. If you do try to alternate radios, there are a lot of switches to throw, and it is very easy to get confused as to which frequency is the active one and which is the previous one. What it all boils down to is that the number two radio is really there as a backup, and any other miscellaneous use you have for it is fine, but don't try to intergrate it with normal ATC communications.

SQUELCH AND VOLUME

A nice thing about the radio system installed in the Falcon 20 was that you couldn't turn the volume all the way down. As long as the switch was thrown for that radio, no matter how low you turned the volume, you could still hear *something*. This was nice because the volume does sometimes get accidentally turned all the way down, and ATC can go crazy trying to get a hold of you before you realize it has been a long time since you heard anything and think to check the volume.

If it has been real quiet for awhile, check the squelch. If the volume was turned down too low to hear, or the radio has quit working, you should discover it when you check the squelch. (You won't hear any noise.) If you find that the volume *was* turned all the way down, "fess up" to it—it's not the end of the world, but an entire Center may be doing handstands trying to work around you and the sooner things get back to normal the better.

If the volume is okay, wait a little bit longer—usually just when you reach maximum nervousness somebody else will ask why it's so quiet, saving you the trouble. If you just can't stand it anymore, ask for a radio check. Nine times out of ten the controller will come back "Five by five, how me?"—but better safe than sorry. If he doesn't answer you, ask if anyone else on the frequency can relay a message; if someone else answers, explain your problem and see if they can get a better frequency from ATC for you. If *nobody* answers, try another radio. If that doesn't work, try FSS on 122.2, first on that radio, then on the other, and then again on 121.5. If that doesn't work, turn up the volume on the *nav* receiver—FSS may be trying to relay messages to you that way. If nothing works, and you are in VFR conditions, land and cancel. If you are IFR, continue as last cleared per detailed radio inop procedures described in FAR 91.127c and the Airman's Information Manual.

If you haven't thought about those procedures since you took your written, this is a good time to review them.

MEMORY TRICKS

I have found that when ATC throws two things at me at once, that I can handle both without too much problem. An example would be "32 Xray, turn 30 degrees to the right. Climb and maintain one zero thousand." I can usually remember both of those things long enough to say "Thirty degrees to the right. Out of nine for one zero thousand. 32 Xray." Once I say it out loud, it sticks pretty well in my head too, although I would immediately reset the heading bug 30 degrees and the altitude alerter to 10000 (or write it down if I don't have an alerter). But if he throws *three* things at me: "Turn 30 degrees to the right; climb and maintain one zero thousand; contact Memphis Center on 135.5," it gets a lot tougher. One memory trick is to read it back in reverse order. You're supposed to read it back in the same order, but I read somewhere— and it seems to work—that your brain can remember a list of things better if you say them in reverse order. The controllers prefer you to read a clearance back in the same order (and I prefer not to get more than two instructions at once), but it isn't required, and I've never heard a controller complain about it.

If you don't like changing the order, then read back what you can and ask again for the rest: "32 Xray, right 30 degrees, out of nine for one zero thousand, and say again Memphis Center." If there are any controllers reading this, I personally think you'll save time in the long run by not giving out more than two instructions at once. It goes a lot smoother.

Another memory trick is to visualize the numbers in the air somewhere as the controller says them. Just kind of draw them out there in space somewhere. It may not work for you, but I have found that I can hang on to a bunch of numbers better if I can visualize them this way than I can just trying to keep them in my head long enough to answer him or find my pencil and get it all written down.

SIMULTANEOUS TRANSMISSIONS

One last thing, and this is important: *Listen* before you talk. Airborne VHF is FM—Frequency Modulation. There are many advantages in using FM over AM (Amplitude Modulation), but one of the *disadvantages* is that two people can't talk at once. When they do, the two transmissions cancel each other out, resulting in a very loud squeal. When two people transmit on an FM radio at once, the following results: 1) Neither transmission is received by the intended recipient; 2) If one of the senders was ATC, nobody knows who he was talking to; 3) Since the senders can't hear what the other receivers actually receive, neither of the two senders knows he was blocked.

In other words, it creates all kinds of confusion, mainly because the parties involved don't know there's a problem. This usually leads to more confusion as everybody else tries to help them out—an Alphonse and Gaston act. If two aircraft call at once, let ATC straighten it out; don't add to the confusion with your two bits. But if you know it was ATC that was blocked, sometimes a quick "Blocked" will do the trick. This is short enough to not wipe out any reattempts, and lets ATC know right away that he didn't get through. But the important point is to *listen* first and make sure no one else is talking before you do, so this sort of thing doesn't happen.

Once in a great while, two people block each other just by chance—two people both listen, hear nothing, and both decide to start talking at exactly the same moment. It would be nice if the radio manufacturers could come up with some kind of listening device that would alert you to this condition, but it's a difficult problem because it is hard for an airborne radio to receive and transmit at the same time—the transmitter antenna is so close to the receiver antenna that a direct transmission would destroy the receiver. With current technology, occasional simultaneous transmissions are inevitable.

But most of the time simultaneous transmissions are avoidable. Most of the time they happen either because somebody just switched frequencies and started immediately talking without listening at all, or had the volume turned down and didn't know anybody else was already talking. Sometimes it happens because someone down low keeps trying to establish radio contact before he is high enough to hear ATC. He can't hear ATC talking so he just keeps calling, wiping out everybody else within range. Try to find out how high you have to be to pick up Center, and wait until you get up there to start calling. A lot of this is just courtesy and common sense. Remember, this is a big party line, and not a very good one at that, and it takes a lot of cooperation on everyone's part to make it work.

RADIO PROCEDURES: THE KEY TO THE SYSTEM

The point of proper radio procedures is clarity and understanding—communication that is positive and absolute. The backup, to prevent serious errors resulting from inevitable misunderstandings, is verification. The goal is fluency with the language—the radio language. The way to get that fluency is to listen, imitate, and practice. Fluency with the radios leads automatically to fluency with the instrument system as a whole. The communication system is the heart and soul of the instrument system. The pilot who knows how to communicate is well on his way to mastery of his craft.

Chapter 9

Emergency and
Abnormal Procedures

A pilot's job has two parts. One part is flying the airplane; the other part is being prepared to deal with emergency and abnormal situations. Since major malfunctions are fairly rare, dealing with abnormal and emergency situations is usually seen as separate from the normal task of getting the airplane safely from A to B. The two tasks *aren't* separate; the ability to be able to deal with emergency and abnormal situations at any given moment is an integral and extremely important part of the pilot's job. But as long as airplanes continue to become more and more reliable and failures continue to be less and less common, this apparent separation is inevitable. The bulk of this book is concerned with flying airplanes safely and routinely from A to B. But "flying airplanes safely" also means being prepared for the *non*-routine, and that's what this chapter is all about.

When a system malfunction occurs, the pilot must analyze the situation, reconfigure the aircraft to minimize further damage or danger, and optimize the remaining performance and capabilities of his aircraft. In the early days of aviation, when aircraft systems were relatively simple, the pilot was expected to know his aircraft well enough to be able to handle any failure or problem by relying on a combination of memory, experience, and ingenuity.

But as airplanes became increasingly complex, total reliance on the memory, experience, and ingenuity of the pilot became unacceptable. The systems became too complex to reasonably expect the average pilot to be completely familiar with each and every detail, and the adverse consequences of faulty procedures became unacceptable. Failure, for instance, to bring a functioning generator back "on line" in an open cockpit, VFR-only aircraft was of little consequence, but as aircraft became increasingly dependent upon a reliable source of electrical power for navigation, communication, lighting, and the control of other systems, a consistent and reliable solution to the temporary loss of that power became imperative. This is just one example—in an "all-weather" environment there are *no* inconsequential systems.

Not only is complexity a problem, but *people* can be a problem, too. Not all pilots are equally experienced or ingenious, and relying on these qualities to solve whatever problems arise often leads to more problems. There will always be a place for a human being as the final arbiter in an aircraft, but most problems can be anticipated, and most problems have an optimum solution which is best determined ahead of time.

CHECKLIST-ORIENTED PROBLEM SOLVING

The aviation community has attempted to deal with these combined problems of complexity and human variability since the white silk scarf left the cockpit. Led by the military, the airlines, and the better corporate flight departments, a two-part strategy based on detailed emergency and abnormal procedures checklists, and backed up by regular and thorough training in the use of those checklists under simulated failure conditions, has evolved.

The pilot of a complex Transport Category aircraft is no longer expected to be able to resolve problems as they arise based on his ingenuity alone, nor is he expected to be able to react solely from memory to each and every possible failure. He is only required to solve himself those rare but theoretically possible problems that cannot be anticipated, and he is only expected to be able to react from memory to those items which are so critical that his response must be virtually instantaneous—i.e., those items that cannot even wait for a checklist to be picked up and referred to. Very few items in an airplane are *that* critical, but those that are must be identified, memorized, and practiced. The rest wait for the checklist. This reduces pilot workload to an acceptable level, regardless of the complexity of the aircraft, and it results in much higher rate of successful problem resolution for all aircraft.

This doesn't mean the pilot has become a robot—no checklist

can every be made complete enough to cover ever possible contingency. The pilot still has to have a general understanding of the systems in order to handle those situations that do not fit a checklist. But it does mean that a large part of the troubleshooting and repairman functions of the pilot have been replaced by the use of checklists, freeing the pilot to do what he does best—fly the airplane.

So far, this philosophy of checklist-oriented problem solving has not filtered down below the airline and corporate turbine level to a significant extent. Most general aviation owner and renter pilots have read the manufacturer's owner's handbook for their aircraft, and most have a general idea of the aircraft systems and the manufacturer's recommendations for dealing with various emergency and abnormal situations. But very few of them are aware of the need for specific checklists for each emergency and abnormal situation that can be anticipated.

This is too bad, because the typical general aviation aircraft today is as complex as the airliners of the previous generation when the emphasis on the use of checklists for problem solving began. Personal aircraft have reached the point in sophistication where they require checklists for emergency and abnormal situations, and the part-time owner or renter pilot who does not have access to regular simulator training and systems ground schools especially needs something he can count on in a crunch.

The best device so far invented for that purpose is a checklist.

CHECKLIST PREPARATION

Unfortunately, it is impossible for me to provide you with a set of checklists that will cover each and every system for each and every airplane—airplanes vary too much. But I *can* give you an idea of what areas should be included in any set of emergency and abnormal checklists, and an idea of what sorts of things should be included in each of those areas. With this information for background, you should be able to go to your Owner's Handbook and Flight Manual and make up your own systems checklists based on the information contained in those publications.

If you own or fly a fairly modern aircraft—one manufactured within the last six or seven years or so—your Operating Handbook and Flight Manual will follow the GAMA (General Aviation Manufacturers Association) Handbook Specification Number 1. Specification Number 1 is a standardized format for all aircraft information, and is a tremendous improvement over the mishmash of information that was provided prior to this specification. If your aircraft has such a manual, your job will be fairly simple. The emergency procedures information is already tabbed with a red marker in your standardized handbook. All you have to do is mark the memory items with a red pen and add additional tabs to help locate specific problems.

If you do not have a centralized location in your Owner's Handbook for this information, the best thing to do is create your own emergency and abnormal situations checklists. It is a lot of work, but there is no better way to really get to know your aircraft systems than this—and I think you will be glad you did it once it's done. I *know* you'll be glad you did it if you ever have to use one.

Physically, these checklists don't have to be anything fancy— a small looseleaf binder with plastic inserts for each of the emergency and abnormal situations, appropriately tabbed for quick referral, will do nicely. Or you might be able to get everything on the front and back of a couple of pieces of heavy paper—one for emergencies, with red borders; another for abnormals, with black borders—and have them laminated so they'll hold up. Whatever works. The only physical requirements are that you have something you can store within easy reach, such as in a side pocket or under the seat, and that it be easy to use. In a true emergency situation, stress is going to be a significant factor and you want to be able to get to the checklist without difficulty—and once you have it in your hand, you want to be able to instantly locate the appropriate part.

In creating your own checklists, it is very important that you transfer the information from the appropriate parts of the Flight Manual and Owner's Handbook accurately and without "editorial license." The temptation is awfully great, as long as you are making up your own checklist anyway, to make your own changes too. If you *do* make changes, you are wandering in the area of the unknown—the realm of the test pilot. Follow the Flight Manual *exactly* (because those are legal limitations), and avoid the temptation to make changes to the manufacturer's recommendations. Very often there is more to a specific recommendation than meets the eye, and making what seems like a perfectly simple and obvious change for the better may come back to bite you later. If you *really* think you have a better way, write the manufacturer and see what he says, but be very careful about making changes on your own.

EMERGENCY VERSUS ABNORMAL

It is important, as you go about this task, to differentiate between emergency and abnormal situations. The difference between an *emergency* and an *abnormal situation* is that in an emergency situation, the safety of the flight is in immediate jeopardy, and generally some sort of corrective action must be taken immediately—usually from memory, if not instinctively. An abnormal situation, on the other hand, is simply something that is not a normal occurrence. An abnormal situation requires corrective or compensating action, but the safety of the flight is not immediately jeopardized and time is not so critical. Generally, in an emergency situation, you use the checklist after the fact—both to *check* that you have accomplished the memory items correctly, and to "clean up" the non-critical items. In an abnormal situation, you have time to get the checklist out and to use it as your guide from the beginning.

The Operating Handbooks tend to call anything an emergency, but this isn't technically correct and has several disadvantages. Emergencies are important enough to be kept separate from abnormalities, especially since in an emergency, the appropriate response or responses very often must be memorized. "Abnormals" deserve their own section too, mainly to keep them manageable—there can be a lot of abnormal situations, and it's nice to keep them separate from the truly critical situations. This is the way it is done with Transport Category aircraft—emergency checklists in one group and abnormal checklists in another—and I think you would be well advised to do the same. It is also the way we will divide up the situations in this chapter.

MEMORY ITEMS

To expect a pilot, under stress, to do anything from memory is asking a lot, so it is important to restrict the memory items to only the most critical elements of real emergencies. The following are generally accepted as "real" emergencies: engine fires, engine failure (for jet aircraft, engine failure is usually not an emergency, but for propeller-driven aircraft it is), propeller overspeed, cabin smoke or fire, electrical smoke or fire, electric trim runaway, forced landing, ditching, rapid depressurization (pressurized aircraft), emergency descent, failure of all generators, and spins. Not all of these will pertain to all aircraft, but this list should cover all the emergency situations for most aircraft. These are not the only things that can go wrong with an airplane, of course, but in each of these situations, either the immediate safety of the flight is jeopardized or memory items are required.

It is possible that your particular aircraft has other systems or characteristics that could result in other emergency situations. Use your Flight Manual as your guide, and if you wonder whether a particular situation is an emergency or not, ask yourself if the situation is one that jeopardizes the immediate safety of the flight and/or requires immediate action from memory. If the answer is "yes" in either case, then it's an emergency.

EMERGENCY CHECKLISTS

I want to talk about each of these emergencies specifically and in some detail so that you can go to your Flight Manual and Handbook and have a pretty good idea of what you want to include in your own emergency checklists. I have also included a hypothetical checklist for "Engine Fire" to use as a model in creating your own checklists.

Engine Fire

If this isn't an emergency, I don't know what is. Not only is the engine not going to work very well if it's on fire, but fuel runs all through the aircraft, creating an ideal situation for setting the entire airplane on fire. (One of the advantages of using kerosene for fuel [Jet A] is that it doesn't vaporize very well, while avgas is extremely volatile, even explosive.)

The engine failure part is the least important part of this emergency. The first priority is to get the fire stopped, and that means shutting off the supply of fuel. It may also be possible to snuff the fire out with increased airspeed. Check your manual for the recommended procedure, but it will probably involve mixture to cutoff and fuel selector off, and these fuel cutoff items should be done from memory. Then there will be clean-up items, which go on the checklist after the memory items—things like mags and master off (something electrical probably started the fire). For single-engine aircraft, the checklist should include a referral to the forced landing checklist (because that is now your next problem), and for twins a referral to the engine failure checklist to ensure that the failed engine is properly secured.

Figure 9-1 is a typical emergency procedures checklist for engine fire. Use it as a model only—the chances of it fitting your aircraft exactly are slim. I made it up simply as an example to show

```
Phase I:

        1. Mixture—IDLE CUTOFF
        2. Fuel Selector Valve—OFF
        3. Heater/Defroster—OFF

Phase II:

        4. If fire continues, increase airspeed.
        5. Notify ATC.
        6. Magnetoes—OFF
        7. Generators—OFF
        8. Battery—OFF
        (Single-engine aircraft): Refer to Forced
        Landing Checklist. (Multi-engine aircraft): Refer
        to Engine Failure Checklist. Land immediately.
```

Fig. 9-1. Typical emergency procedures checklist for engine fire. Phase I items are memory items; Phase II items are checklist items, to be done after memory items have been done and checked.

you a suggested format and to illustrate the general principles. This is the kind of thing you want to develop for your specific aircraft for each emergency situation.

The items marked "Phase I" are memory items. "Phase II" are non-memory items to be accomplished using the checklist, after having checked to be sure that all the memory items have been taken care of. (That's why they call it a *check*list.)

Engine Failure

The most important consideration in any engine failure situation, for any airplane, is to maintain control of the aircraft. I'm not going to go into basic flying techniques in this chapter—that's a job for your flight instructor. I *do* want to help you develop a checklist so that after the engine failure, and once the aircraft is stable and under control, you can do whatever you can to restore power—and, if that is impossible, to clean up the aircraft for either unpowered or single-engine flight.

For any aircraft, if there is any question whatever about the performance of an engine prior to liftoff, *abort*. I don't think you really have to have a checklist for this, but you should know what configuration the manufacturer recommends for maximum braking effectiveness.

For a single-engine airplane, if the engine fails after liftoff, the most important consideration (after maintaining control) is to attempt to restore power. If smoke is coming out of the engine, or the cowling and windows are covered with oil, or there is any other sign of a mechanical failure, you obviously are not going to be able to restore power. But if the engine seems to have quit for non-mechanical reasons, you want a checklist to help you try to get it going again.

Fuel and ignition are immediately suspect as culprits. Check your manual and see what the manufacturer recommends: switching fuel tanks, turning on boost pumps, and mixture to full rich are standard responses. For ignition, try the left and right magnetos separately, or whatever the manufacturer recommends. You won't always have time to refer to the checklist if this happens, so these all should be considered memory items. When you do have time, you can refer to the checklist to make sure you haven't forgotten anything.

A checklist is particularly helpful after a partial power loss—with a partial power loss you probably *will* have time to dig out a checklist, and a partial power loss is also fairly likely to respond to corrective action such as switching tanks, turning boost pumps on or off, and isolating magnetos.

For a multiengine airplane, the emphasis after an engine failure is on configuring the aircraft to optimize the performance of the remaining engine. Getting the bad one started again isn't nearly as important as maintaining control and gaining—or at least maintaining—altitude with the remaining engine. Again, airplanes vary as to the best way to clean them up, but in general, the gear should come up as soon as a positive rate of climb has been established, the flaps as soon as altitude and airspeed allow, and the engine shut down and feathered as soon as control is established. Refer to your manual for the recommended procedure for your aircraft.

The engine failure checklist for a twin will be mostly memory items except for the final "clean-up" items—i.e., down to such items as turning the fuel pump and generator off on the failed engine, and crossfeeding procedures. But it is very important to have the entire procedure on the checklist for two reasons: one, it will help to fix the procedure in your memory, and two, once things are under control it is very important to go over the checklist from the top making sure nothing was overlooked. In the excitement, it is awfully easy to overlook even major items such as raising the flaps, and impossible to remember all the clean-up items. You probably won't remember to close the cowl flaps on the dead engine, for instance, and shouldn't be expected to. If "Cowl Flaps—CLOSED" is on the Engine Failure checklist, you won't have to remember to close the cowl flaps or any of the other non-essential clean-up items. The only thing you have to remember is to use the checklist.

The last part of the checklist should be a reminder of any accessories unique to one engine, and the consequences of losing them. For instance, some airplanes have only one hydraulic pump. If the engine that drives that pump goes, the hydraulics also go. What are the consequences of losing hydraulic power? Will the gear still retract? What other systems use hydraulic power? If you lose an engine, you also lose the generator once the prop is feathered. What are the consequences of reduced generator capacity? Don't count on your memory—in an emergency situation your memory will be reduced to primordial innocence.

Propeller Overspeed

The rotational stress placed on a prop is directly proportional to the speed with which it rotates, and the stress increases exponentially: A small increase in prop speed results in a large increase in the stress. If the prop control fails, the blades will normally fail to flat pitch and the prop speed will increase. If this happens at cruise, the prop rpm will usually zoom past the redline. The prop won't stay together long at rpm over redline (take a good look at what's holding the blades to the hub on your next preflight), so immediate action is necessary. If the prop control is broken, you won't be able to reduce the rpm with that, but you can reduce power—and this should be done immediately and from memory. You may have to bring the power back almost to idle before the rpm drops below redline, but that's less of a problem than having the prop come apart.

Once the rpm is under control you have time to refer to the checklist, which should tell you to check the oil pressure (the lack of which probably is what caused the prop control to fail and the propeller to overspeed). Then the checklist should provide a note to see the checklist for forced landing for single engine airplanes, or possible precautionary shutdown for twins.

Cabin Smoke or Fire

The greatest danger in these situations is usually asphyxiation and smoke blindness. Fires can be put out, but smoke is much more difficult to deal with. If you have oxygen available, your first reaction to smoke of any sort should be to don the mask. Then, if you have smoke goggles (don't laugh—more on this), get those on. Now you can breathe and see.

If you don't have oxygen or smoke goggles, the only thing you can do to clear the smoke is increase the ventilation and hope you can see and breathe well enough to find the checklist and isolate the source so the smoke will clear. If that doesn't work, you should think about an emergency descent: Get the thing on the ground before it gets any worse.

The reason smoke goggles are so important is because your eyes will involuntarily close if exposed to enough smoke, and wild horses won't get them open. Picture yourself sitting there in your aircraft, the smell of smoke everywhere, trying to fly the airplane, and your eyes are closed and won't open. If you can't find smoke goggles through normal aviation supply channels, try safety goggles with the ventilation holes taped over—probably cheaper that way anyway. Every airplane should have a set within reach of the pilot.

The checklist should remind you to use the fire extinguisher if flames are visible (in the excitement, it's easy to forget that you even *have* a fire extinguisher), and to increase the ventilation if there is smoke. The checklist should then ask you to determine whether the fire or smoke is electrical or non-electrical in origin, and divide into two parts, one for each of these situations.

Electrical Smoke or Fire

If the smoke or fire is electrical in origin, attempt to isolate the faulty system. Sometimes the source will be obvious, but if it isn't, the basic method for finding it is to turn the master electrical switches off (battery and generators), and pull all the circuit breakers. Then turn the electrical switches back on—nothing should happen with all the breakers pulled, but if the smoke returns, turn the switches back off. Occasionally there are one or two electrical items protected in some fashion other than with circuit breakers, and one of those items *could* be the source of the fire. Assuming nothing happens when the electrical switches are turned back on, reset the breakers in order of importance until you smell or see smoke again—that's the bad circuit.

The checklist should also remind you to think about terminating the flight early unless you are certain you have isolated the faulty system and can operate safely without it. (This isn't out of the question at all; suppose one of the radios burns up. Once that circuit has been isolated and the smoke has cleared and ATC has been notified, there is no reason why the flight cannot be continued.)

Non-Electrical Smoke or Fire

If the smoke is non-electrical in origin it will most likely be environmental of some sort—heating, air conditioning, or pressurization. The checklist should remind you to try to determine the source and either put it out, turn it off, or isolate it—normally by turning off all fans and air outlets.

Trim Runaway

This applies only to airplanes with electrically powered trim systems. Occasionally the trim will continue to move toward the full nose-up or full nose-down position after the trim switch has been released. This can lead to serious problems, particularly in the nose-up situation. The reason it is considered an emergency and not an abnormality is that, while it is usually possible to stop the runaway, it is not always possible to correct the out-of-trim condition. The trim sometimes stays stuck wherever you have stopped it. Therefore, prompt action is important. It is most dangerous on airplanes that adjust the trim by changing the position of the entire horizontal stabilizer. In this case, overpowering the trim by muscle power won't completely solve the problem, because the position of the stabilizer in the out-of-trim position will limit the range of elevator effectiveness.

If your aircraft has an electric trim system, it is very important that you know what the manufacturer recommends or requires you to do for your aircraft in the event it runs away. The *general* procedure is to maintain control of the aircraft by overriding the trim as much as possible with muscle power, and use opposite trim on the electric trim switch to stop the runaway. Opposite trim will usually either pop the trim circuit breaker, cancel the malfunctioning switch, or neutralize the trim movement, stopping it at that position.

On some systems you will have to hold the opposite trim until you can find the circuit breaker and pull it, or it pops itself. All of this varies from aircraft to aircraft. For your checklist, the first item will be the recommended procedure to stop the runaway (a memory item), followed by the recommended procedures to correct or disengage the faulty system.

Forced Landing

This isn't the worst thing that can happen in an airplane, but you'll never convince the passengers of that. A forced landing means simply that you have lost all power, either because of engine failure, fuel starvation, or engine shutdown. Forced landings are possible emergencies for any airplane, regardless of the number of engines. (They're just much less likely with more than one engine.)

The common sense part—like trying to get to an airport or suitable emergency landing site with enough altitude to make a proper approach and landing—doesn't have to go on the checklist, and of course the checklist won't do you any good if you lose all power right after takeoff. But assuming the failure occurs at altitude, a checklist can be very helpful.

The checklist should list the proper configuration and airspeed for maximum glide, along with the steps to take to configure the aircraft for maximum crash survivability. This would normally include turning the fuel off, mixture to cutoff, mags off, a note about the flaps and gear (normally flaps down for minimum ground contact speed and gear down for long and smooth terrain, up for short or rough), and master electrical switch off. The checklist should also remind you to transmit a Mayday message, squawk 7700, and tighten all seat belts and lock all shoulder harnesses if possible. You also want to brief the passengers on how to open the doors and exits, and what to do if you are incapacitated.

Ditching

Ditching is very similar to a forced landing situation, and many of the same considerations apply. The differences are: Power is available in a ditching situation; you always ditch gear-up; to maximize the flotation time you may not want to open the main door. (But then again, you may not have any choice if that is the only way out, or the only door the raft will fit through.)

The main difference is the first one: power available. If it is certain that you are going to run out of fuel prior to reaching land, it is better to deliberately ditch with power available than to let the tanks run dry and attempt a forced landing on the water. With power still available, you have the advantage of being able to keep the descent rate to a minimum in order to touch down on the water at a very flat angle. This enormously reduces the chance of flipping over or diving into the water. Nonetheless, just prior to impact you still want to shut everything down—generators, battery, and fuel—just as you would for a forced landing. A note at the bottom of the checklist to ditch parallel to the swells and on the crest is a helpful reminder. (Think of the swells as parallel runways.) Unless the precarious fuel situation catches you completely by surprise, you should have plenty of time to prepare the aircraft and passengers for the ditching, using the checklist to ensure completeness.

If power is not available, then this becomes a forced landing situation, only over water. In this case you would want to use both checklists, the forced landing and the ditching checklists. The only real difference between a forced landing over water and over land is that you always keep the wheels up for a water landing and you want to make sure you can get to the raft and have a plan for getting it out the door and into it.

Rapid Depressurization

For a pressurized airplane capable of operating at the higher flight levels, this is one of the major emergencies. I have heard that when the door blows off a fully pressurized airplane, it sounds just like a cannon going off. The cockpit immediately fogs up, and everything loose in the airplane blows out the door—including people. (This is why, in an airplane I can move around in, like a Falcon 20, I never hang around the main door on my way to the coffeepot or the back of the airplane. Doors *do* blow off and people really *have* gone right out the door.)

Without supplemental oxygen, the time of useful consciousness at the higher flight levels is a matter of seconds. There is literally *no* time to pick up a checklist—and it may have gone out the door anyway. So the first item, for any pressurized airplane, is mask on and oxygen selector to 100 percent. (Not all masks have selectors, but if they do they should be left in the 100 percent oxygen position; as soon as the mask goes on this should be checked.) Getting the mask on is the most important thing—you can forget everything else as long as you get the mask on. If you don't get the mask on in time, you will pass out, and that's that until the airplane descends on its own through something like 20,000 feet or so (assuming it does descend on its own and assuming you're still alive).

There are a bunch of things to do in a rapid depressurization situation, and they should all be done quickly, so usually a memory system of some sort is developed for each airplane. In the Citation, for instance, you start by sweeping the cockpit from the left side panel rear to pick up the quick-donning oxygen mask and hit the switch for manual passenger mask drop, then left side panel forward to switch the mike to the oxygen mask, then front panel left side for ignitors, on to front panel center for the seat belt sign and transponder to 7700, then center console for throttles to idle and speed brakes extended. This orderly sweep of the cockpit helps a lot in remembering all the necessary items. Then you call for the checklist to make sure you didn't skip any.

If you are flying a pressurized airplane, I think it is very important that you try to develop a similar kind of memory system for your aircraft also—either a sweep or memory aid using easily remembered letters. The initial items for any pressurized airplane are: masks on and 100 percent oxygen selected if you have that option; communications selected to oxygen mask; passenger oxygen checked on, dropped manually as a standard back-up; no smoking. This much by itself won't solve the problem, but it will keep everyone alive and maintain communications.

Emergency Descents

Emergency oxygen is not intended to be used other than to allow enough time to maintain consciousness while descending to an altitude where oxygen is not required. You have no idea how long the emergency supply will last, nor are you assured, at the higher flight levels, that the oxygen flow from the masks will be adequate. Therefore, if the failure is catastrophic—a door or window blowing out—immediately initiate an emergency descent. If the depressurization is rapid, notify ATC and then initiate the emergency descent. If the depressurization is gradual, notify ATC and request an immediate clearance to 10,000 feet. If he doesn't give it to you right away, ask again and stress the urgency—the depressurization may not stay gradual for long.

Emergency descent procedures also vary from airplane to airplane, but they all involve reducing the power to idle, creating drag (which includes adjusting the props to high rpm), rolling the airplane to the manufacturer's recommended bank angle to reduce the wing loading, and pushing the nose over to achieve a target rate of speed that depends on the recommended configuration. The idea is to get the airplane down at the fastest possible rate. Whatever the manufacturer recommends is what you should use, and you should memorize it.

If you must initiate an emergency descent, the priorities have to be oxygen and aircraft control. But if at all possible, you also want to notify ATC. This should be done both over the radio—"32 Xray, emergency descent, out of Flight Level 330 to the left"—and also by squawking 7700 on the transponder. You are going to go through a whole bunch of altitudes, and ATC needs to know about it.

It helps a lot to have two pilots when you go through this drill. There is an awful lot to remember, and it is all important. I've been through it in the simulator many times. In each case I know that sometime during the training it is coming, and I have studied for it in advance; I still usually miss at least one item. I've also watched other pilots go through the drill, and very few remember every single item with any regularity—there is a lot to do in a very short period of time.

As a single pilot, your job is even harder. You have to know what the priorities are and use the checklist to cover the rest. Even though everything on the checklist is important, and even though everything should be done from memory, realism dictates that as long as you can get the mask on and start the airplane coming down, there will be time to get the checklist and do the other items. But don't get so excited that all you do is dive the airplane. That won't do it. And don't use "being realistic" as an excuse for not trying to do it all from memory. But, in all honesty, the only part that is *absolutely* critical is getting the oxygen mask on. The rest is just critical.

If the depressurization was a result of a structural failure that may have reduced the integrity of the airframe, you may not want or be able to descend at the maximum recommended airspeed. If, for instance, a prop blade or turbine wheel came loose and ripped a hole in the cabin, you may have to baby the airplane down. If you have the mask on and start it down, even slowly, you should be able to get low enough before the oxygen runs out to at least maintain consciousness. The key is to get it started down.

Depressurization is not the only reason for an emergency descent. Fires, uncontrollable vibrations, and progressively worsening structural failures are others. So even if your airplane is unpressurized, you should have an emergency descent checklist modeled on the above, but you can omit donning the oxygen mask—you will either be low enough you won't need it or will already have it on.

If your manual does not describe an emergency descent procedure, try this one: power to idle, prop forward, bank 45 degrees, either gear *down*, target speed of maximum gear extended speed, or gear *up*, top of the yellow airspeed arc in smooth air, top of the green arc in less-than-smooth air. Experiment to see which configuration gives you the maximum rate of descent. (Pick a good day to try this and make sure you clear underneath first.) You don't have to bring the power all the way back to idle for comparison purposes, but if you really want to know the actual maximum rate of descent, the power will have to be reduced to idle. This isn't the best way to treat an engine, but if you have the engine temp stabilized as cool as possible prior to reducing the power, the stress should be minimal.

Failure of All Generators/Alternators

This means failure of *the* generator on most single-engine airplanes, and failure of both generators on most twin-engine airplanes. This is only marginally an emergency; it could almost be considered an abnormal situation, but with everything turned on and all generating power gone, the battery in most airplanes will usually only last a few minutes, so time is important. Probably the only real memory item is to remember to use the checklist.

The checklist should include whatever information you need to verify that the generators are indeed off-line, and the procedure for attempting to reset them. If the resets fail, it should then remind you to reduce the electrical load as much as possible. A list of nonessential items is helpful here: pitot heat (takes a huge amount of juice), secondary navs and coms, all the lights, and the turn-and-bank. (For items not having switches, pull the controlling circuit breaker.) Anything you don't *have* to have—which is normally everything but one nav and one com, the transponder, and any electrically operated primary gyro instruments—should be turned off, at least initially. If the juice lasts until final approach, you can always turn the pitot heat, landing lights, flap and gear controls and so on back on for the landing. If it doesn't last, you will have to lower the gear manually (and remember that the gear indicator lights won't work). This should be noted on the checklist, along with a reminder to notify ATC of the problem and request a vector or descent to VFR conditions.

A note listing all the items which *will* operate without electrical power is a reassuring one at the bottom of this checklist also. Possibilities include: the engine, compass, altimeter, airspeed indicator, vacuum-operated gyros, vertical speed indicator, wind-up clock, and one or two of the engine instruments. The easiest way to find out what works and what doesn't—a very useful lesson—is to fire your airplane up on the ground and then turn the battery and generators off. Whatever is still working is what you have left after the battery runs down.

Spins

The recommended procedure to recover from a spin, for your aircraft, should be on the emergency checklist, not because you will have time to dig it out and use it, but because it will help to fix the procedure in your head and be useful for review purposes.

The classic spin recovery procedure is: opposite rudder, stick neutral, power idle; when the rotation stops, rudder neutral and pull out gently from the dive. Airplanes respond differently to spins, though—it depends a lot on how the airplane was designed, so do whatever the manufacturer recommends. If the manufacturer prohibits spins, believe it. If spins are prohibited, it means either that the airplane was never fully spun in the test program and nobody really knows what it will do in a fully developed spin, or that it is possible, with certain weight-and-balance situations, to enter a spin from which recovery is impossible.

ABNORMAL CHECKLISTS

So much for emergency procedures. Abnormal situations don't require an immediate memorized response, so the more situations you can think of and prepare for ahead of time with a checklist the better. The checklist serves two important functions: One is to help troubleshoot the situation, and the other is to provide the best and most complete response. No matter how well you may know your aircraft systems, there is no reason not to have a checklist to at least back you up, but the smart thing to do when an abnormal situation arises is to go straight to the checklist and let the checklist systematically take you through a troubleshooting analysis, if appropriate, and solution. This is the error-free way to do it.

Here are some typical abnormal situations: generator failure (when more than one generator is available), starting problems, loss of hydraulic pressure, flaps stuck or split, precautionary shutdown, single-engine operations, no nosewheel steering, brake failure, pitot heat inop, fuel pump inop, low fuel pressure, low oil pressure, high oil temperature, high cylinder head temperature, gear problems, overpressurization, heater inop, door not latched, vacuum pump failure, static system clogged, and induction icing.

I'm not going to go into the same detail with each of these that I did with the emergency situations, but I do want to give you an example of a situation that requires troubleshooting prior to being able to take the proper corrective action and show you what that kind of checklist might look like. I also want to point out some general principles to follow when making up abnormal procedures checklists, and I will make some comments about some of these situations. With that you should be able to do a pretty good job of making up your own abnormal procedures checklists.

Generator Failure

Figure 9-2 is a sample abnormal checklist for generator failure—an electrical problem. People always have trouble with electrical systems, myself included, and this is one of the best situations to use a checklist. A generator (or alternator) can fail—or appear to fail—in several different ways. Just because a warning light comes on doesn't mean that all generating power has been permanently lost.

Electrical systems vary enormously; you will have to make up your own based on the manufacturer's recommendations for your particular airplane. But this is an example of the kind of thing you want to create: something that helps you troubleshoot the problem, and then directs you to the proper corrective action depending on the outcome.

I don't believe in troubleshooting for the sake of troubleshooting. Leave that to the mechanics. If you have an idea what the problem is, fine, but the main idea is to *solve* the problem, not identify its cause. If, for instance, you were using the checklist in Fig. 9-2 after a generator warning light had come on, and you discovered that the voltage read zero, and you attempted to reset the generator but the light came back on, don't worry about trying to figure out if it was the generator itself that failed, or the voltage regulator, or the gauge, or something else—just turn the switch off like the checklist says. You've done all you can. Let maintenance figure out what needs fixing. If you spend the rest of the trip trying to figure it out, you'll probably mess something else up.

GENERATOR FAILURE

Generator warning light ON.

1. Check circuit breaker.
2. Check generator switch ON.
3. Check voltmeter.
   a. Zero voltage.

   > Atempt reset—Switch to OFF, then ON.
   > If light stays off, continue to use generator.

   > If light comes back ON, select generator OFF, proceed to Step 4.

   b.Voltage normal.

   > Reset not possible. Select generator OFF. Proceed to Step 4.

   c. Voltage high.

   > If higher than 30 volts, select OFF. Proceed to Step 4.

   > If less than 30 volts, continue to use generator. Monitor voltmeter. Report to maintenance.

4. Generator selected OFF.

   > a. Reduced load on remaining generator to 100 amp.

   > b. Review emergency checklist for double generator failure.

Fig. 9-2. Typical abnormal procedures checklist for generator failure. At item number 3 the checklist branches into three troubleshooting possibilities, with a recommended action for each condition. There are no memory items.

For any system for which a circuit breaker is a part of the system, the first step on the checklist should be to check the circuit breaker. You'd be surprised how many problems can be solved by pushing a circuit breaker back in. If it pops again, wait a minute or so for the breaker to cool and try it one more time. If it pops the third time, hold it in. *No, don't do that;* that's an old joke. The general rule for circuit breakers is: You get two tries per circuit breaker; after that, leave it out and proceed with the rest of the checklist.

If the system incorporates a switch, checking that the switch is ON should be part of the checklist. Switches very often get knocked off, and it's pretty frustrating trying to troubleshoot a system that is turned off. You may say these two checks are obvious, but I can't tell you how many times a checklist has helped me catch a popped circuit breaker or switch knocked off.

Here are some quick points on some of the other abnormalities:

Loss of Hydraulic Pressure

Most general aviation aircraft have pretty simple hydraulic systems, so the loss of hydraulic pressure is not nearly so serious for them as it is for larger transport aircraft (where the flight controls are generally hydraulically boosted). In fact, in most cases the only thing the hydraulic system operates is the gear. In any case, the loss of hydraulic pressure is not in itself a problem—it's the *systems* you lose that are a problem. So the main point of this abnormal checklist is to note which systems are affected, and refer you to those checklists (i.e., "See Landing Gear—Manual Extension checklist").

Flaps Stuck or Split

Flaps stuck (after takeoff) are not a problem for non-Transport Category aircraft, except that your airspeed is limited whenever any flap is extended and cruise performance is reduced due to the additional drag. The checklist should have a listing of what the speed restrictions are for each increment of flaps, and a reminder of the reduction in altitude and range capability, with the suggestion that a return to the departure point or takeoff alternate be considered.

Flaps split—where one side has a greater flap extension than the other—is a serious problem. Assuming the airplane is within lateral balance limits (i.e., you have observed all restrictions on fuel balance from side to side), you should be able to control the airplane even with one side of flaps full down and the other all the way up. But you want your checklist to cover whatever procedures the manufacturer recommends for your particular aircraft to try to get them unsplit—this is no way to try to fly an airplane. In most cases, if the flaps cannot be unsplit, it is better to go back to the last setting so they are at least the same on each side. Then refer to the Flaps Stuck checklist.

Precautionary Shutdown

It helps on this checklist to have a list of possible reasons for shutting an engine down. This will help you make the decision to go ahead and shut one down if that is what is indicated, and slow you down from unnecessarily shutting one down for various false alarms. Good reasons for shutting an engine down are: rapidly rising oil or cylinder head temperatures with the oil pressure dropping; both oil and cylinder head temps rising rapidly; any temp over redline that cannot be reduced and which is confirmed as not a gauge problem; bad or worsening vibration; uncontrollable prop speed. The question isn't one of saving the engine—the engine is probably shot already. Rather, it is one of whether the risk of the situation getting catastrophically worse and causing structural damage to the airplane is greater than the risk of operating without the engine. Then the checklist should have an orderly, set-by-step procedure for shutting the engine down and cleaning it up, with a referral to the Single-Engine Operations checklist.

Single-Engine Operations

A reminder of crossfeeding procedures is a good idea here, as is a note on the single-engine service ceiling at various weights if that information is available, and a reminder of the best single-engine rate of climb speed.

Pitot Heat Inop

If you don't have a warning light installed for Pitot Heat Inop, you probably won't know the pitot heat is inop until the airspeed goes completely haywire. Since erroneous airspeed indications can be very hard to identify, I think a warning light is a great idea, but if your airplane doesn't have one, be very skeptical of airspeed indications that don't seem quite right.

If you aren't sure whether the pitot heat is working or not, turn it off and look for a drop in load, and then turn it back on and look for a rise. If nothing happens, the pitot heat is inop. If it is inop, disregard all airspeed indications in icing conditions.

An old instrument flying adage is: Power plus attitude equals performance; any given attitude and power setting will result in a given airspeed and rate of climb (positive, negative, or zero). If you know, for instance, that a nose-level attitude and 1800 rpm results in an approach speed of 80 knots and a descent rate of 500 fpm, then you don't really need an airspeed indicator, do you? As long as the attitude is set to nose-level and the power is set to 1800 rpm, the airplane will settle at 80 knots and 500 fpm (or very close to it), with or without an airspeed indicator. This is where "knowing your airplane" pays off. (This is also where a note to check the circuit breaker pays off.)

Gear Problems

This is an important checklist, and the more complicated the system, the more important it is. You particularly want to know what all the various possible light combinations mean if your system has both an unlocked or intransit light, and green, gear down-and locked lights. You can get some pretty confusing indications. Does a warning light mean not locked up, in between, or not locked down? What does it mean if you get both a warning light *and* three green lights? On some airplanes, this just means there is a problem with the intransit circuit, but the gear is definitely down and locked. On others, *anything* other than just "three green" implies a locking problem. What precautions does the manufacturer recommend you take whenever there is any abnormal gear indication? What is the step-by-step manual extension procedure? Finally, what is the recommended procedure for a gear-up landing?

Heater Inop

An airplane cools off fast at 20 and 30 below, and it doesn't take long to get so cold you literally can't fly the airplane. If there is any way to get a failed heater started again, you want to know what it is, and you want it on the checklist so you don't have to waste time looking it up in the book.

Vacuum Pump Failure

What instruments and systems are vacuum-operated? Make up a list, with backup instruments, so when it happens you don't have to experiment or guess.

Static System Clogged

A clogged static system results in erroneous airspeed, altimeter, and vertical rate indications. The checklist should remind you of the alternate or emergency static source location. It should also either list or direct you to the airspeed compensation chart for the alternate source, or advise you of the amount of error that can be expected.

PROFESSIONALISM

It's a lot of work to make up an emergency and abnormal checklist for each of these situations, but it is extremely worthwhile, and I can't think of a better way to truly master the systems in your airplane. A checklist-oriented solution to problem solving is the professional way of dealing with emergency and abnormal situations, and, in my opinion, it is one of the main reasons that flying on a professionally flown aircraft is so much safer, statistically, than on a nonprofessionally flown aircraft. ("General aviation"—which includes corporate aviation but which is predominately private aviation—had an accident rate *60 times greater* than the airlines in 1984, according to preliminary figures from the National Transportation Safety Board: 0.164 accidents per 100,000 hours for the airlines, verses 9.8 per 100,000 hours for general aviation.)

The airlines certainly aren't safer just because their pilots are getting paid—the airplane couldn't care less whether the guy manipulating the controls gets a paycheck or not. Professionals aren't supermen or geniuses either, but they *do* have checklists to help them out when things go wrong, and they *have* been trained to use them. There's no reason why you can't do the same thing.

If nothing else, I hope this chapter has caused you to review and rethink your attitude toward emergency and abnormal situations. The professional doesn't just *hope* nothing ever goes wrong, and he doesn't just *assume* that if it does his experience and general knowledge of the systems will be enough in itself to solve the problem. Most professionals are smart enough to know they're not that smart.

One of the more obvious but frequently overlooked differences between a professional pilot and an amateur pilot is that the professional flies a lot more. He flies enough that, over the years, a lot of these emergency and abnormal situations actually occur. He only has to scare himself once or twice by responding in an erratic and non-systematic way to learn that things *will* go wrong and that ingenuity and his superior nerves alone won't always save the day.

The ground school instructor I had when I was studying for my ATP written told us a story about two different times he, as an Air Force navigator, witnessed crews conducting actual precautionary engine shutdowns. The first time, as soon as a warning light came on, everybody in the cockpit started trying to solve the problem at the same time—only everyone had a different idea of how to do it. Somehow they managed to shut the wrong engine down, had to get it going again, and finally got the desired one shut down before anyone thought to use the checklist—and then discovered that they had done it wrong and had to retrace their steps and do half of it over again.

The second time, with another crew, the engineer announced the warning light, and the Aircraft Commander called for the "Engine Shutdown" checklist. The copilot picked up the checklist and made the callouts, while everybody in the cockpit (including the navigator, as per procedure) verified that the Aircraft Commander had his hand on the proper control for the proper engine prior to moving it. Within a matter of seconds the engine was shut down, the clean-up and crossfeed items attended to, and everybody went back to drinking coffee and looking out the windows.

That's the way it's supposed to be done, but to do it takes two things: a checklist and self-control. A good place to start is with the checklist.

Chapter 10

Proficiency

Pilots talk a lot about "proficiency." The word gets used in a variety of ways, but usually "proficiency" means "maintaining basic flight proficiency." That's jumping ahead a little, though, because before proficiency can be *maintained*, it has to be *acquired*. Proficiency thus has two parts, the first being the acquisition of the knowledge and skills essential to safe flight, the other being the maintenance of that knowledge and those skills through training and practice.

The first chapter, The Basics, tried to cover the areas that a serious pilot should be familiar with, and described the standards he (or she) must achieve to function smoothly and properly in the aviation transportation system. That chapter, was mostly about the *acquistion* of proficiency. This chapter, Proficiency, is mostly about *maintaining* that proficiency.

That first chapter was somewhat simplified. It was necessary, at that point, to simply list and describe basic flying skills and their allowable tolerances; there was no practical reason to go into any more detail until those skills and standards were established. If Chapter 1 described the basic skills, then this chapter describes the manner and method of achieving and maintaining those skills—and that is what we call, in flying shorthand, "proficiency."

THE PROCESS

While it was necessary at some point to list the skills and standards necessary to achieve minimum levels of proficiency, that doesn't mean that "proficiency" is simply a matter of achieving a certain minimum level of skill and then maintaining that level. Proficiency is more complicated than that.

If you think back to some experience in your life that was particularly meaningful and satisfying, but very demanding—some activity you became very skilled at and were very proud of, such as an experience on a winning team, or some special challenge or training in the military, or some aspect of your work that you became especially skilled at—I think you will see what I mean by "proficiency" not being a simple matter.

If you reflect back on this accomplishment, you will probably remember that you were very proud of yourself, and when all was said and done you were very glad you had undertaken this project, but that there had been moments of serious doubt and discouragement along the way. In addition, at some point after you had achieved your goal you probably realized that you had, in fact, achieved a higher level of skill than the minimum needed to just get the job done, but you probably also remember that as soon as this particular experience was over—the team broke up, or you left the military, or your job changed—your newly acquired skills deteriorated almost instantly from the peak that you had achieved. In fact, as time went by, it probably seemed that *all* the skill and knowledge—skill and knowledge which had taken so much effort to acquire—disappeared and there wasn't much you could do to hang on to it.

Even now, though, you are probably quite certain that you could go back to that activity, and, with a little review, be just as good at it as you ever were—and maybe even be just a little better. Specific facts and essential details tend to be forgotten very quickly once we quit reinforcing them with daily use. But the important parts of an accomplishment—the physical skills, the general principles, the lessons of experience—stay with us forever, and the specific facts and essential details come back quickly.

Flying well is one of these demanding but satisfying experiences. If you have been flying for a while now, you know that achieving true proficiency is an awful lot of work and is frequently very discouraging, but, having achieved it, you know that there is a lot to be proud of and you would gladly do it again. You know that having achieved real proficiency in aviation, your level of accomplishment is actually greater than needed to just get the job done, but you also know that it is your extra level of accomplishment that gets you through the tight situations. You know that peak levels of skill can only be achieved with great effort, and only maintained at a peak for very short periods of time—that you have to fly almost all the time to maintain a peak, and even then the non-routine aspects fade from inevitable neglect—but you also know that having achieved a peak of proficiency, you can tolerate a little bit of slippage. You know that if you were to quit flying, it wouldn't be too long before you had forgotten all the essential facts and figures, but you also feel that with a little effort they could be reacquired very quickly.

This *process* we go through whenever we achieve a high level of skill and competence in some area, which I have tried to break down into its component parts, is really what I think "proficiency" is all about. I want to use this process as the structure for talking about the specifics of proficiency—what, as a pilot, do you *do* about proficiency?

ACQUISITION

As it is with any difficult but worthwhile activity, basic proficiency doesn't come easily, nor in the case of aviation, does it come cheaply. There is a lot of work involved before anyone can achieve minimum levels of competence. It takes time and study and practice before you can consistently keep the altitudes within 100 feet and the headings within a couple of degrees and the speeds within a few knots and before you really know an airplane's systems and don't have to fumble for switches or worry about forgetting little things or having to look everything up. There are no shortcuts to acquiring proficiency. It is slow, it is discouraging at times, and it is expensive. But proficiency, in anything, has to be built on a foundation of fundamental competence. Before you an sit down with the orchestra, you have to achieve basic mastery of the instrument.

MARGIN OF SAFETY

When you have truly mastered the fundamentals, your level of skill will in fact be much better than it "needs" to be. When you are really comfortable with your airplane and with the instrument system, and you look back on what you have accomplished, you will find that you have in fact achieved much more than the minimum. Minimum levels of competence seem unreasonably high when you are just starting out—which is good, because it forces you to work hard to achieve them. And in working hard to just reach the minimum, you inevitably do more than you need to.

It is very important that this "extra" level of skill beyond the minimum be achieved, because that is where the safety factor comes from. If you have only just mastered the basics to minimum standards, there is no way to allow for extraordinary or demanding circumstances. This is just common sense again. You have to achieve at least minimum standards, but to be sure of never dropping below those minimums you have to be better than just minimum—there has to be a "cushion" to fall back on.

In practical terms, I don't think this extra margin is anything you have to consciously worry about. You don't, for instance, have to raise your personal minimum standards to be sure of staying within the legal minimums. The legal minimums are demanding enough in themselves; if you can meet those standards (plus or minus 100 feet and 5 degrees and so on), you will already have the necessary skills to do *better* than that—the highest hurdle will already have been jumped. You will know that you have gone beyond the minimum when you don't have to struggle or even think about holding altitude and heading and speed. One day you will be flying along and you will realize that, without working at it, everything is within limits and there is no reason why it can't always be that way. At this point, you have *acquired* proficiency.

CHECKRIDES

Now we get into the critical area: *maintaining* proficiency. One of the deficiencies of Part 91, I think, is the lack of a requirement for regular recurrency training and checkrides. Any pilot-in-command operating under Parts 135 or 121 (the regs that cover air taxi operators, the commuter airlines, and the major airlines) has to have a checkride every six months. In addition, any pilot-in-command of a Part 25 (Transport Category) aircraft has to take a checkride every 12 months, regardless of what part he operates under. (I think this is at least a partial admission, on the FAA's part, that there is a need for a requirement for regular checkrides under Part 91 also.) The checkrides basically cover the normal, abnormal, and emergency operation of the systems, the usual airwork, single-engine procedures, and a series of approaches.

Proficiency checkrides normally aren't quite as tough as an initial checkride for a type rating, but they *can* be, and at any rate they don't miss by much. I don't know many professional pilots who really get a kick out of taking checkrides, but I also don't know any who aren't in favor of them—at least in principle.

I know of very, very few instances where pilots have "busted" a check. It does happen and it *can* happen to any pilot at any time if he has a real bad day or the examiner is determined, for some perverse reason, to "bust" him, but it is rare. The point of a checkride is not to weed out bad pilots. That may be the official reasoning, but that's not the *real* reason. The real reason for checkrides is to force a pilot to regularly bring his level of competence up to a peak. No matter how many checkrides you take or how experienced you are, the pressure is always "on" when you have a checkride due. That pressure is what forces a pilot to open his (or her) books, review his abnormal and emergency procedures, pay attention during the training sessions, and generally do whatever he can to bring his abilities up to a peak so he doesn't embarrass himself on the checkride.

RECURRENCY TRAINING

It's a tough system, but it works. Every time I go to recurrency training, I ask myself why I'm doing it. But I always get through it, and I am always a much better pilot coming out than going in. I also know that no matter how lazy I am between checkrides (I always mean to get my manuals out a lot more often than I do), and no matter how undemanding or routine the flying is between checks, my overall flying won't deteriorate *too* badly, because on the average I am going to be "back in the wringer" every four months, and in any case no longer than every 12 months. The result, for most professional pilots flying Transport Category airplanes, is that while their proficiency varies from checkride to checkride, it starts at an elevated level because of the fairly intense initial training and testing for the type rating, and it never drops very far below that level because of the frequent checks after that. This is true "maintenance of proficiency." I don't like taking checkrides, but I do think they are necessary evils for safe flying.

Part 91 doesn't have a requirement for either regular recurrency training or for checkrides (except for pilots of Transport Category airplanes). The requirement for a Biennial Flight Review is a step in the right direction, but the interval is too long and it isn't a checkride—it's a "review" (as opposed to a "test"), which means there isn't the same incentive to prepare for it as there is for a checkride. The Part 91 pilot enjoys freedom from checkrides, but as a result, the total responsibility for maintaining his proficiency falls on him.

MAINTAINING PROFICIENCY

Assuming you have achieved basic mastery of the airplane, including its systems and procedures, and can operate comfortably within the limits of the instrument system, the question becomes: "How do you maintain that basic proficiency, and how do you stay current in your emergency and abnormal procedures?"

I've already said that I think the best answer to that question is regular recurrency training with checkrides to keep you honest. Unfortunately, formal recurrency training for pilots of personal aircraft is limited at this point, but it does exist, for some types, and the major training organizations are working with the aircraft manufacturers to add aircraft to the list of aircraft ground school/simulator programs all the time. (I don't want to mention names, because there are several good training organizations, but the one that is probably the best known is the one with the slogan, "The best safety device in any aircraft is a well-trained pilot.") If your airplane is one for which formal ground school and simulator training is available, you are very fortunate. Going to school is the easiest and best way possible to maintain your proficiency. Sign up right now to go twice a year. Write it off as just another one of the fixed costs of aircraft ownership.

SIMULATOR TRAINING

The reason simulator training is the best way to maintain your proficiency is because simulator training is much more complete—and, in an ironic way, simulator training is also much more *realistic* than flight training. Simulator training is more complete because every conceivable situation can be simulated, practiced, and analyzed, and it is more realistic because there are many abnormal and emergency situations that cannot be realistically simulated in an aircraft, either for reasons of safety, or for practical reasons: engine fires, gear failures, hydraulic failures, trim runaways, total electrical failures, dead stick landings, brake failures, prop overspeed, fuel leaks, and so on, and so on. The reason the military, the airlines, and the top corporate flight departments believe in using simulators for initial and recurrent training is not because simulators are cheaper than airplanes for training. (In some cases they are, but that's simply a side benefit.) The reason they use simulators is because simulators are *better* than airplanes for training.

If your airplane is not one for which regular recurrency training is available, be patient—it may be soon. In the meantime, you need to do what you can, assuming you have succeeded in acquiring at least basic proficiency, to maintain that proficiency.

FREQUENCY

Probably the first and most important single thing a pilot can do to maintain his proficiency is to fly a lot. There simply is no substitute for regular flying. When I haven't flown for even a week, I can tell when I do get back that I am not quite as proficient as I was before. The switches and knobs don't fall to hand as they should, the checklist doesn't go as smoothly, my eyeballs have trouble finding things, key numbers don't leap into my head, and so on. It comes back fairly quickly, but even after just a week away I can tell. It's hard to say what "regular" flying is, and too much flying can sometimes be a problem too, but I would guess that something like three to four times a week is optimum.

Certainly I think you need to fly several times a month to even hope to maintain your basic proficiency. I don't know how many "several" is, but it's more than two or three. This may mean having to take the airplane out of the hangar and fly it even though you don't have anywhere to go, but there *are* things you can do to get more out of the flying you have to do anyway.

A "flight" is a cycle: startup, taxi, takeoff, climb, cruise, descent, approach, landing, taxi, shutdown. You have to go through this cycle for every flight, regardless of the length. As far as proficiency goes, the number of *cycles* is much more important than the number of *hours*. So, to help maintain proficiency, break up your flights. From the viewpoint of maintaining proficiency, two 250-mile legs are better than one 500-mile leg. The time spent sitting at altitude with the autopilot on really doesn't do much for your proficiency, but an extra takeoff, descent, and landing does. Two legs may be less efficient than one, but that's a small price to pay to keep up your proficiency.

If you own your own airplane, you have an advantage over the renter pilot in that the only significant operational expense, over and above what you have to pay for anyway, is fuel. If your aircraft is maintained on a system based on hours-in-service (and I think it *should* be), as opposed to a simple annual inspection, there is an additional expense for maintenance each time you fly, but the hourly cost is relatively small. The biggest hourly expense is fuel. Most of the other big bills have to be paid whether you fly or not:

insurance, annual inspection, hangar fees, and interest expense. Depreciation is also a big expense, but depreciation is generally a direct reflection of the age of the airplane and doesn't increase much with time on the airframe; in fact, less than 300 hours per year may be a liability. Each hour you fly also puts your engines that much closer to overhaul time, but most engines are overhauled due to lack of activity, which results in corrosion and premature wear, not because they have run out of time. In this case, more frequent flying may even *save* you a little money.

The point is, that most of the bills have to be paid whether you fly or not. For all practical purposes, if you own your own airplane, you can fly for very close to the price of the fuel—you're going to have to pay most of the other bills in any case. So fly it. If your airplane holds four, but you have six who want to go, make two trips. If your partner lives 25 miles away and needs to go with you on a trip, don't make him drive to your airport; fly over to his and pick him up. It may not make perfect sense economically and it may not even save any time, but you have the airplane, a good part of the cost of ownership is paid for, and the more you fly it, the better. Any excuse to fly is more economical than going up just to practice. If you find you can't afford to be this proficient, that's another question—you may have too much airplane. But you certainly can't afford not to be proficient.

The pilot who rents has to look at that big hourly fee everytime he thinks about flying some where. Very often that's all it takes to kill the idea, and he finds himself flying less and less, and pretty soon his proficiency is gone. This really is the wrong way to look at it. It does cost a lot to rent, but in most cases renting still doesn't cost as much as the total cost of owning an airplane. The break-even point for owning over renting usually doesn't come until after 300 to 400 hours of operation a year. So the plus side for the renter pilot is to take all the money he saves not owning an airplane and use it for rentals. The pilot who rents needs to fly just as much and just as often as the owner pilot does. The airplane doesn't know or care whether you have an equity interest in it or not—it simply insists on being flown by a proficient pilot.

Flying as much as you can is the single best thing you can do to maintain your proficiency. But you know and I know that no matter how much you fly it won't be enough. Flying for the non-professional always has to be squeezed in between job and family, and it's usually a tight fit. It's like going to the doctor for a physical—you never get enough exercise to satisfy him. But the doctor also knows that if he doesn't nag you a little bit, you'll exercise even less. So I'm nagging you a little bit: *Fly.* Fly every chance you get. Look for reasons to fly. If you have to, fly even when there isn't any reason. To get the most out of your flying, plan each flight carefully, even the short ones. You get much more out of one flight done properly than five done poorly or out of habit. Make each flight count, and *fly as much as you can.*

SYSTEMS

Flying all the time is the key to maintaining proficiency in the basic skills, but there is another part to proficiency and that is proficiency with the aircraft systems. We have already gone into the specifics of a variety of abnormal and emergency situations, and came to the conclusion that a checklist is the best tool for dealing with these problems. But having a checklist and being able to use it are two different things. Proficiency means being able to read the checklist and do what it says while flying the airplane in its emergency or abnormal condition. Proficiency also means having a thorough understanding of the systems so you can deal with the situations that don't fit the checklist. Regular flying, unfortunately, doesn't do a thing for these situations, because abnormal and emergency situations are not a part of regular flying.

One of the things you can do to maintain your proficiency in abnormal and emergency procedures is get your Operating Handbook and Flight Manual out and read them—or at least parts of them, with some regularity. Every time I get my manuals out I find things I had either forgotten about, never knew, or remembered incorrectly. (Remembering incorrectly is probably *more dangerous* than not knowing at all.)

I think one of the things we learn as we get older is that self-discipline is the hardest form of discipline; people actually do us favors when they *require* things of us, and don't do us favors when they allow us to discipline ourselves. The FAA requires me to study my manuals at least every 12 months for each aircraft I am typed-rated and current in—which is really doing me a favor. I might not always "get around to it" if they didn't. The FAA would probably actually be doing *you* a favor if it were to require *all* Part 91 pilots to study their manuals on a 12-month basis, instead of just pilots flying Part 25 aircraft. But it doesn't, so you're going to have to discipline yourself. If the pages of your manuals are starting to stick together, you aren't reading them enough.

PROCEDURES TRAINING

So now you're flying all the time and really doing a good job of maintaining your basic flying proficiency, and you read your manuals regularly and know your systems and abnormal and emergency procedures pretty well. What else can you do? One thing is to sit in the airplane with the abnormal and emergency checklists and go over each of the procedures. Pick an emergency or abnormal area at random, drill yourself on the memory items, and then go to the checklist, making sure you understand it and can find everything listed quickly and accurately. It's a good idea to actually move the controls, turn the knobs, throw the switches, and so on. This sometimes reveals things you *thought* you knew but don't—it is awfully easy to just *assume* you know where everything is, when in fact you don't, or do but can't figure out how to get the door open or the knob to turn, or whatever. In addition, actually doing it helps fix the procedure in your memory.

If your FBO has a power cart that supplies the correct voltage to your airplane, and your airplane has an external power receptacle, you can hook up the cart and power all your systems (except the engines, of course) without draining the battery. This allows you to turn your airplane into a specialized sort of simulator known as a "procedures trainer."

The simplest form of a procedures trainer is a full-size picture of the cockpit layout. As you go through the procedures, you point and touch the appropriate switch. These are very often used in formal ground schools for initial training.

The next step up in sophistication is a model cockpit, with real switches and levers to move, but no power—nothing actually happens. The next step is to power the instruments so that the lights and indicators go on and off as various switches are thrown, and the last step is to hook the procedures trainer up to a computer so that the gauges and indicators respond to the movement of the switches and levers.

In hooking your airplane up to a power source you have a third-level procedures trainer—which isn't bad at all. You can go through all the procedures and, as you throw the switches and levers in response to the checklist, in many cases something will *happen*—lights will go out or come on, electrical loads will rise and fall, warning flags will appear, and so on. (Don't move the gear switch—I know that probably goes without saying, but I don't want some clown to say I didn't actually tell him not to try to raise the gear on the ground.) It may sound dumb to think about sitting in the airplane by yourself "playing pilot," but if it is, the word hasn't gotten to *professional* aviation yet—you can go to any airline or corporate training center and see pilots sitting in little paste-up airplanes talking to themselves and pointing to pictures of switches.

FLIGHT TRAINING

All of this is great, but there's still one part missing, and that's getting into the airplane (assuming, again, that you don't have access to a simulator) and actually going through the procedures. I think every pilot who doesn't have access to simulator training, regardless of the type of airplane he flies, should go up twice a year with an instructor who has a lot of experience with his particular airplane—even if his particular airplane is a Champ.

Single-Engine

Obviously, in the case of a Champ, you wouldn't spend too much time on emergency procedures because there aren't very many in a Champ. (There are some, though—a Champ can have an engine fire too). But you can do some airwork—a good exercise is maneuvering from minimum controllable airspeeds through partial stalls to full, accelerated stalls—and you can work on the maneuvers requiring precision, such as short and soft field takeoffs and landings. A good instructor will also throw in a couple of unexpected engine failures and will know of a runway somewhere in the local area that is marked to simulate a short field. It is nice to know how short a field you can get one into if you have to. All of this, to one degree or another, applies to all single-engine operations. For instrument-rated pilots, the training should also include a review of instrument approach procedures and at least one hold.

Multiengine

For multiengine pilots, the emphasis will be on instrument work, single-engine operations, and aircraft systems (since the aircraft systems are invariably fairly complex in multiengine aircraft). This doesn't have to take all day—many elements can be combined. For instance, on one approach the instructor can simulate a gear problem—the gear never acts up on good days—and on another approach, fail an engine.

I know this kind of a drill is a lot of work and mostly not too much fun, but the fact is that you asked for it when you decided you wanted to fly a multiengine airplane. You get a lot of performance and utility out of a sophisticated twin, but the price you pay for that utility is the requirement to be able to fly it safely. Your capabilities have to match the airplanes. The more sophisticated the airplane, the more flying you have to do, the more work it is, and the more self-discipline it takes to stay with it. For the part-time pilot without access to simulator training, maintaining proficiency in a sophisticated multiengine airplane can be a real challenge.

In general, therefore, to maintain proficiency you have to fly a lot, you have to study your manuals regularly, you have to sit in the airplane once in a while and practice your emergency and abnormal procedures, and you have to fly with somebody who is really on top of the airplane and who can give you a good workout in it every six months. (If you fly less than four or five legs per month then you probably ought to reduce this interval to four months.) If you do all of these things, I think you can be confident that you are doing all you reasonably can to maintain your proficiency. You will also be doing more than 99 percent of all other non-professional pilots are doing, and you deserve to take real pride in your ability to maintain proficiency in a demanding skill above and beyond your primary profession or occupation.

LOSS OF PROFICIENCY

The *loss* of basic proficiency is a distressing but sometimes unavoidable occurrence. Partner problems, special assignments, transfers, kids, other interests—lots of things can lead to long periods of flying inactivity. It doesn't take very long to become very rusty. The first thing to go is the ability to recall important numbers, followed by precision with instrument procedures. Then proficiency with and knowledge of the aircraft systems starts to fade away into a vague blur, and after a year or so it's hard to remember *which* system operated the gear or the flaps, much less *how*. The mind seems to be programed to "dump" information we aren't using in order to save memory capacity for new areas—even when we don't want it to.

The good news is that it comes back very quickly, especially the physical aspects, so don't worry about it very much. When I was working as a flight instructor, someone would occasionally come in who hadn't flown for 25 or 30 years. It was amazing how fast the basic ability to fly the airplane came back to these pilots. The knowledge part was pretty much long gone, but the physical manipulation of the airplane came back very quickly, and the rest didn't take nearly as long to "retrieve" as you might think. Our long term memory may dump a lot of stuff when we quit using it, but it seems to leave an imprint of some sort so that it can be filled in again very quickly.

If you have to quit flying temporarily, my advice to you is to accept the fact that your proficiency will deteriorate very rapidly, and that there isn't much of anything you can do about it. You can attempt to stay proficient by reviewing your manuals, and reading the flying magazines and books, and hanging around the airport, but all you're doing is delaying the inevitable at best—and you may be deluding yourself into thinking you are still as proficient as you ever were. I think you're better off just putting it out of your head and not worrying about it. Don't plague yourself with guilt or resolutions you can't keep. If you want to be able to fly again someday, use your energy and time to do whatever you have to do to be able to fly again rather than struggling to try to maintain an *illusion* of proficiency.

The knowledge that the loss of proficiency is not irreversible or permanent should give you the peace of mind to pursue your other priorities until flying can reenter the picture. This is true whether your break from flying is six months or six years. The bulk of the loss occurs very quickly—within a year—and any additional time after that results in very small increments of additional loss. In fact, the biggest problem after a year away is not "rustiness" (the further deterioration of proficiency), but obsolesence—things change and you have that much more catching up to do when you come back.

REGAINING PROFICIENCY

The process of regaining proficiency is exactly the same process as acquiring proficiency in the first place, only greatly accelerated. The parts that you have not forgotten you will recognize immediately and be able to skim over. The parts that need work won't need nearly as much work to bring back as they did to acquire in the first place.

I decided recently to try my hand at gliders again, after 10 years away. I told the instructor that I had had some previous instruction and experience with gliders, but that I didn't really know how much I remembered, so I wanted him to assume I was a new student and take it from there. In fact, I was surprised how much I did remember, but I was also surprised at some of the things I had forgotten—such as how to use my feet for coordination. (Jets have short wings that don't generate much adverse yaw, and the yaw dampener takes care of what little rudder is needed anyway, so my feet had gotten very lazy.) Starting from scratch was the right thing to do. It put everything in the right order—the instruction had continuity—and we didn't skip anything. And it came back very quickly.

If you decide to get back into flying after some time away, you should start with the regulations, then basic VFR airwork, then concentrate on the airplane and its systems, go on to IFR procedures, and finally emergency and abnormal procedures. If you've been away less than a year this process won't amount to much more than what you would do every six months anyway. If you've been away longer than that, it may take several sessions, but the important point is that you don't have to learn to fly all over again. It does take a little work, but a lot less work than it takes to worry or fuss over it for a year or two trying to stay "sort of" proficient. At any rate you are being honest with yourself this way: When you quit flying, you know you lose your proficiency; when you start again, you know you need a little help to get it back. There can't be anything halfway about proficiency. A little bit of proficiency can be a dangerous thing.

EXCUSES, EGOS, AND REWARDS

Proficiency will always be a problem for part-time pilots. Generally, all of their instruction and flying has to come out of their own pockets, and they usually aren't able to fly as much as they really should to maintain their *basic* flying skills—much less to maintain proficiency with emergency and abnormal procedures. But the biggest problem is getting part-time pilots to understand that neither the system nor the airplane will make allowances for them—there is no handicap system in aviation. The system is not very tolerant—it demands instrument proficiency; and airplanes are not very forgiving—they demand competence. Neither gives any points for extenuating or mitigating circumstances. Serious flying is like playing hardball with the big kids: If you want to play you can, but you play their game or you don't play at all, and if you get hurt you can't complain to them; they didn't ask you to play in the first place.

There isn't any way to sugar-coat the importance of proficiency. The lack of basic proficiency among pilots of personal aircraft is a serious problem, and general aviation has the accident record to prove it. There is no reason why a part-time pilot cannot also be a proficient pilot, as long he realizes that proficiency doesn't happen automatically and he is willing to work at acquiring and maintaining it.

Flying is not a "normal" thing for human beings to do. In fact, it is potentially a very dangerous thing to do. What makes it safe is pilot proficiency, and proficiency is not something you are born with, although your ego will try to tell you otherwise.

Airplanes are supposedly dumb, mechanical beasts, but they have an uncanny way of finding and punishing pilots who let their egos control their actions. But airplanes also have a way of rewarding pilots who respect both their capabilities and their dangers. That reward comes in the form of reliable transportation and enormous self-satisfaction—and self-satisfaction is the best ego-trip of all.

Chapter 11

Judgement

I didn't sleep much the night before I took the test for my Private Pilot's License. I was nervous to begin with, and the nearest examiner was 60 miles away, which meant that before I could even take the test I had to fly cross-country to an unfamiliar airport, so I had a lot to think about that night.

I wasn't up to confessing my anxiety to my flight instructor, but since failure seemed to be the most likely outcome, I thought a little bit of prep work was in order. So when I got to the airport, I said something stupid like, "I sure hope he isn't big on turns-about-a-point or any of that kind of stuff."

I was looking for reassurance, of course. I should have kept my mouth shut. If my instructor had said, "I wouldn't count on it. He's a real S.O.B. about turns-about-a-point. You might as well just throw up right now and get it over with," it would have been bad enough. But what he said was *worse*.

He said, "Don't worry about the airwork. He assumes you can do the maneuvers. What he wants to test is your judgement."

"My judgement?" I said. "I think I left that at home."

What's "judgement?" I've got two plotters, three computers and four pencils, and he wants judgement. I had never even heard the word used before in an aviation context. All the time I had spent to get to this point, the Great Private Pilot Checkride, and I had never once heard the word "judgement" used—and it turns out *that's* what he wants to test. This is going to be funny, I thought. I can't wait.

Somehow I got my little airplane over to the appropriate airport, and the flight test itself turned out to be very typical and predictable. We did the usual assortment of airwork, cross-country procedures, and takeoffs and landings; I did some of it well, some of it not so well, some in between, and the examiner—whose name was Santa Claus, if I remember correctly—signed me off.

But that word bugged me for years: *judgement*. It had the aura of something vague and mystical, maybe even something only rare individuals were born with—something the rest of us mortals could only envy, like "charisma" or "brilliance." I knew it had something to do with maturity, and that was good, because I could only get more mature—but would that be enough? Somehow I knew it wouldn't be. Somehow I knew that "judgement" was more than just maturity.

INSIGHT

Finally one day, years later, sitting in my car waiting to pull out into traffic, it hit me what "judgement" was. "Judgement" was knowing whether to shoot out in front of the next car or wait for a bigger opening. *It was as simple as that.* After years of driving, it was something I did unconsciously—something we all do unconsciously. Every time we pull out into traffic we unconsciously make a decision, a decision based on our experience, our skill, our training, and our discretion. We call the sum of that decision making process our "judgement." Terrific. I'm ready to take the test now, sir.

This was really a big breakthrough for me, because it took a lot of the vagueness out of judgement. It meant that judgement wasn't something like "wisdom," which maybe, if you were smart enough, and you lived long enough, you might obtain but couldn't do much about. Judgement was something that—to a certain extent, at least—could be learned and acquired. In fact, the more training you took and the more experience you got, the better your judgement would get.

JUDGEMENT AS LEARNING

A brand-new student driver has very little idea when to pull out into the traffic. He or she hasn't learned yet to estimate distances and speeds—closing rates—nor does he have a good "feel" ıor how the car responds: "If I step on the gas, can I count on the car to go right now, or is there a hesitation or sluggishness to contend with?" The student driver has neither good nor bad judgement—he has *no* judgement. He is dependent upon the instructor telling him when it is okay to go. After some instruction and some practice, he starts to get a better idea for himself—he starts to acquire some judgement. When he goes to take his driving test, this is one of the things the examiner looks for: Does he have a good sense of when it's safe to pull out and when it isn't? It is a skill in the sense that it is something that can be learned and something that gets better with practice and experience, but it is called "judgement" because it isn't just a physical skill, it also is a mental process. A decision has to be made.

FLYING AS JUDGEMENT

Flying has many analogous situations. In fact, flying is not so much a series of physical manipulations as it is a series of judgements. The physical part is usually the easy part, but that's the part in pilot training that gets all the attention. How hard is it—physically—to go around, for instance? Not hard at all. All you have to do is push the power lever all the way up and change the pitch attitude, then raise the gear and flaps. But making the *decision* to go around—exercising that judgement—there's the hard part.

Exercising good judgement is really what being a good pilot is all about. But that's not what most people think. Most people think that the physical manipulation of the controls is what being a good pilot is all about. That's why the passengers always pay so much attention to the landing. They think the landing is the most difficult and critical part of the flight, and if the pilot does that well, he must also do everything else well. It just isn't so. The most difficult part of the flight is not the landing; the most difficult part is making the proper judgements so that you arrive at a point where a safe landing can be made.

Certainly there are physical demands made upon pilots: gusty, crosswind landings, circling approaches to minimums, single-engine takeoffs, difficult situations visually, such as flying at dusk, or night approaches over water—they all require considerable physical skill. But by and large, once you have mastered the basics and have enough experience to be comfortable with the airplane, the physical act of flying the airplane is the easy part.

Professional pilots call the guys who are physically skilled at manipulating the airplane "good stick-floppers." As you can probably tell from the choice of words, it is not an unequivocable form of praise. This isn't because pilots don't respect guys who are naturally skilled at flying the airplane; it is because the description "good stick-flopper" is usually used to "damn with faint praise." It frequently means something else more important is missing—like experience, maturity, or judgement. If a pilot is truly a good pilot in all respects, another pilot will simply say, "He's a good pilot." Normally, "He's a good stick-flopper" translates into "He handles the airplane well, but his decision-making ability leaves something to be desired." It's the aeronautical equivalent of describing your date as having a "good personality."

I toss that out about the "stick-floppers" to illustrate the importance professional pilots place on judgement verses physical skill with the airplane. Because an airplane is an unwieldy and unforgiving sort of beast—much more so than a car, for instance—the physical aspects get a lot of attention, and rightly so, at least in training. It isn't easy to learn to fly and there are always things you can learn to do better, and areas that get rusty if you don't stay in practice. But in terms of the priorities for safe flying, judgement—the part you do with your head—ties up about the first 90 percent, and flying the airplane—the part you do with your hands and feet—gets the remaining 10 percent.

GRAY AREAS

The part about judgement that is so hard to get a grip on—and this is what threw me for a loop about it for so long—is that decision-making in aviation is not a black-and-white thing. It seldom is in any endeavor, of course, but some things are much more black-and-white than others. Deciding whether to buy or rent an airplane, for instance, is a fairly straightforward process of projecting usage and playing with some numbers. The final decision (assuming emotional considerations can be left aside) doesn't involve much judgement. But because judgement in aviation is seldom black-and-white, it can't be reduced to a mechanical process, or handed over to a computer, or simplified into "rules of thumb." Only a human being can exercise judgement.

Judgement is a very complicated thing. Judgement can be learned and experience helps a lot, but ultimately a human being has to make a decision that in many cases could be argued either way—there may not be an absolute right or wrong to it. Even the final outcome won't necessarily prove the decision right or wrong. Lots of things turn out all right even though the decision behind them was wrong. The kid, for instance, who pulls out directly in front of a loaded cement truck, tires squealing and rocks flying, and just makes it, still made a lousy decision. He exercised very poor judgement, but since it turned out all right, it is hard to prove that what he did was wrong. About the only time a decision is *proven* wrong is when things actually *do* turn out badly—the cement truck crunches him—and fortunately, that is rare. Sooner or later bad judgement tends to catch up with you, which is why teenage drivers have such a terrible driving record compared to older drivers, but the fact that nothing has gone wrong *yet* doesn't prove the existence of good judgement.

ESSENTIAL ELEMENTS

I think the best way to get a grip on what is, after all, a fairly slippery question is to look at a couple of flying situations requiring the exercise of judgement, and examine the part each of its components—knowledge, experience, skill, and discretion—plays in that process.

Wake Turbulence

One area where judgement plays a major role is in avoiding wake turbulence. One of the first things a student pilot learns is that all airplanes generate wingtip vortices which are very turbulent, and the degree of that turbulence is in direct proportion to the weight of the aircraft, and is in indirect proportion to the speed. Therefore, large airplanes on final (i.e., heavy and slow) will generate the most severe wake turbulence, and are to be treated with the most respect. But the exact degree of "respect" is a matter not of law or science but of judgement. The controller's rule is to allow at least three miles between any two airplanes, increasing the separation to five miles if the airplane in front is a "heavy" (over 300,000 pounds). But these are just minimums for controllers to use. As the pilot, in visual contact with the traffic ahead, you can increase or decrease this separation at your discretion. So how do you decide?

In making a decision, several elements are involved. There is the technical element: knowledge of wake turbulence theory. There is the element of experience, which is just a way of saying personal, firsthand knowledge of wake turbulence. There is the element of pilot skill. And finally, there is the intangible element of discretion. Whenever "judgement" is involved, there comes a point after the knowledge, experience, and skill have been plugged into the equation where a human being has to exercise his discretion, and the decision that results reflects to a large extent what kind of person he is.

The first step is the knowledge part. This can't be skipped, but often is. Often a pilot goes straight to the question of how much distance, in this case, he feels he should put between himself and the "heavy" in front based on a purely arbitrary decision or guesswork or what he just read in a magazine or heard somebody say. If he doesn't get any bumps, he says he exercised good judgement; and if he does, he says the guy in front slowed up and didn't tell anybody.

You can't make judgements arbitrarily—not good ones, anyway. Good judgement has to be based on fact to make any sense, so the first step, in this case, is to find out as much as you can about what is known about wake turbulence and what the best current thinking is to avoid it. This means reading all the available literature including the *Airmen's Information Manual* and the appropriate sections from your flight training handbook, and it means having received instruction in the techniques of wake turbulence avoidance. This then forms a basis of fact and knowledge about the subject so your decisions can be based on reality and not myth, or wishful thinking, or the war stories of the heroes who hang around the airport lounge.

The next part is experience. With a knowledge of the facts and theories on the subject under your belt, you have the basis for forming sound guidelines for avoiding wake turbulence: three to five miles separation and always above and upwind of the glide path of the aircraft in front. Experience will then reveal whether those initial guidelines are good ones or not.

Experience is just self-instruction—the School of Life. One smooth, quiet morning, when you get rolled 90 degrees following a little DC-9 by seven miles, you will know that five miles doesn't always do it. Another day, when it is not so smooth and you are following an even bigger airplane, and you accidentally drop below the glideslope and don't feel any wake turbulence at all, you will have learned that turbulence can do a pretty good job of breaking up wingtip vortices. This doesn't mean you can disregard considerations of wake turbulence when it's bumpy, but it does mean you have learned, from personal experience, how to modify the guidelines—to allow extra room when it is smooth and that turbulence can, in some cases, be beneficial. Experience has *improved* your judgement.

Pilot skill is the least important factor in exercising good judgement. If you are flying an airplane that you have hundreds of hours in and are very comfortable with, and you have some experience with wake turbulence with that airplane—maybe just getting into the burbles of turbulence around the edges once or twice—then maybe you can safely accept the minimum separation. But no amount of skill is going to make you immune to the dangers of wake turbulence. Pilot skill is the least important variable in the judgement equation.

A known lack of skill, on the other hand, can cause you to modify your judgement substantially. If you've only flown a couple of ILSs before, and the controller has you four miles behind a jet and you aren't completely confident you won't drift below the glideslope slightly, you could tell the controller that you would like more separation. He can do it as long as you don't wait until the last minute to pop it on him. It may cost you an extra turn or two, or he may even have to take you out of line and bring you back in again at a point where there are no jets in front of you. In the worst case, it might cost you 10 minutes. If you know you lack skill in a certain area, then good judgment dictates extra caution. Ten minutes is a very small price to pay for a smooth and safe flight.

The part that makes judgement different from simple decision-making is the human element. Whether we call this element maturity, discretion, or wisdom doesn't really matter. The fact is that since exercising judgement is not a matter of black-and-white or right-or-wrong, the judgements that are made reflect, to a large extent, the personal makeup of the pilot involved. To the extent we need a name for that personal element, we are going to call it "discretion."

This all goes back to the oldest cliche in aviation: "There are old pilots and bold pilots, but there are no old and bold pilots." Some pilots are bolder than others. Two pilots can have identical training, experience, and skill, and one will decide that three miles behind a "heavy" is okay but the other wants five miles. As long as both land without incident, both decisions are correct. But the one five miles behind showed better judgement. It is of course possible to be unnecessarily conservative; 10 miles behind would probably be excessive, but no one can argue with five miles. The guy who consistently elects the "bolder" course of action is consistently exposing himself and his passengers to a higher degree of risk, and in so doing is reducing his chances of making it to "Old Pilot" status.

This human element is the variable that makes judgement such an unwieldy concept. I can't change your personality, and regardless of how mature you are, you are less mature at your present age than you will be 10 years from now—and there is nothing you can do to accelerate that process. All I can do is identify for you the elements that make up "judgement," encourage you to do the best you can with the elements that *are* under your control—knowledge, experience, and skill—and hope that you either know already or will someday learn the virtue and wisdom of following the path less bold. In this specific example, that means following three miles behind any jet and five miles behind a "heavy" is an absolute minimum and any separation you can get beyond that is better—and, in some cases, essential.

Circling versus Crosswind

Let's look at another example. You have just completed an ILS approach and have broken out at circling minimums. The tower has given you the option of landing straight in, but with a gusty 15 to 20 knot crosswind, or circling to a shorter runway that is aligned with the wind. The airport is surrounded by mountainous terrain, and the circle will be tricky, with minimum visibility (two miles) and the approach end of the desired runway hidden by a hill for the first half of the circling approach.

This is a tough one, because neither choice is very good. (Unfortunately, that's the way it usually is in the real world.) There are a lot of elements at work here. Nobody likes to circle if he can help it—it takes a lot of concentration and work to do a good circling approach under the best of circumstances and this is the worst of circumstances. Flying along just under the clouds and just above the terrain at a relatively slow airspeed is inherently riskier than a straight-in approach—it's very tempting to take the easy way out and just go straight in. But in so doing you take on a gusty crosswind which is itself difficult and somewhat risky.

So what is the "right" thing to do? What does the "Smart Set" do under these circumstances?

Let's break it down into the essential elements. First of all: knowledge. You know that a circling approach, if flown properly, provides marginal but still safe separation from the terrain. You know that the degree to which it is safe or not safe is completely dependent upon your skill as a pilot. You know that a mistake could well be disastrous—few survive 120-knot impacts. You also know that gusty, crosswind landings are tricky and routinely result in damaged aircraft ("pranged" is the euphemism most commonly encountered), but are seldom fatal.

Experience: You have done a few circling approaches to minimums in the past. They have all turned out well, but your experience tells you they are demanding and unforgiving, and particularly disconcerting when the approach end of the desired runway cannot be seen until towards the end of the circling maneuver. You have a lot of experience with crosswind landings and know that there is a big difference between a steady crosswind and a gusty crosswind, and that for a gusty crosswind, the size of the gust factor is the key determinant. In short, you know that 15 knots gusting to 20 is manageable, where 10 knots gusting to 30 might not be.

Skill: You feel equally skilled in each maneuver, but a higher premium is placed on skill in the circling maneuver. Since you don't feel especially skilled in one over the other and are confident you *could*, if necessary, do either safely, skill is not a factor in this case in exercising your judgement, but you lean towards the crosswind landing.

Personal element: What kind of person are you? Are you conservative and careful and don't care much if the passengers think you're a lousy pilot because the crosswind landing you attempt is bumpy, lands the airplane "crooked" (on the upwind wheel) and sets down hard? Or are you the kind who takes real pride in a successful circling approach under difficult conditions, especially if you can give the passengers a smooth ride with a squeaker landing? Do you worry about the consequences if worse comes to worst and decide that a "pranged" airplane is better than an "inadvertent contact with the ground," or do you think that question is irrelevant because you are completely confident that you can handle either situation? Are you the impatient type who wants to get on the ground as fast as possible, or do you enjoy the challenge of a tough circling approach?

Let me say quickly that this situation can be argued both ways. If you are very knowledgeable, experienced, and skilled at circling approaches, good judgement might dictate that you elect the circling approach, thus eliminating the difficulties of the crosswind landing. (The problem with gusty crosswind landings is that even the most experienced pilot can be "embarrassed" by one once in awhile, because no one can "see" the wind and the right one-two punch of gust and sheer can catch anybody.) But for most pilots I would say the crosswind landing would be preferable, because the "downside risk"—the worst-case scenario—for the crosswind landing is so much smaller than it is for the circling approach. But whereas there can be good reasons for doing it either way, there can also be bad reasons for doing it either way. Bad judgement is anything you decide on the basis of laziness, luck, a desire to impress your passengers, or impatience.

What if the crosswind is 10 gusting to 30? Now you *have* to circle, right? Not necessarily. You could go to your alternate, or if the condition is temporary, as it might be if a thunderstorm were passing overhead the airport, you could go somewhere else and hold for a while. Good judgement sometimes means remembering there are other choices.

THE HARD CALLS

The two toughest situations for making judgement calls are when nobody else is around to help you out, and when everybody else is doing something else. Let's look at them separately.

You show up at the airport and the runway is covered with three inches of light snow. All the plows are broken and the airport manager says it will be at least three hours before he can start plowing. You have never taken off on anything but a dry runway before and have no idea what effect the snow will have on acceleration and aren't too anxious to try to find out. The local 19-year old flight instructor says, "Hey, give it a try. The snow's dry—it won't bother you. You shouldn't have any trouble at all." (Why did he say "shouldn't?") The chief mechanic, who doesn't fly at all but who has formed an opinion or two in his 30 years of turning screws, just shakes his head and walks off.

Nobody has taken off since the snow started to fall. You have nothing to go by. One person thinks you'll have no problem and another thinks you're crazy. If you don't go, one of them will think you're a sissy, and if you *do* go, the other will think you're a fool. Wouldn't it help if somebody else would go first? Then if it works out without any problem you could follow him and act like you planned on it all along; if he ends up in the snowbank at the end of the runway you can thank your lucky stars you had enough sense not to try such a foolhardy deed.

So what do you do with a tough call when you have no experience to guide you and no example to follow? The answer is obvious: Take the safest way out regardless of the cost or inconvenience. The advice of others who are not in your place is cheap and unreliable. Putting up with the snickers of the resident experts is no fun, but you have to play your own game.

The same principle applies when everybody else is doing something you have misgivings about. It's awfully hard, for instance, to cancel or postpone a flight into possible icing conditions when everyone else is going, but if it doesn't seem right, *don't do it.* I know I sound like your mother telling you that "just because everybody else does it doesn't make it right," but every now and then a guy makes a *true* hero out of himself when he doesn't follow the pack and one of the pack gets hurt. The Eastern Airline Captain at DCA who pulled out of the takeoff lineup to go back for a *second* deicing, when the next plane off stalled on takeoff, hit a bridge, and ended up in the Potomac, is one—and there are others.

I have made the opposite of a true hero out of myself, on occasion, when I have not followed my instincts—and it's not a nice feeling. One night at LaGuardia, after waiting in line for takeoff for close to two hours, I took off into a whole bunch of thunderstorms. It didn't seem right at the time, but plane after plane—the vast majority of them airliners—had gone in regular procession in front of me, and I hadn't heard a single adverse report, so I figured that the situation had to be better than it looked.

The takeoff was fine—fairly smooth; we didn't even start to lose ground contact for 4,000 or 5,000 feet. The radar showed an area of heavy precip directly over the departure path, but everybody ahead was going through it without any problem, so again I rationalized that it had to be all right.

Well, it wasn't. The only warning we got were two small bumps, and then, for about 15 seconds, the kind of turbulence that, even with the belts tight, lifts you right out of your seat and throws everything all over the cabin. We got tossed around so much that I lost my grip on the control column and couldn't get a hold of it again, nor could I get to the autopilot button, so for several seconds we were literally being blown about like a leaf on the wind. Once we got through the area of heaviest precipitation it was smooth sailing for the rest of the trip, a good part of which was spent trying to come up with a good explanation for what happened, because our passenger, who just happened to be the Chief Pilot's boss (i.e., my boss's boss), wanted to know.

All I could do was apologize for the awful ride and tell him that no one else had had any problem, but he knew and I knew that the explanation was weak. Between the time the airplane right in front of us went through that area and the time we did—a matter of three or four minutes—the cell must have built up to severe proportions. I would like to have been able to say that it was just "one of those things"—an Act of God; something unavoidable. But it wasn't. If you take off into thunderstorms, you have to expect that once in a while some "funny" things will happen. The fact that "everyone else" seems to be cheating the odds can't change that. I exercised poor judgement that night (and so did a bunch of other pilots who happened to get away with it, but that's not the point). It's tough to say no when everybody else is doing it. Watch out for this one. It's a real sucker hole.

CONSERVATISM

When it comes to making good judgements, knowledge and experience are invaluable—no matter what the situation, the pilot who knows something about the situation and has some firsthand experience with it will be in a position to make a better decision than the pilot who doesn't. In addition, the more experienced and knowledgeable the pilot, the more likely he is to make a conservative decision.

Experience almost always tempers judgement in a conservative direction, and knowledge almost always leads to an awareness of hidden dangers, which in itself leads to conservatism. Since there are no shortcuts to experience, the only way to accelerate the process of acquiring good judgement is to expand your knowledge, and to *be* conservative, even if you don't fully understand why. Experience will, in time, teach you why being conservative was smart.

When I first started flying professionally, I frequently found myself questioning the decisions of the captains. I've never been a "hotdogger," but sometimes it seemed like the "old guys" deliberately went out of their way to be conservative—unnecessarily so. After all, enough is enough. But the more I flew, the more I found myself agreeing with these guys. They were still pretty conservative, but they didn't seem to be *unnecessarily* conservative anymore. Now that I have been a captain for awhile, I find that it's the quality of some of the *copilots* that seems to be the problem; some of them are still too anxious to take chances when they don't know what they're doing, and I can tell that they think that I'm too conservative, when I know I'm not. Fortunately, being conservative is a Captain's privilege. As the Pilot-in-command, it is your privilege also.

THE REAL TEST

Examiners do try to test judgement, but testing judgement is a very hard thing to do. An examiner can test your knowledge and your skill, and can assess your experience, and in so doing can get a rough idea of what your judgement is like, but it is very hard to find out what kind of *person* you are in the space of a short flight test—and without that information, an accurate assessment of your judgement is impossible. Despite what my flight instructor said, examiners don't test judgement; airplanes do. Good luck on your test.

Chapter 12

Professional Aviation

Professional pilots are frequently approached by non-professional pilots about flying. Typically they say something like: "I really envy you. I mean, I have a good business [or job, or practice], but it's a rat race: 12 plus hours a day of hassles and headaches. The suppliers are at me from one side and the customers from the other. The only thing I really enjoy is flying. I'm thinking of getting out of it and going full-time as a pilot—like you. You aren't tied to a desk or an office, your hours are flexible, you get outdoors a lot, the pay's not bad, and besides, I've made lots of money and I'm old enough to know by now that that's not what it's about, and when you're in your airplane you're your own boss. No reports, meetings, phone calls, arguments—just doing what you like to do and getting paid a little bit for it too. I'm serious about this. I've been thinking about it for quite a while and I may just do it." Variations on this theme are "I know it's too late for me, but I sure do envy what you're able to do. If I could do it over again, I'd go into flying too," and, "I'm thinking about law school, but what I really want to do is fly."

I know what you're thinking. You think I'm going to ridicule these people and their hopelessly naive and romanticized picture of what the professional pilot's life is like. I'm not. I'm also not going to tell you that professional aviation is the most wonderful occupation in the world. No puff pieces here. (The name of this book is *not* "So You Want to be a Professional Pilot"). But I get asked about professional flying, both by high school and college-age people thinking about careers, and by older, potential career-switchers often enough to know that it is a serious question demanding a serious and balanced answer.

If you are one of these people (and most pilots are, at least at one time or another), I want to give you the best possible and most accurate answer I can because, after all, this is your life we're talking about. But I want you to understand that all I can do is tell you what *my* experience has been. No matter how objective I may want to be, what I'm telling you is how it looks from this side of these eyeballs. Take it and use it for whatever it's worth.

BACK-DOOR ENTRY

The way I got started in professional flying is not at all typical, but it's not at all uncommon either, and it may well relate to your situation. As I explained earlier in the chapter Aircraft Limits, I started taking flying lessons just after college while I was in the Army, just for fun. I had no intention of making a career of aviation at the time.

After the Army I went to graduate school to study art history; I thought I wanted to work in museums. My first year in museum work—in which I discovered that the bulk of museum work is administrative and clerical, that I needed a Ph.D. (four to five more years of graduate school), and that there were about 30 qualified applicants for every museum job—convinced me that that wasn't what I wanted to do, but as much as I loved flying, I had very little idea how to get from Private Pilot to Professional Pilot, especially at the advanced age of 26. So I decided to try being a professional photographer instead, because I had always like photography and had been taking pictures since I was a kid and therefore thought I was already qualified for that profession.

People in their twenties often make mistakes, but I seemed to be trying for some kind of record. I quickly found out that calling yourself a professional photographer doesn't make you one. So, as a backup, I decided to start using my Veteran's Benefits to get my Commercial license and Instrument rating.

One of my favorite sayings (attributed to Winston Churchill) is: "It is occasionally useful to recognize the obvious." I had thought about flying for the military, way back when I was in college, but didn't because I didn't want the extra commitment: five years or more to fly for the Air Force or Navy, instead of two for the Army;

this was during the Vietnam era, and I knew I was going to have some sort of military obligation. (Those extra years seemed so important then and so unimportant now.) Then I thought about going to civilian flight school right after the Army, but didn't quite have the courage to do it and went to graduate school instead. (Another two years down the tubes. So much for the years I saved not going into the Navy or Air Force.) Then, when museum work looked like it wasn't going to work out, I thought about flying again, but decided against it to try photography. I think I had what psychologists call a "block." I think it was sitting on top of my shoulders.

Anyway, one day I was down at the airport, waiting to do some instrument dual, when I had a brief conversation with a professional pilot that somehow hit me alongside the head hard enough that I was finally able to recognize the obvious. He was a laid-off TWA or Pan Am pilot (I can't remember which) flying a Baron for a construction company. We struck up a conversation, and I explained that I was working on my Instrument rating and wanted to get my Commercial and multiengine ratings too, and that I was a photographer but what I really wanted to do was to get an airline job, but nobody was hiring (as evidenced by the fact that he was laid off) and I figured by the time they did hire again, I would be too old.

He said, "How old are you?", and I said, "Twenty-six."

He said he didn't think that was too old. He asked if I had been to college and I said yes, and he said, "There are a whole bunch of airline pilots who were hired after the War [WWII] who will be approaching retirement age in the next five years, and the industry won't stay in a slump forever anyway. There is going to be a lot of hiring in the not-too-distant future, and if you get your ratings right away, you should be in good shape to get hired."

I said, "But don't you need thousands of hours and military experience to get hired by an airline?" And he said, "No, not necessarily. There's no predicting exactly how *anyone* gets hired, but with a college degree, the ratings, and *some* time you should have a good shot at it—but you should get going on it right away."

Well, it changed my life. All of a sudden I realized that even though it was a long shot, I still had a chance at an airline career. I knew the chances weren't great, but they were *possible*, and I felt that motivation and concentration on that goal would give me a tremendous advantage over the dabblers and doubters.

I was both right and wrong, as it turned out, and he was both right and wrong too, but it all worked out all right anyway, and I hate to think what might have become of me if I had kept struggling away as a photographer. (Probably the same thing eventually—I think it was just a matter of time before *something* broke my "block," but more time would have been wasted.) The part I was right about was that I did have just as good a shot at becoming a professional pilot as the next guy (and so do you), and the part I was wrong about was that I did not, in fact, have a very good shot at an airline job per se. The timing was wrong for me. The big block of former WWII pilots who were going to retire over a fairly short period of time never seemed to materialize. I suspect there was just too much attrition and assimilation over those 30 to 35 years for anything like a recognizable "block" to have existed anymore, and to the extent retirements did increase, they were easily absorbed without creating any great hiring boom. When the airlines did start to hire in large numbers, the competition was so fierce that my flight instructor rating and a couple thousand hours wasn't even a start. By the time I had some jet experience and a type rating they weren't hiring again, and when they started hiring again after *that* I was basically too old: Most airlines prefer pilots under age 35 or so, although they won't say so. The airline part of my goal never worked out.

Am I bitter about that? Not in the least. Nobody promised me anything; I knew the risks from the beginning and accepted them. But more importantly, I'm not bitter because I discovered that professional aviation means more than just flying for the airlines. I worked hard, got my ratings, got some experience, and I didn't get an airline job, but I did eventually get a very good corporate job and I had a great time getting there. Not that there weren't moments of anxiety, but aviation is one place where patience, flexibility, and hard work can produce tangible results—maybe not all the time, but they do enough of the time to make it a good bet. Clean living pays off. I really believe that.

What would I do if I could do it over again? I would probably make just as many mistakes as I did the first time, only they would be different ones. But if I *could* do it again, knowing what I know now, I would probably try to go to Navy flight school, and if that worked out I would try to make a career out of the Navy, and if it didn't work out I'd try for the airlines, only this time I would have the kind of training and background the airlines were looking for and would have a much better shot at it.

STARTING OUT

That's what *I* would do. If *you* are just starting out and you want an aviation career and are still young enough to go into the military and can get into flight school, maybe that's what you should do too. (Either the Navy or the Air Force, or possibly the Army for helicopters—I think the decision as to which branch of the service to choose is strictly personal preference.) But you don't *have* to go to a military flight school to be a professional pilot and if you can't for one reason or another—too old (usually 27) or wear glasses or didn't go to college—it just means you need another plan, that's all.

If you are already a Private Pilot and are thinking of career switching (or fantasizing, at any rate), the "can you" part is easy: Yes, you can—at almost any age, with almost any background, in any part of the country. You may not get an airline job but you can be a professional pilot. But the "should you" part—that's another question.

Let's take the easy part first, the "can you" part. I will tell you how you can become a professional pilot if you want to. Then we'll go on to the harder part, the "should you."

CREDENTIALS

The minimum legal credential to be a professional pilot is a Commercial license with an Instrument rating. Eventually you will also need a multiengine rating and an ATP (Airline Transport Pilot's license), but those can wait. Your first goal, if you want to be a professional pilot, is to get your Commercial license with Instrument rating.

If you have the time and the money, the best way to get that training is at a full-time school with an approved program. That is obviously the quickest way, and it is also one of the best ways because the training is generally very good, you can concentrate on it without distractions, and in the long run it may be cheaper than stretching it out on an hourly basis at home. If you can't take the time to do that, or don't have that kind of money saved up, you can still do it on an hourly basis at your home airport. It may take a while, but it can be done. One way or another you have to have a Commercial license with an Instrument rating just to get in the running.

With a Commercial license and an Instrument rating you have, at least in theory, the necessary credentials for an entry-level position in corporate or charter aviation, but in practice those credentials won't be enough. You will also need a multiengine rating (there aren't too many flying operations utilizing only single-engine aircraft), and you will need several hundred if not a couple thousand hours of flight time. Therefore, in addition to the basic ratings, you need some "time."

FLIGHT TIME

In the beginning, the *amount* of flight time is more important than the *type*—you need raw time in your logbook. After a couple thousand hours, more single-engine time isn't going to help much, and at that point you can start worrying about how much multiengine time, turbine time, instrument time, "heavy" time and so on you have, but in the beginning you want to concentrate on the amount of flight time per se.

With only a couple of minor exceptions, the only way to get that time is as a flight instructor. The exceptions are crop dusting, banner towing, glider towing, and giving rides, but even these are usually not available to brand new Commercial pilots because of insurance restrictions. When I started out as a flight instructor, I couldn't give rides until I had 500 hours—which is pretty silly considering how much more difficult instructing is than giving rides, but that's the way it is. So for all practical purposes, you might as well plan on being a flight instructor initially and for a couple of years thereafter, and you therefore should plan on getting your CFI (Certified Flight Instructor) rating at the same time as you get your Commercial and Instrument. The sooner you get your CFI the better, because then you can start having the money come in instead of go out. Once you get used to having someone else pay for your flying, it's awfully hard to spend your own money on it again.

FLIGHT INSTRUCTING

Flight instructing is a great experience. I look back on my years as a flight instructor as some of the most satisfying and fun-filled years of my life. Even though I made all of about $7,000 my first year, and even though I swept a lot of hangar floors, cut a lot of grass, and fueled a lot of airplanes, I really loved what I was doing. I was making a living doing what I wanted to do, and every time I flew I was getting experience that someone else was paying for. Every time I soloed a student or got someone to understand something they were having trouble with before or saw the smile on someone's face after they had passed their checkride, I felt just great. I was a part of the process of turning people into pilots. I still can't think of any other segment of aviation that gives such immediate and tangible rewards.

So don't say you'd like to try your hand at aviation but you can't stand the thought of being a flight instructor for several years. There may be other reasons why you can't do it, not the least of which are financial—you will have to spend several thousand dollars to get your ratings and won't make enough initially to live on, much less pay back any loans—but don't miss the chance to try it because you think you won't like flight instructing. If you aren't going to like it, you will find that out long before you complete all your ratings, and if you do stick with it long enough to get your CFI, I'm sure you'll like teaching as much as I did.

The reason I'm so sure about that is because I have never met a former flight instructor who didn't have the same experience. It's just a real shame flight instructing doesn't pay any better than it does, but if it did, learning to fly would be even more expensive than it is, fewer people would fly, fewer flight instructors would be hired, and you'd have just as much trouble getting a job as a brand new flight instructor as you do now getting any other flying job. At least as things stand now, you can almost always find a job instructing, and it does pay *something*.

THE MULTIENGINE RATING

After you've taken the first steps and are working as a flight instructor, the next rating you need is a multiengine rating. Without a multiengine rating you are going to be a flight instructor forever—which, as I said, isn't so bad but you probably can't live on that kind of money forever, and besides, I know you want to fly bigger and "better" airplanes just like I did (and everyone else who hasn't done it yet does). So you might as well start planning on it from the beginning.

Multiengine training is expensive by the hour, but it doesn't take too many hours, so the overall cost is relatively low as ratings go. In addition, as a working pilot you can usually work out "deals" of one sort or another, either with your employer or someone you get to know once you're "in the business." But it is still going to cost several hundred dollars, which at this point in your career may be awfully hard to come up with. All I can say is, the sooner the better anyhow. This aviation pump takes a lot of priming. No matter how bleak your chances are of getting any multiengine time, they are *zero* without the rating. With the rating you can sometimes get the right seat on multiengine charter flights and then you can legally log the time as second-in-command. With the rating you may get to ferry a multiengine airplane or two, and with the rating you may get to know an aircraft owner who wants you to fly his twin once in awhile. Without the rating, these kinds of opportunities are going to pass you by.

You just never know what might come along that you can take advantage of if you have the rating that you might miss otherwise. I once talked a reluctant student of mine who had just gotten his Commercial, Instrument and CFI into getting his multiengine rating, even though he didn't think he needed it yet. I ran into him four years later at Houston Hobby getting out of the right seat of a Learjet. He'd been working as an instructor in the area, had made some contacts, and eventually had gotten a job with this particular company. Without that multiengine rating and whatever multiengine time he had been able to scrounge, he never would have had a chance. Nobody hires someone to fly the right seat of anything on the condition they get their multiengine rating "right away." So the sooner you get it, the better as far as your aviation career beyond flight instructing goes.

MULTIENGINE TIME

The first 25 to 50 hours of multiengine time is real hard to come by, because that amount of time—at $100 per hour and up—is too expensive for most people to buy, and because of insurance restrictions, hardly anyone will let you fly their multiengine airplane without at least that much time. It's a real Catch-22, but as a flight instructor with a multiengine rating, hanging around the airport full-time, you will be in the best situation to find those opportunities that do exist. You'll find a way. Everyone else does, somehow, but it is a big hurdle. Just remember: Without the rating, you can't even start.

ADDITIONAL INSTRUCTOR RATINGS

If you work at an airport that has a lot of instrument and multiengine students, by all means get instructor ratings to cover those areas too; that's the best way to get instrument and multiengine time. But if you work at the typical small airport, the vast majority of your instruction will be primary flight instruction, and the additional expense of getting those ratings may not be justified. At any rate, you can wait and see; you don't need to get them right off the bat. If it looks like there are opportunities there, it isn't too big a deal to add those capabilities to your basic instructor's certificate at a later date, and if there aren't many opportunities for instrument or multiengine instruction, you will have saved yourself a bunch of money.

INSTRUCTOR GOALS

With a CFI and a multiengine rating you are in position to do some serious "time building." "Time building" has a bad reputation, because there are, unfortunately, instructors who are *only* interested in time building and aren't at all interested in instructing. That's too bad, not just for the many students they go through—and they go through a lot, because it doesn't take the average student too long to sense when his flight instructor is only doing what he's doing to build time—but it's also too bad for themselves, because a bad attitude and/or unmitigated self-interest always catches up with you in aviation. Aviation is a very small world—*very* small. People remember these things. It may not seem small when you are starting out, but it is—and don't *ever* forget it.

By "serious time building" I mean having a good idea of what your goals are so you can get the most efficiency out of the time you do accumulate as a flight instructor. There is no reason why you can't be a perfectly good flight instructor and still focus on your goals, as long as you keep your priorities straight: instructing first, time-building second.

THE ATP

The ATP is a required license only for Captains (Pilots-in-Command) operating under Part 121 (the major airlines), but it is, for all practical purposes, required for any corporate job, and it is a very desirable license to have when applying for any flying job—charter, commuter, or cargo.

The hourly requirements to be eligible to take the written and flight tests for an ATP are given in FAR 61.155, and are fairly complex, but the parts that normally will concern you are: 1500 total hours flight time as a pilot, 500 hours cross-country time, 100 hours of night time, and 75 hours of actual or simulated instrument time. You want to meet, if possible, each of the specific hourly requirements (500 hours cross-country, 100 hours night, etc.), while you are building your first 1500 hours of total time.

This means that while you are working towards 1500 hours of flight time (and remember that *all* flight time counts towards that 1500 hours including dual received, dual given, glider time, second-in-command time, and so on), keep the other parts in mind and do what you can to keep those times in proportion. As a flight instructor they won't necessarily "take care of" themselves. Most of your flying as a flight instructor will be VFR in the local area: airwork and pattern work. You probably won't get a whole lot of cross-country time, certainly not a third of the total time (1500 total hours are required and 500 cross-country) as a flight instructor. But there are a couple things you can do to maximize your cross-country time. One is to remember that any flight over 25 nautical miles with a landing is a cross-country. (Actually, the FAA does not define cross-country time, except for student pilots, but to avoid problems later—you have to have your logbook inspected in order to take the ATP written—I would use this student pilot definition.) You may be just running a spare part over to the next airport, but if it's more than 25 nautical miles away, you can log the time as cross-country time. If you take a student to a nearby airport (but more than 25 miles away) and in the course of the lesson make at least one landing, you can log it as a cross-country even though the object of the lesson was not cross-country instruction. This might happen if you went to another airport to practice short field takeoffs and landings, or flew to a tower-controlled airport for instruction in radio procedures.

After you've been around for a while you will probably start to get to do some single-engine charter. This is where you can really add up the cross-country hours, so don't be bashful about getting in line for those trips. Every little bit counts and you don't want to get 1500 hours of total time and still be 200 hours short on your cross-countries if you can help it.

Getting the required night and instrument time can also be a problem for a flight instructor. The regs require that all private pilot applicants have three hours of night time with 10 takeoffs and landings, but there is no law that says they can't have more. I think it's a good idea to do a short night cross-country with students, just to give them an idea of how vastly different night VFR cross-countries are from day cross-countries. (I also think it's a good idea to be honest with them and explain that the regs only require three hours of night time, and that you won't require more of them either, but that you feel that additional night time is very valuable.) With the required night instruction plus an occasional charter that runs into some night time, you should be able to make the night time "come out even."

One of the best ways I found to get instrument time, other than as an instrument instructor, is in riding along with instrument-rated owner pilots who are smart enough to know that they are not current enough or proficient enough to go IFR by themselves and therefore like to take an instructor along to help. You act as pilot-in-command and keep them from getting in trouble, giving them as much help as they ask for or need while generally letting them do the actual flying—the "fun" part, for them. You can meet some great people this way, have a lot of fun yourself, get to travel some, and it's very productive "time:" actual IFR time *and* cross-country time. (Or better yet: IFR cross-country *night* time—in a multiengine airplane. It can happen.)

The important thing in all of this is to remember to log all the possible time you can—in all the possible ways—so that you can qualify to get your ATP at the earliest opportunity. You can't even take the written until you have those hours.

The ATP Written

There is nothing, however, that says you can't study for the ATP written ahead of time, and you should, because the written is the hard part of the ATP—a real bear. It requires, for one thing, a lot of memorization of the regs in Part 121, which pertain only to airline operations. A typical question might be something like: "How many flight attendants would be required on an aircraft that seats 123 passengers and has 97 on board?" It also has a lot of very tricky and hard-to-read performance curves taken from the flight manuals of transport category aircraft, and it has some very complicated weight-and-balance stuff involving shifting loads. A lot of people bust it, even two and three times, and even after taking three-day review courses. My point is not to discourage you; everybody who really wants to pass it does and you will too. My point is that you have to study for it and the sooner you start the better, so that when you *do* qualify to take the test, you are ready.

The ATP Flight Test

The flight test for the ATP is pretty straightforward. The tolerances are less than for an instrument checkride, but other than that there is nothing new. You'll do the usual airwork, maybe a hold, some approaches including a missed approach and a single engine approach, and that's about it. You'll be scared to death anyway, just like I was, but the point is that it isn't anything new, whereas the ATP written is.

With an ATP, you're ready to type up a resume and start looking. A great job probably won't come right away, but with an ATP rating you separate yourself from the great mass of pilots with Commercial licenses into a fairly small group of pilots who are entitled to call themselves "ATPs." It won't guarantee jobs, but it will open doors that are otherwise boarded shut. Just the fact that you made the extra effort to get the license will indicate your motivation and conscientiousness. You'll hear all kinds of things from the local experts about how an ATP is useless and nothing but a prestige item, but don't believe a word of it; it's mostly sour grapes and ignorance. Trying to get a good flying job without an ATP is like trying to run a marathon with ski boots on. With the ATP, you have a good shot at a variety of flying jobs, and depending a little bit on luck—but much more on how flexible and persistent you are—you will eventually succeed.

So, back to my original question: "Can you or anyone else who has a least a Private Pilot's license become a professional pilot?" The answer is "yes." I just told you how, and you can do the whole program, through ATP, in three years. Figure 12-1 shows how it breaks down.

First Year

Commercial, Instument, CFI, Multiengine ratings.
Start work as CFI.   500 hours

Second Year
Continue working.   500 hours

Third Year

Continue working, study and take ATP written, take ATP flight test. Start looking for position as a line pilot.
                                                500 hours

                                        Total 1500 hours

Fig. 12-1. From Private Pilot to Airline Transport Pilot in three years. A typical program.

Once you have accomplished these basic goals, you will want to think about taking the Flight Engineer written if you want to try for the airlines; if you want a job in corporate aviation, you will probably need a basic type rating—Learjet or Citation. But these things can wait, and you'll find out all about that stuff once you start working, so I'm not going to go into that. In the beginning, keep it simple, but keep at it.

It *can* be done; if you are truly motivated, you can be a professional pilot. The real question is: "Should you do it?" And the real answer is: "I don't know." I can't answer that for you, but I can give you an idea of what professional aviation has meant to me, the pluses and the minuses, and maybe that will help you in some way to come to a conclusion that is appropriate for you.

I always like to end on an upbeat note, but if I am going to give you both the pluses and the minuses *and* end on an upbeat note, I have to start with the minuses. Just remember, there is a plus part coming.

THE MINUSES

With few exceptions, a career in professional aviation means a life of continuous financial insecurity. You will have to struggle for every job you ever get, it will never pay enough to make you financially secure (the days of the $150,000 per year airline job are disappearing rapidly and will be gone by the time you get there), and worst of all, you can be laid-off at any time, no matter how secure the company or the airline—and you probably will be, sooner or later. In other words, you will probably never make enough money to be able to create a financial cushion, yet you can expect to find yourself suddenly one day out on the street with no job, no money, having to start from scratch with nothing but your resume and your "tickets" and a bunch of other guys wanting the same jobs you do.

I once said to another pilot, strictly off the top of my head, "I'll bet you can't name a single corporate pilot over 50 who hasn't been laid off at least once in his career. I know I can't." He couldn't either. I've tried the same question on other pilots since then, and no one has been able to come up with a single pilot over 50 that he personally knows who hasn't been laid-off at least once. By the time a pilot has been flying for 25 to 30 years, it is almost a certainty that somewhere along the way he has been the victim of a cutback or a flight department closing. There are probably a few who have been spared that I don't know about, but on the other hand, I knew several pilots who have been laid off *more* than once.

The airlines haven't been any better. Almost all airline pilots who have been hired within the last 15 years or so have been laid off at least once, and some have spent more time furloughed than working. Don't think you can pick the right airline and be safe, either. Who would have thought 15 years ago that Pan Am would be in financial trouble and that Braniff and Continental would both be bankrupt? If you can accurately predict the airlines that will be around 15 years from now, I'd like to hear from you. I am going to make you a partner. You and I are going to be very rich. We may even get to go on the *Today* show and talk to Jane Pauley. There may be a little more job security with some of the airlines, but not much. It's still very risky business.

You might as well accept the fact that flying as a career will never make you rich—in fact, it may not even make you "comfortable"—and you might as well accept the fact that there will almost certainly be setbacks. Even after struggling to "get there," it may be taken away again. The good news is that most pilots do find work again after being laid-off. The experience you have at that point and the contacts you have made (remember what I said about aviation being a very small world) are tangible assets. But it often takes as long as a year to find something else.

If you think it won't necessarily be this way in the future just because it has always been this way in the past, then you just aren't being realistic. The first thing to go whenever a company runs into trouble is a pilot or two, and the first department to be liquidated when a financial crunch comes is the flight department. Sometimes a flight department is closed for no good reason at all except that a "new guy" wants to make a grandstand play for the benefit of the directors and stockholders. For the airlines, deregulation has made the job of getting hired easier, but it has also made the job of picking the right airline a crapshoot—I know some guys who are on their third airline. If you can't live with some degree of insecurity and aren't willing to pay the price of financial hardship to fly, then maybe you should think about making your living some other way and just fly as a hobby.

In addition to financial insecurity, flying can be very tough on families. Unless you fly for a scheduled airline, your schedule—to the extent you have one at all—will be erratic and unpredictable. A sensible social life is just about out of the question. A "day off" usually means a day you didn't end up actually flying but might have. About the only time off you can really count on is vacation time, and employers are notoriously stingy with vacation time for pilots—two weeks after the first year is normal, possibly going up to three weeks after five to seven years, if you're lucky. Your wife won't be able to accept invitations with any assurance that you will be there, and won't be able to plan parties except for close friends who understand when you don't show. Weekends are very often just two more days to fly. You will miss most of your kids' school events, games, and birthdays, and you will miss your wedding anniversary and your wife's birthday (and if your wife says she understands, I think your wife is a good sport and a lousy liar). In short, you will not be there for many of the moments that make family life memorable. Worse things can happen to a family than having their father or husband off working when something important to the family is going on, and if you are happy and earning a decent living and proud of what you are doing, the rest of the family will almost certainly adapt and understand. But time away from home is a real problem, and you should look it square in the eye before going on.

One of the advantages of being a flight instructor is that you seldom have overnights. The same cannot be said for the rest of aviation. I have slept in more strange beds and eaten more dinners away from home than I care to think about. But that's not the real problem. The real problem with overnights is the effect on your family (which is why you will frequently hear it said that flying is a game for the single man or woman). Life goes on for your family in your absence, but without your help. A lot of people have to travel besides pilots, but for pilots it's a way of life—which means your being away from home a good part of the time is also a way of life for your wife and kids, and if you and/or they can't accept that, then you should probably do something else.

I remember a military pilot telling me he was going to get out of the military and try to get on with the airlines, but he said if he didn't get hired by an airline he was going to get out of aviation, because the only thing left after the airlines was corporate aviation and in corporate aviation you ended up having to do things like take the boss' shirts out and he just didn't need to fly that badly. I've never taken shirts out, but I have done a lot of things that have nothing to do with flying airplanes—such as clean them, fuel them, load baggage, babysit kids going along for the ride, serve dinners (nobody "made" me, but if the passengers ask for hot dinners to be put on, and they don't even know where the oven is, *you* figure out who's going to get the steaks out), and so on. Some companies are better than others about the "related duties," but they all have some.

What this guy didn't know, though, is that first of all, there is more to aviation than the airlines and corporate flying, and secondly, even airline pilots do more than just fly airplanes. There is a lot of paperwork and record-keeping in a Part 121 operation for one thing, and for another, unless an airline Captain was very lucky, he would almost certainly have started his airline career as a Flight Engineer—and Flight Engineers don't even get to fly. In addition, some of the newer, low-cost airlines (the ones doing the bulk of the hiring) require their pilots to double as dispatchers and ticket agents. So the grass isn't always greener. No matter what kind of flying job you get or want, don't be so naive as to think the only thing you are going to do is fly airplanes.

If you get into charter or corporate flying, you're going to spend an awful lot of time hanging around airports, and normally they won't be the fun kind where you can walk around and peak inside interesting local airplanes or watch the hawks soar or take in the scenery, but the noisy, dirty ones, shut up in a "pilots' lounge" (which usually means a couple of beat-up chairs and a broken TV). There always seems to be more time to kill than you need just to rest up, but less than you need to go anywhere interesting or do anything useful. Waiting around, doing nothing, is an occupational hazard of corporate and charter aviation. As the saying goes, "We fly for free and get paid to wait." It's demoralizing, and it gets real old. If you ever *do* start getting used to it, there's something wrong.

If I've been calling you a "he" all through this book, but your real name is "she," your chances at an *airline* job have never been better, but you're going to have a real problem in corporate aviation. Chief Pilots and Flight Department Managers are very reluctant to hire women pilots because of the large amount of time pilots spend together on the road. They just don't want to take a chance on problems, and the truth is that the ones who usually make the biggest stink are the wives of the pilots who already work there, and Chief Pilots get enough trouble from that quarter as it is (see paragraph above about flying and families) without adding to the complaints. It isn't fair, it isn't right, and it may get better in the future, but women pilots in business aviation have a real problem at this time. Focus on the airlines and commuters.

That's the worst of it. Any job has its minuses, and now you know what the minuses are for professional aviation.

THE PLUSES

The best part of the good side of professional aviation is that the "getting there" can be as much fun as the "being there." Whether you go into the military to fly or start out as a flight instructor, despite the anxieties and uncertainties, it is all great fun. Ask any established professional pilot, and if he's being honest and not trying to be funny or cute, I think you'll find that he agrees with me. I have been in professional aviation for over 10 years now, and I have had some of the greatest experiences a person can have—and my case is not unusual. I have seen most of the United States, both from the air and on the ground, and a good part of Canada and the Caribbean. I still get a real kick out of being able to start out in the morning from my own home town and within a few hours be in a completely different part of the country— especially if it's somewhere I haven't been before. The travel part of flying is one of the parts I like best.

I have also had the opportunity to meet some great people. There is something about aviation—and I don't mean just the flying end of it, but also the service and support end also—that attracts interesting, hard-working and honest people—good people. The passengers in most cases are great people also. The trust and appreciation they give you, as their pilot, is one of the most rewarding parts of the job. I have also had the thrill of flying celebrities, politicians, and sport legends, and I now know for a fact that famous people are among the nicest people you can ever hope to meet.

I have eaten Mexican food in El Paso, French food in Palm Springs, German food in Milwaukee, and Cajun food in Lou'siana. I've skied at Vail, ridden a motorbike in Bermuda, and sailed a Sunfish in the Bahamas. I've experienced the thrill of being part of a front page Wall Street Journal story when a deal was announced after a late-night "mission" to buy or sell a subsidiary company, and I was copilot on a Citation that took Jack Welch, who is now the CEO of General Electric, to company headquarters when he found out that he had made the cut for the final five in contention for the top job. (He was so nervous going down he ate every stick of gum in the airplane, and so excited coming back he jumped around in the airplane like a little kid getting his first airplane ride.) All in all I've had a great time, and a good part of it came before my "heavy iron" days. You don't have to fly a jet for a big corporation to have fun flying airplanes.

Mostly, I'm just humbled by it all. I am humbled by how fortunate I have been as a pilot, and how lucky I am to have been born at a time and in a country where it is possible to do the things I have done. When I was three years old my father used to take my little brother and me down to Washington National Airport, and he'd put dimes in the turnstile and we would go out on the observation deck and watch the DC-3s and DC-6s and "Connies" come and go. I can remember thinking that airplanes had to be about the greatest things in the world, and that if I could just someday even drive one of the little tugs that pulled the baggage carts I'd be happy forever.

That observation deck is still there, and Washington National is still my all-time favorite airport to fly to, and you can still put your dime in the turnstile and watch the airplanes come and go—the best 10¢ show in the world. The tugs haven't changed much, but now the airplanes are mostly DC-9s and 727s. The last time I was at DCA I was driving a Citation, someone named Henry Kissinger was in the back of the airplane, and I was looking *up* at the observation deck. Aviation has been very good to me, and I don't know why.

I hope somewhere in this book that I have been able to help you in even a very small way, as partial repayment for the many pilots before me who have helped me in very large ways.

Good luck. And be careful. When all is said and done, this is just airplanes we're talking about. It's not worth dying for.

Index

Index

Other Bestsellers From TAB